THE UNIVERSITY OF NORTH CAROLINA
SESQUICENTENNIAL PUBLICATIONS

THE GRADUATE SCHOOL

DISSERTATIONS AND THESES

THE UNIVERSITY OF NORTH CAROLINA
SESQUICENTENNIAL PUBLICATIONS

Louis R. Wilson, DIRECTOR

CHRONICLES OF THE SESQUICENTENNIAL

THE UNIVERSITY OF NORTH CAROLINA, 1789-1835:
A Documentary History

THE CAMPUS OF THE FIRST STATE UNIVERSITY

THE GRADUATE SCHOOL: RESEARCH AND PUBLICATIONS

THE GRADUATE SCHOOL: DISSERTATIONS AND THESES

STUDIES IN SCIENCE

STUDIES IN LANGUAGE AND LITERATURE

A CENTURY OF LEGAL EDUCATION

A STATE UNIVERSITY SURVEYS THE HUMANITIES

SECONDARY EDUCATION IN THE SOUTH

IN SEARCH OF THE REGIONAL BALANCE OF AMERICA

STUDIES IN HISTORY AND POLITICAL SCIENCE

LIBRARY RESOURCES OF THE UNIVERSITY OF NORTH CAROLINA

RESEARCH AND REGIONAL WELFARE

PIONEERING A PEOPLE'S THEATER

UNIVERSITY EXTENSION IN ACTION

BOOKS FROM CHAPEL HILL

THE GRADUATE SCHOOL
DISSERTATIONS AND THESES

Edited with a Foreword

BY

JAMES L. GODFREY
Associate Professor of History

FLETCHER M. GREEN
Kenan Professor of History

W. W. PIERSON
*Professor of History and Political Science
and
Dean of the Graduate School*

CHAPEL HILL
THE UNIVERSITY OF NORTH CAROLINA PRESS
1947

Copyright, 1947, by
THE UNIVERSITY OF NORTH CAROLINA PRESS

FOREWORD

This compilation of thesis and dissertation subjects, a volume in the publications of the Sesquicentennial Celebration, is offered as an evidence of the vigor and growing importance of the work of the Graduate School of the University. As it covers a span of sixty years and lists the research for advanced degrees of some twenty-five hundred men and women, it was thought that no University celebration could be complete without recognition of the training, discipline, and endeavor of this group embodying so much of the highest and best in the University's efforts.

The plan of the volume is simple. The departments of instruction offering advanced degrees are listed alphabetically; within each department the holders of the degree of Doctor of Philosophy are listed first under the year in which the degree was granted, and following this a similar list is included for the degree of Master of Arts. In the frequent instance of more than one student receiving the same degree in the same year the recipients are listed in alphabetical order.

In addition, it should be pointed out that beginning with the year 1919 the director of the research has been listed following the title of the thesis or dissertation. Such an inclusion requires no justification, but is a mark of appreciation to the graduate faculty for the patience, skill, and devotion to scholarship which must always mark the relationship of graduate faculty to graduate student. It is regretted that directors before 1919 are omitted. In so many instances it was impossible to establish the directors of research before that date, that it was thought best, in the interest of uniformity, to leave out these "pioneers" who worked, all too often, in obscurity.

It is with gratification, however, that we point out a recent and happy inclusion. Two degrees, both doctorates, have recently been granted by State College, one in Agronomy and the other in Plant Pathology, and are listed here in recognition of the position of the Graduate School in the Consolidated University. This is taken as a happy omen that research in agriculture and the mechanical arts will soon supplement in value that undertaken in arts and sciences at Chapel Hill.

In conclusion, one regret must be stated. It cannot be claimed that the list is complete, despite efforts to make it so. The records of the Graduate School and of the departments, the resources of the library, and the memory of man have all been utilized, but anyone dealing with records going back over two generations will be aware of the gaps that can and do occur and will appreciate the difficulty of absolute assurance in the matter of completeness. It is hoped that our fears are largely groundless and that no necessity will arise for these apologies, which we offer in advance.

>James L. Godfrey
>Fletcher M. Green
>W. Whatley Pierson, Jr.

May 1, 1946
Chapel Hill, N. C.

DEPARTMENT OF AGRONOMY
(State College)

Ph.D.
1943   N. S. HALL. A Laboratory Method for the Artificial Alteration of Alumino-Silicates.

DEPARTMENT OF ANATOMY

M.S.
1942   A. J. ATKINS. A Comparative Study of the Yolk Sac in Amniotes with Particular Reference to the Cytology of the Yolk Digesting Cells. W. C. George.

DEPARTMENT OF ART

M.A.
1942   R. A. KOCH. Roger van der Weyden and the Sculpture of His Time. Clemens Sommer.

M. E. MUNCH. The Landscape in Giovanni Bellini's Work: A Catalogued Study. Clemens Sommer.

1944   I. M. DAVIS. Andrea del Castagno's Famous Men and Women. Clemens Sommer.

HELEN FITZ-RICHARD. The Contribution of Renaissance Art to the Genesis of the Violin: A Typological Investigation. Clemens Sommer.

M. DE L. A. MERENO-ENRIQUEZ. Inconography of the Devil in Renaissance Painting. Clemens Sommer.

ERIKA WEIGAND. Classical Traits in Masaccio's Painting. Clemens Sommer.

DEPARTMENT OF BIOLOGICAL CHEMISTRY

Ph.D.
1941   B. D. WEBB. Studies in Quinine: A Method for Its Estimation in Blood and Urine: Effect of Hookworm Infection upon the Blood Levels and Urinary Excretion in the Dog. J. C. Andrews.

1943   C. E. ANDERSON. The Absorption and Metabolism of Quinine in the Animal Body. J. C. Andrews.

1944   W. E. CORNATZER. Physiological Studies on Metabolism and Absorption of Quinine. J. C. Andrews.

A. DE T. VALK, JR. Studies in the Metabolism of Quinine. J. C. Andrews.

1945   MRS. M. M. MCEWEN. Studies on the Effect of Vitamin B-Complex Deficiency on the Metabolism and Absorption of Quinine. G. C. Kyker.

8   DISSERTATIONS AND THESES

M.S.
1940   A. B. SAMPLE. The Extraction of Proteins from
            Aqueous Solutions by Means of Emulsification with
            Chloroform. J. C. Andrews.

1941   W. E. CORNATZER. Fractionation of Proteins by
            Emulsification with Immiscible Solvents. J. C.
            Andrews.

1943   D. P. LEWIS. Silicostungstic Acid as a Quantitative
            Reagent for Alkaloids and other Nitrogenous Substances. J. C. Andrews.

            E. L. LYNCH. Determination of Quinine in Biological
            Materials by Turbidimetry and Fluorimetry. J. C.
            Andrews.

DEPARTMENT OF BOTANY

Ph.D.
1923   H. R. TOTTEN. Description, Life History, and Mycorhizal Character of *Rhizopogon parasiticus*.
            Coker and Totten n.sp. W. C. Coker.

1924   J. N. COUCH. Sexual Reproduction and Variability
            in the Genus *Dictyuchus*. W. C. Coker.

1930   V. D. MATTHEWS. Studies on the Genera *Nematosporangium* and *Pythium*. W. C. Coker.

1936   A. G. LANG. Some Observational and Theoretical
            Considerations of Spermatogenesis in *Marsilea
            quadrifolia*, with Special Reference to the Structure of the Spermatozoid and the Evolution of the
            Nucleolus. J. N. Couch.

            VERA MILLSAPS. The Structure and Development of
            of the Seed of *Paulownia tomentosa* Steud. and
            Cynoglossum amabile Stapf and Drumm. W. C.
            Coker.

1938   T. E. SMITH. Host Range Studies with *Bacterium
            solanacearum* E.F.S. R. F. Poole.

1939   A. C. MATHEWS. The Morphological and Cytological Development of the Sporophylls and Seed of
            Juniperus virginiana L. W. C. Coker.

            LELAND SHANOR. Studies in the Genus *Olpidiopsis*
            (Cornu) Fischer. W. C. Coker and J. N. Couch.

1940   G. A. CHRISTENBERRY. A Taxonomic Study of the
            Mucorales in the Southeastern United States. J. N.
            Couch.

            J. A. DOUBLES, JR. A Taxonomic Study of the Myxomycetes of North Carolina. W. C. Coker and J. N.
            Couch.

Ph.D.

1941   A. J. WHIFFEN. Culture Studies in the Chytridiales with Relation to Growth on Synthetic Media and Decomposition of Cellulose. J. N. Couch.

1942   L. S. OLIVE. Cytology, Morphology, and Parasitism of *Thekopsora Hydrangeae* Magn. W. C. Coker.

B. E. SMITH. The Dicotyledonous Flora of Darlington County, South Carolina. W. C. Coker.

M.A.

1912.   J. A. McKAY. Cleistogamy.

1914.   H. R. TOTTEN. I. Development of the Seed in *Mayaca Aubleti;* II. Development of the Seed in the Cleistogamic Flower of *Specularia perfoliata.*

1922   J. N. COUCH. Spore Formation and Discharge in Some Genera of Water Molds. W. C. Coker.

1925   J. V. HARVEY. A Study in the Water Molds and Pythiums Occurring in the Soils of Chapel Hill. W. C. Coker.

1927   V. D. MATTHEWS. Studies on Saprolegniaceae and the Genus *Pythium.* W. C. Coker.

P. M. PATTERSON. Fertilization and Oogenesis in *Achlya colorata.* W. C. Coker.

1930   N. B. ELIASON. Development of the Seed in the Morning Glory (*Ipomaea purpurea*) and in Dodder (*Cuscuta arvensis*). W. C. Coker.

REBECCA WARD. Seed Development in *Hibiscus esculentus.* W. C. Coker.

1931   A. C. MATHEWS. The Seed-Development in *Pinus palustris* (Long Leaf Pine). W. C. Coker.

1932   N. Q. HENRY. The Seed-Development in *Cuscuta arvensis.* W. C. Coker.

1933   M. L. VARDELL. Seed Development in *Spigelia marilandica* L. W. C. Coker.

1934   RUTH SCHOLZ. Studies in the Leguminosae of North Carolina: Part I. Some Diverse Forms and Peculiarities Found in Certain Species of the Family Leguminosae; Part II. The Structure and Development of the Seed of *Strophostyles umbellata* (Muhl.) Britton. W. C. Coker and H. R. Totten.

B. E. SMITH. A Taxonomic and Morphological Study of the Genus *Cuscuta,* Dodders, in North Carolina. W. C. Coker.

M.A.

1936   J. R. RAPER. Heterothallism and Sterility in *Achlya* and Observations on the Cytology of *Achlya bisexualis*. J. N. Couch and W. C. Coker.

E. M. WELLS. The Structure and Development of the Seed in *Cimicifuga racemosa*. W. C. Coker.

1937   D. D. RITCHIE. The Morphology of the Perithecium of *Sordaria fimicola* (Rob.) Ces. and De Not. J. N. Couch.

LELAND SHANOR. Observations on the Development and Cytology of the Sexual Organs of *Thraustotheca clavata* (de Bary) Humph. W. C. Coker and J. N. Couch.

L. M. STEWART. Studies in the Life History of *Nitella hyalina* Agardh. W. C. Coker.

1938   G. A. CHRISTENBERRY. A Study of the Effect of Light of Various Periods and Wave Lengths on the Growth and Asexual Reproduction of *Choanephora cucurbitarum* (Berk. and Rav.) Thaxter. W. C. Coker, J. N. Couch, and J. E. Adams.

J. A. DOUBLES, JR. Myxomycetes of the Chapel Hill Area. W. C. Coker.

F. K. FOUST. Studies on *Rozella* and *Pleolpidium*. J. N. Couch.

J. G. LEITNER. New Species of *Achlya* and *Apodachlya*. W. C. Coker and J. N. Couch.

1939   H. T. COX. A New Genus of the Rhizidiaceae. J. N. Couch.

W. C. HEWITT. Seed Development of *Lobelia amoena*. W. C. Coker and H. R. Totten.

MARY W. WARD. Studies in Aquatic Fungi: I. Observations on a New Species of *Thraustotheca;* II. Observations on *Rhizophlyctis rosea* (de Bary and Woronine), Fischer. W. C. Coker and J. N. Couch.

A. J. WHIFFEN. The Cytology of *Octomyxa Achlyae*. J. N. Couch.

1940   M. G. BURTON. Oogenesis and Fertilization in *Pythiopsis intermedia*. W. C. Coker and J. N. Couch.

*L. S. OLIVE. Studies in the Genus *Gymnosporangium*. W. C. Coker.

H. I. WILBURN. Seed and Fruit Development in *Smilax*. J. E. Adams.

---

* Master of Science.

M.A.
1941   Lane Barksdale. The Pedicellate Species of *Trillium* Found in the Southern Appalachians. J. E. Adams.

H. E. Orr. Gametogenesis and Fertilization in *Pythium pulchrum*. J. N. Couch.

A. W. Ziegler. Gametogenesis of *Achlya recurva* Cornu. J. N. Couch.

1942   E. G. Setzer. Sporogenesis in *Isoachlya anisospora* (de Bary) Coker. J. N. Couch.

1943   C. F. Hendricks. Observations on the Development and Cytology of *Blastocladiella cystogena*. J. N. Couch.

1944   R. E. Allen. Four Ascosporic Species of *Aspergillus* Found on Tea Leaves. J. N. Couch.

H. S. Sherwin. Some Wild Yeasts Found around Chapel Hill. J. N. Couch.

DEPARTMENT OF CHEMISTRY

Ph.D.
1883   W. B. Phillips. Part I. Rate of Reversion in Superphosphates Prepared from Red Navassa Rock; Part II. North Carolina Phosphates.

1885   E. A. De Schweinitz. (No title available.)

1887   H. B. Battle. (No title available.)

1894   Charles Baskerville. Comparison of the Methods of Separation and Estimation of Zirconium.

1901   J. E. Mills. Molecular Attraction.

1903   R. O. E. Davis. The Atomic Weight of Thorium.

1909   Stroud Jordan. Condensation of Chloral with Primary Aromatic Amines.

1914   J. T. Dobbins. Action of Ammonia on Solutions of Arsenic Triiodide in Organic Solvents.

1915   V. C. Edwards. 1, 4, 5, 6-Tetrahydroxynaphthalene: I. A New Case of Desmotrophy; II. A Series of Bromine Derivatives.

W. L. Jeffries. The Function of "Cooking" Fossil Resins in Varnish Manufactures.

1916   C. B. Carter. Action of Ammonia on Arsenic Triiodide.

V. A. Coulter. Studies on the Resine of *Pinus heterophylla*.

Ph.D.

1919   J. W. SCOTT. Halogenation of Juglone, a New Type of Naphthalene Dye. A. S. Wheeler.

1921   T. M. ANDREWS. New Derivatives of 2, 3, 8-Tribromojuglone. A. S. Wheeler.

I. W. SMITHEY. The Bromination of 2-Amino-p-cymene. A. S. Wheeler.

1922   I. V. GILES. 5-Chloro-2-amino-p-cymene and Derivatives. A. S. Wheeler.

1923   S. C. SMITH. Part I. The Constitution of Dichlorohydroxy-ethylidene-bis-nitroanilines; Part II. The Reaction of Dichloracetic Acid with Aromatic Amines. A. S. Wheeler.

1924   H. M. TAYLOR. The Bromination of 2-Amino-p-cymene and Certain Azo Dyestuffs. A. S. Wheeler.

1926   F. P. BROOKS. The Nitration of 2-Amino-para-cymene. A. S. Wheeler.

H. D. CROCKFORD. Heat of Fusion of Some Nitrotoluenes. J. M. Bell.

C. R. HARRIS. 2,6-Nitro-amino-p-cymene and Certain New Azo Dyes. A. S. Wheeler.

E. DE W. JENNINGS. A Study of Gossypol and Some Bromine Derivatives of 2,6-Diamino-p-cymene. A. S. Wheeler.

S. C. OGBURN, JR. The Analytical Reactions and a Scheme of Separation of the Platinum Metals. J. M. Bell.

1927   B. G. CARSON. Bromination of Naphthazarine. A. S. Wheeler.

S. C. COLLINS. Study of Ammonia Complexes of Lithium Chloride. F. K. Cameron.

L. F. P. CUTLAR. New Derivatives of 2-Amino-5-bromo-p-cymene. A. S. Wheeler.

1928   R. W. BOST. Para-cymylene-2,5-diamine. A. S. Wheeler.

W. M. LOFTON, JR. Emulsification of Tars and Asphalts. F. C. Vilbrandt.

H. G. PICKETT. The Sulfur Factor in the Synthetic Methanol Reaction. F. C. Vilbrandt.

1929   W. M. MEBANE. The Solubility of the Phosphates of Calcium in Aqueous Solutions of Sulfur Dioxide. J. T. Dobbins.

Ph.D.
1929 R. D. NORTON. Grignard Reactions in the Paracymene Series. A. S. Wheeler.

1930 D. R. ERGLE. The Bromination of 1,5-dihydroxynaphthalene. A. S. Wheeler.

J. B. GALLENT. The Composition of Satin White. F. H. Edmister.

R. A. LINEBERRY. The Ceramic Properties of Certain North Carolina Clays. F. K. Cameron.

1931 G. G. ALBRITTON. A Comparison of the Behavior of the Tartrate and Oxalate Solutions of Columbium and Tantalum Oxides. F. H. Edmister.

R. M. BYRD. A Study of the Soda-Alum System and a Volumetric Method of Determining Sodium. J. T. Dobbins.

A. E. HUGHES. The Action of Sulphur Dioxide on the Phosphates of Calcium. F. K. Cameron.

H. A. LJUNG. A System of Qualitative Analysis for the Anions. J. T. Dobbins.

W. J. MATTOX. The Chlorination of 1,5-dihydroxynaphthalene. A. S. Wheeler.

J. P. SANDERS. The System: Lithium Sulphate-Aluminum Sulphate-Water and Quantitative Determination of Sulphate, Aluminum and Lithium. J. T. Dobbins.

1932 M. W. CONN. Synthesis of Certain Thiophanes and Their Behavior in Hydrocarbon Solutions. R. W. Bost.

T. L. KING. The Nitration of 2,6-Dibromo-1,5-dihydroxynaphthalene. A. S. Wheeler.

1933 JACOB ADDLESTONE. A Study of the Soda-Alum System. J. T. Dobbins.

B. L. JOHNSON. A Study of the Aging of Rubber. F. K. Cameron.

1934 D. J. BRAWLEY. The System: PbO_2-$PbSO_4$-H_2SO_4-H_2O. H. D. Crockford.

A. T. CLIFFORD. A Study of Cellulose from Various Sources by Means of X-Rays and Darkfield Microscopy. F. K. Cameron.

E. W. CONSTABLE. The Diverse Equilibrium Behavior of Ferric Sulfate. (First Report). F. K. Cameron.

Ph.D.

1934 J. N. LECONTE. Some Quinoline Derivatives from 2-Amino-p-cymene. A. S. Wheeler.

S. D. SUMMERFORD. Studies in Agitation: The Suspension of Sand in Water. A. M. White.

J. O. TURNER. The Identification and Uses of Mercaptans and Disulfides. R. W. Bost.

1935 H. O. FARR, JR. Activity Coefficients of Lead Chloride in Solutions of Barium Nitrate: An Investigation Concerning the Debye-Hückel Ion Size Parameter. H. D. Crockford.

1936 A. L. ALEXANDER. Some Chemical Compounds Obtained from the Destructive Distillation of Tobacco. R. W. Bost.

DAN FORE, JR. A Study of the Reactions of Organic Disulfides, with Particular Reference to Their Detection and Determination. R. W. Bost.

A. R. MACORMAC. Utilization of the Whole Cotton Plant, Extraction of Oil and Making of Pulp. F. K. Cameron.

H. A. TANNER. Some Studies of Porous Metal Membranes. Edward Mack.

L. C. THOMAS. A Study of the Soda-Alum System. J. T. Dobbins.

W. W. WILLIAMS. A Study of the Methods of Formation and Properties of Aliphatic Sulfonic Acids. R. W. Bost.

1937 H. L. EDWARDS. A Scheme of Qualitative Analysis Involving the Use of Organic Reagents. J. T. Dobbins.

J. K. HODGES. The Sulfonation of Certain Aliphatic Hydrocarbons. R. W. Bost.

J. C. LOFTIN. The Activity Coefficients of Lead Chloride in Aqueous Solutions of Mannitol: An Investigation of the Ion Size Parameter. H. D. Crockford.

N. L. SIMMONS. The Precise Measurement of Gas Viscosities by the Oscillating Disk Method. Edward Mack.

J. H. WOOD. A Study of the Action of Inorganic Sulphides upon Aldehydes and Related Compounds. R. W. Bost.

1938 M. E. KAPP. A Semi-micro Scheme of Qualitative Analysis for the Anions. J. T. Dobbins.

CHEMISTRY

Ph.D.

1938 S. B. KNIGHT. The Decomposition of Ammonium-Deuterium Chloride. E. C. Markham.

G. C. KYKER. A Study of the Preparation and Properties of 6-Halogen Substituted Carvacrylamines and Derivatives. R. W. Bost.

DAVID MILNE. The Growing and Processing of Whole Cotton. F. K. Cameron.

P. M. NICHOLES, JR. Activity Coefficients of Lead Chloride in Aqueous Solutions: An Investigation Concerning the Effect of Temperature on the Debye-Hückel Ion Size Parameter. H. D. Crockford.

J. A. SOUTHERN. A Semi-micro Scheme of Qualitative Analysis. J. T. Dobbins.

1939 W. F. BARTZ. The Action of Aqueous Sulfur Dioxide on the Oxides of Aluminum, Iron, and on Minerals Containing Them. F. K. Cameron.

BERNARD BERGER. The Autoxidation and Gum-forming Tendencies of Certain Hydrocarbons. R. W. Bost.

P. H. BURDETT. The Influence of Electrolytes on the Ballo-electric Effect (with Special Consideration of Textile Mill Wastes). F. K. Cameron.

B. R. CLANTON. The Flotation of Colloidal Suspensions (with Special Consideration of Textile Mill Wastes). F. K. Cameron.

S. F. CLARK. A Synthetic Approach to the Constitution of Natural Tannins. Alfred Russell.

J. E. EVERETT. Studies on Certain Thiocarbonyl and Sulfonium Compounds. R. W. Bost.

G. C. HOLROYD. Direct Processing of Whole Cotton. F. K. Cameron.

P. H. LATIMER, JR. Preparation of Certain Aliphatic Sulfonic Acids and Their Derivatives. R. W. Bost.

W. W. OWEN. The Permeability of Regenerated Cellulose Film to Carbon Dioxide. Edward Mack.

1940 W. G. SINK. Voltage Studies of the Lead-Acid Storage Cell. H. D. Crockford.

A. P. SLEDD. The Synthesis of 2-iso-Propyl-5-methyl-sulfanilamide and Some of Its Derivatives. R. W. Bost.

Ph.D.
1940   L. C. SURPRENANT. Concentration of Sulfur Black Dyes by Froth Flotation (with Special Consideration of Textile Mill Waste.) F. K. Cameron.

S. A. WIDEMAN. Activities of Sulfuric Acid in Water, Water Ethanol Mixtures, and in Ethanol. H. D. Crockford.

1941   E. R. ANDREWS. Some New Alkyl and Alkamine Esters of Phenylthiocarbamic Acid. R. W. Bost.

E. M. BEAVERS. Factors Influencing the Flocculation and Precipitation of Bentonite Hydrosols. F. K. Cameron.

C. V. CANNON. The Photolysis of Azomethane. O. K. Rice.

E. G. COBB. Constitution of Natural Tannins: Coloring Matters Derived from o-Hydroxyacetophenone, m-Hydroxyacetophenone, and p-Hydroxyacetophenone. Alfred Russell.

G. F. DEEBEL. Some Derivatives of the Isomeric Nitro- and Amino-benzene Sulfonic Acids. R. W. Bost.

J. W. DUCKETT. Some New N^1-Isocyclic-Sulfanilamides. R. W. Bost.

H. C. GULLEDGE. Synthesis of Vicinal Substituted Resorcinols. Alfred Russell.

W. L. HADEN, JR. An Investigation of the Photolysis of Acetaldehyde in Intermittent Light. O. K. Rice.

W. B. HAPPOLDT. Coloring Matters Derived from Anthracene-9-aldehyde. Alfred Russell.

J. H. LANGSTON. Studies in Sulfone Formation. R. W. Bost.

LEE LEISERSON. The Relationship of Molecular Structure to Wetting Activity. R. W. Bost.

H. C. SCHULTZE. Sulfonium Derivatives of Omega Halogenated Ketones. R. W. Bost.

1942   H. A. BERNHARDT. The Determination of the Entropy of Certain Ions by E.M.F. Measurements. H. D. Crockford.

G. B. BUTLER. Preparation of Polyhydroxybenzophenones and Related Compounds. Alfred Russell.

J. R. FRYE. Synthesis of Certain Polyhydroxychalcones. Alfred Russell.

Ph.D.

1942   R. L. KENYON. Synthetic Tanning Materials: Condensation Products of Sulfonated Alkyl Dihydroxy Diphenyl Sulfones with Formaldehyde. Alfred Russell.

L. B. LOCKHART, JR. The Oxidation of Unsaturated Hydrocarbons by Molecular Oxygen at Elevated Temperature and Pressure. R. W. Bost.

V. L. SIMRIL. The Sorption of Water Vapor by Polymers. S. E. Smith.

C. P. TEBEAU. Heteropoly Salts of Columbium and Tantalum.' F. H. Edmister.

1943   W. F. AREY. A Study of the Preparation and Properties of Polychlorinated Aryl Ethers. R. W. Bost.

D. L. COOK. Some Physical and Chemical Properties of Ketene and Ketene Dimer. O. K. Rice.

A. H. GERMANY. The Nitration of Acenaphthene and Related Compounds. R. W. Bost.

E. A. KACZKA. The Toxic Principles of *Ichthyomethia piscipula* (Jamaica Dogwood). Alfred Russell.

J. A. KRYNITSKY. A Study of the Preparations and Properties of Some Highly Chlorinated Hydrocarbons. R. W. Bost.

F. S. PERKERSON. A Study of the Problem of Bonding Rubber to Cellulose Fibers. F. K. Cameron.

A. C. SANTORA. A Study of the Factors Affecting the Alkylation of Naphtalene. R. W. Bost.

J. C. SPECK. The Acyloin Condensations: Formation of the Aliphatic Acyloins and Reactions of the Related Alpha Diketones. R. W. Bost.

W. G. TEBBENS, JR. Chemical Constitution and the Tanning Effect. Alfred Russell.

LOCKE WHITE, JR. Part I. The Thermal Reaction of Hexafluoroethane in Quartz; Part II. The Validity and Application of the Wells and Gerke Method of Particle Size Determination in Aerosols. O. K. Rice.

1944   L. A. BASS. Reactions of Polyhydroxybenzophenones with Metal Ions. J. T. Dobbins.

W. T. DYE, JR. A Study of the Hydrolytic Stability of Organic Halogenated Compounds. R. W. Bost.

Dissertations and Theses

Ph.D.

1944
J. L. TAYLOR. The Isolation and Identification of Tannins Present in Domestic Dwarf Sumac (*Rhus copallina* L. Alfred Russell.

E. E. TOWELL. The Action of Aromatic Ortho-Diamines with Alpha-Diketones. R. W. Bost.

T. S. TUTWILER. Investigation of the Properties of Synthetic Organic Ion-Exchange Resins. Alfred Russell.

1945
E. S. GILREATH. A Semi-micro Scheme of Qualitative Analysis for the Cations without the Use of Hydrogen Sulfide. J. T. Dobbins.

J. F. MASI. Hydrogen-Ion Activities and Spectrophotometric Indicator Constants in Mixed Solvents. S. B. Knight.

J. W. NOWELL. The Permeabilities of Cellophane Film to Various Gases. Sherman Smith.

O. D. SHREVE. The Polarographic Reduction of p-Nitro-aniline in Aqueous-Ethanol Media. E. C. Markham.

LITTLETON UPSHUR, JR. The Influence of Isomerism on Surface Activity. R. W. Bost.

M.A.

1902
*J. W. TURRENTINE. Preparation of Pure Praseodymium Compounds and the Behavior of Some of Them.

1903
*I. F. HARRIS. Nucleic Acid of the Wheat Embryo.

*RESTON STEVENSON. Neodymium: Its Purification and Its Nature.

1904
*R. A. LICHTENTHAELER. (No title available.)

1905
V. C. DANIELS. Trichlorhydroxyethylidene-Alpha-naphthylamine and Trichlorhydroxyethylidene-Beta-naphthylamine; Also, An Investigation of the Action of Chloral upon Dimethylaniline in the Presence of Zinc Chloride.

1906
*G. A. JOHNSON. Study of the Oleoresins from American Conifers.

E. E. RANDOLPH. (No title available.)

1907
*F. P. DRANE. Oxygen Absorption of Turpentine.

*STROWD JORDAN. (No title available.)

*J. E. POGUE, JR. Comparative Study of Resin and Oleoresin from *Pinus heterophylla* and *Pinus palustris*.

---
* Master of Science.

M.A.
1910   E. J. Newell. Further Application of the Specific Gravity Method for the Determination of Oil in the Cotton-Seed Products.

1911   *Hampden Hill. Effects of Ammonia and of Hydrochloric Acid on Ethyl-phospho-platino-chloride.

T. P. Nash, Jr. Composition of the Resine of *Pinus heterophylla*.

C. S. Venable. Composition of Fused Kauri Copal as Used in the Manufacture of Varnish.

1912   J. T. Dobbins. Action of Ammonia on Arsenic Triiodide.

W. L. Jeffries. Further Studies on the Chemical Composition of Cooked Kauri Copal.

*C. W. Willard. (No title available.)

1913   *J. O. Graham. Isoprene from Pine Oil, and Volatile Oil of *Pinus serotina*.

*B. H. Knight. Distillation of Cottonseed Oil at Very Low Pressure.

L. E. Stacy, Jr. Certain Benzylidine Anthranilic Acids and their Oxazines.

1914   *C. B. Carter. Dammer Resin and Its Constituents.

*V. A. Coulter. Further Studies on the Resine of *Pinus heterophylla*.

*L. B. Rhodes. Further Studies on Hydrojuglon.

*W. A. Rudisill. The Heat of Mixing Liquids.

1917   *T. M. Andrews. Condensation with p-Bromphenyl-semicarbazine.

*F. R. Blaylock. An Oxybenzoate and Oxysalicylate Compound of Zirconium.

1919   *I. W. Smithey. Certain Zirconyl Oxyhalogen Compounds. F. P. Venable.

1920   *I. V. Giles. Some Derivatives of p-Cymene. A. S. Wheeler.

*D. H. Jackson. Preparation and Analysis of Anhydrous Zirconium Sulfate, and the Effect of Time, Temperature and Concentration upon the Rate of Hydrolysis of Zirconium Sulfate and Oxychloride. F. P. Venable.

*Ernest Neiman. Bromination of 2-Nitro-p-cymene. A. S. Wheeler.

---
* Master of Science.

DISSERTATIONS AND THESES

M.A.

1920 S. C. SMITH. Action of Basic Reagents on Schiff's Base: New Complex Ethers Obtained by the Interaction of Chloral with the Nitroanilines and Alcohols. A. S. Wheeler.

1921 *P. R. DAWSON. Derivatives of Dichlorojuglone, 2,8-Dichloro-5-Hydroxy-Alpha-Napthoquinone. A. S. Wheeler.

*H. M. TAYLOR. An Investigation of the Residual Kelp Oils. A. S. Wheeler.

1922 *F. P. BROOKS. Condensation of Acetonyl Acetone with Phenylsemicarbazine. A. S. Wheeler.

*BARNETTE NAIMAN. Derivatives of 2-Bromo-5-hydroxy-1, 4-napthoquinone. A. S. Wheeler.

A. P. SLEDD. The Constitution of Oxyjuglone. A. S. Wheeler.

1923 *J. A. BENDER. A New Ketone Reagent: p-Bromophenylsemicarbazide. A. S. Wheeler.

*E. W. CONSTABLE. The Bromination of 2-Amino-p-Xylene. A. S. Wheeler.

*H. D. CROCKFORD. Determination of the Latent Heat of Various Nitrotoluenes. J. M. Bell.

W. E. GILES. Thermal Evaluation of the By-Product Coke Industry. F. C. Vilbrandt.

*J. L. McEWEN. New Derivatives of Dichlorojuglone, 2,3-Dichloro-5-Hydroxy-Alpha-Napthoquinone. A. S. Wheeler.

*E. O. MOEHLMANN. The Behavior of Acetylacetone with Phenylsemicarbazine. A. S. Wheeler.

*H. G. PICKETT. Study of the Nitration of Orthonitrotoluene. J. M. Bell.

*W. B. SMOOT. Electromotive Force Measurements with Solutions of Hydrochloric Acid Containing Mercuric Chloride and Potassium Chloride, Either or Both. J. M. Bell.

1924 R. W. BOST. Tolylsemicarbazide and Certain Derivatives. A. S. Wheeler.

H. A. DICKERT. Oxidation of Sulphur Dioxide with Potassium Permanganate. F. C. Vilbrandt.

*E. DeW. JENNINGS. The Action of Dichloro-acetic and Trichloro-acetic Acid on Amines. A. S. Wheeler.

---

* Master of Science.

M.A.

1924   MILDRED MORSE. The Chlorination of 2-Amino-p-Xylene and New Azo Dyes. A. S. Wheeler.

J. H. MOURANE. Action of Arsenic Trichloride on Diethylaniline. J. T. Dobbins.

1925   *R. M. BYRD. The Instability of Lubricating Oil. F. C. Vilbrandt.

*R. A. LINEBERRY. A Manufacturing Study of North Carolina Brick Clays. F. C. Vilbrandt.

*G. M. MURPHY. The Basic Copper Sulfates. J. M. Bell.

*K. B. PERINE. The Electrometric Titration of Copper and Zinc. J. M. Bell.

T. T. WALKER. 4-m-Nitrophenylsemicarbazide, a Ketone Reagent. A. S. Wheeler.

1926   JACOB ADDLESTONE. An Electrometric Study of the Reaction between Copper Sulfate and Sodium Hydroxide. J. M. Bell.

B. G. CARSON. Bromination of Naphthazarine. A. S. Wheeler.

*W. H. LEMMOND, JR. Certain Iodo Derivatives of Para-Cymene. A. S. Wheeler.

W. M. LOFTIN, JR. Combustible and Non-combustible Lubricating Oils. F. C. Vilbrandt.

*W. M. MEBANE. The Classification of Cotton by Microscopy. F. C. Vilbrandt.

A. R. SMITH. Substitution of Sodium Compounds for Potassium Compounds. F. C. Vilbrandt.

1927   L. A. BASS. The Quantitative Separation of Asphaltic from Non-asphaltic Bodies in Lubricating Oils. F. C. Vilbrandt.

J. B. BULLITT, JR. The Potentiometric Estimation of Copper, Lead, and Zinc. J. T. Dobbins.

K. H. CRUTCHFIELD. A Study of Unsaturation in Oils. F. C. Vilbrandt.

J. E. DAVENPORT. Stabilization of Hydrogen Peroxide Bleaching Liquors. J. T. Dobbins.

E. S. GILREATH. Action of Sulfur Dioxide on Phosphate Rock. J. T. Dobbins.

A. R. GREENE. The Reclamation of Used Crank-Case Oil. F. C. Vilbrandt.

---

* Master of Science.

DISSERTATIONS AND THESES

M.A.

1927   J. D. McCluer. The Electrometric Titration of Nickel Solutions. H. D. Crockford.

Gladys Morgan. I. A Study of the Esterfication of 3,5-Dibromoanthranilic Acid; II. A Study of 2-Amino-5-chloro-p-cymene Hydrochloride and Its Coupling with Other Amines. F. C. Vilbrandt.

1928   C. E. Anding, Jr. Reduction of 2,6-Dinitro-p-cymene and the Action of Aldehydes on Meta-Diamines Particularly Para-cymylene-2,6-diamine. A. S. Wheeler.

*A. T. Clifford. The System: Lime-Arsenic Oxide-Water at 25 C. F. K. Cameron.

*F. W. Davis. The Winning of Caesium from Its Ore. F. C. Vilbrandt.

J. O. Dunston. Color and Odor Constituents in Menhaden Oil. F. C. Vilbrandt.

*D. R. Ergle. Juglone Studies. A. S. Wheeler.

*J. B. Gallent. The Potentiometric Titration of Fluorine. H. D. Crockford.

*O. B. Hager. Electrometric Studies of the System Indigo-Indigo White. H. D. Crockford.

*H. A. Ljung. Reduction of Nitro-Compounds. J. T. Dobbins.

Andrew Murphy. North Carolina Oil Shale Investigation. F. C. Vilbrandt.

*W. B. Sellars. Acid Mercerization of Cotton. F. C. Vilbrandt.

*R. E. Thomas. Behavior of 5-Bromo-meta-4-xylidine. A. S. Wheeler.

*F. W. Zur Burg. Studies of the Binary Systems of Some Nitrotoluenes with Calculations for the Heats of Fusion of the Components. H. D. Crockford.

1929   *W. V. Harshman. A Study of the Iodometric Process of Analytical Analysis, Especially in Relation to the Determination of Hydrogen Sulfide. F. H. Edmister.

*G. C. Holroyd. The Action of Benzoylacetone on 4-Phenylsemicarbazide. A. S. Wheeler.

*A. E. Hughes. The Binary Systems of Some Nitrotoluenes with Benzoic Acid. H. D. Crockford.

---

* Master of Science.

M.A.

1929 *S. M. MARTIN, JR. The Effect of Benzoic and Acetic Acids on the Freezing Point of Benzene. J. M. Bell.

W. J. MATTOX. Toluene-4-carbithioic Acid and Certain Derivatives. R. W. Bost.

J. G. PARK. p-Cymyl-4-semicarbazide-2 and Certain Derivatives. A. S. Wheeler.

*C. L. THOMAS. Para-cymylhydrazine-2 and Derivatives. A. S. Wheeler.

E. R. WARD. The Solubility of Ferrous Sulphate in Aqueous Solutions of Sulphuric Acid. F. K. Cameron.

1930 *R. F. ABERNETHY. The Chemical Constitution of Shrimp Oil. F. C. Vilbrandt.

*E. M. CHAPIN. The System: Oxalic Acid-Hydrochloric Acid-Water. J. M. Bell.

M. W. CONN. Preparation and Properties of Certain Thiophanes. R. W. Bost.

E. E. HUFFMAN. Pressure Factor in Mercerization. F. C. Vilbrandt.

J. B. JOYNER. The Effect of Equipment Composition in Water Analysis. F. C. Vilbrandt.

*T. L. KING. Some Reactions of p-Cymylhydrazine-2. A. S. Wheeler.

C. R. MCLELLAN. 6-Nitro-2-amino-p-cymene and Certain Derivatives. A. S. Wheeler.

*HAYWOOD PARKER, JR. Iodine Compounds in *Penaeus setiferus*. F. C. Vilbrandt.

*J. H. SANDERS. Color Factors in Cottonseed Oil. F. C. Vilbrandt.

W. F. SMITH. 4-p-Tolylthiosemicarbazide and Certain Derivatives. R. W. Bost.

*W. W. WILLIAMS. Cyclohexyl-carbithioic Acid and Certain Derivatives. R. W. Bost.

1931 H. R. BAKER. Synthesis and Reactions of Tin Tetra-p-Tolyl. R. W. Bost.

*R. H. BELCHER. The Preparation and Properties of Certain Mixed Sulfides. R. W. Bost.

S. C. CUBBAGE. 2-Iodo- and 3-Iodo-para-cymene. A. S. Wheeler.

---

* Master of Science.

M.A.
1931 *J. P. Dosier. 5-Bromo-para-cymylhydrazine-2 and Certain Derivatives. A. S. Wheeler.

*G. H. Fleming, Jr. The Distribution of Sulfur in the Coking of North Carolina Coal. A. M. White.

*T. W. Richmond. The Removal of the Last Traces of Iron from Aqueous Sulfate Solutions. F. K. Cameron.

*Mrs. E. P. Stevens. A Chemical Analysis of *Ipomoea pandurata*. A. S. Wheeler.

J. O. Turner. A Study of Para-Phenylphenacyl Bromide and Dinitro-Chlorobenzene and Their Reactions with Mercaptans. R. W. Bost.

1932 *A. L. Alexander. The Synthesis and Application of New Dyes from 3-Nitro-4-amino-Biphenyl. R. W. Bost.

*D. J. Brawley. The System: $CuSO_4$-$CoSO_4$-H_2O. H. D. Crockford.

*T. B. Douglas. The Free Energy of Ionization of Certain Sulfur-Substituted Acids in Aqueous Solution at 25° Centigrade. H. D. Crockford.

C. V. Harrill. The Chlorination of Para-Cymylene-2, 6-diamine. A. S. Wheeler.

*R. H. Munch. The Vapor Pressures of Certain Ethers and Thioethers. H. D. Crockford.

*H. C. Thomas. The Activity Coefficient of Lead Chloride in Solutions of Cadmium Nitrate. H. D. Crockford.

1933 *W. H. Baskerville. Physico-chemical Characteristics of Iron Precipitates from Aqueous Sulfuric Acid Solutions. F. K. Cameron.

J. M. Early. The Chlorination of 2-Nitro-p-cymene: Studies on 2-cymidine-5-sulfonic Acid with the Preparation of Certain New Azo Dyes. A. S. Wheeler.

*J. C. Loftin. The Decomposition Potentials of Certain Fluorine Compounds. H. D. Crockford.

*G. M. Oliver. Effect of Phosphates upon the Volumetric Method of Determining Sodium. J. T. Dobbins.

*S. D. Sumerford. Studies in Agitation: The Suspension of Sand in Water. A. M. White.

---
* Master of Science.

M.A.
1933 *L. C. THOMAS. A Volumetric Determination of Sulfate Using Organic Reagents. J. T. Dobbins.

1934 A. C. AYCOCK. The Chemical Composition of *Melia Azedarach*. R. W. Bost.

*J. K. COLEHOUR. The Determination of Potassium by Means of Perrhenic Acid. J. T. Dobbins.

*H. L. EDWARDS. Pyridine as a Precipitant for Certain Metallic Ions in Qualitative Analysis. J. T. Dobbins.

DAN FORE, JR. The Chemical Composition of the Oleaginous Constituent of *Melia Azedarach*. R. W. Bost.

R. E. GEE, JR. The Action of 2,4-Dinitrochlorobenzene on Sodium Alcoholates. R. W. Bost.

*F. W. GRANT. Solubility Relationships in the System: K_2SO_4-$CoSO_4$-H_2O at Low Temperatures. H. D. Crockford.

*E. O. HUFFMAN. Recovery of Values from Alunite. F. K. Cameron.

1935 *C. C. HUDSON. Ferric and Ferrous Sulphates in Aqueous Solutions. F. K. Cameron.

*J. E. HUNTER, JR. The Effects of Ferric Sulphate on Aqueous Solutions of Ammonium Sulphate at 25 C. F. K. Cameron.

*W. F. HUNTER, JR. The Destructive Distillation of Peanut Hulls. R. W. Bost.

*W. R. JOHNSTON. The Chemistry of Tobacco and Tobacco Tar. R. W. Bost.

*P. M. NICHOLES, JR. The Photochemical Decomposition of Carbon Disulphide. H. D. Crockford.

*D. A. PICKLER. Ferric and Potassium Sulphates in Aqueous Solution. F. K. Cameron.

*S. A. WIDEMAN. The Dissociation Constant of the Indicator Cymyl-Orange. H. D. Crockford.

1936 E. B. MCDEARMAN. A Study of the Soda-Alum System. J. T. Dobbins.

*C. A. PIGOTT. Certain New Azo Dyes Derived from 2-Amino-p-cymene. R. W. Bost.

*W. B. RICHARDSON. The Nitration of 1,5-Dihydroxynaphthalene. R. W. Bost.

---

* Master of Science.

DISSERTATIONS AND THESES

M.A.

1937
*S. B. KNIGHT. The Composition of the Triple Sodium Uranyl Acetates of Zinc and Cadmium and Their Reaction with Sodium Hydroxide: The Determination of Sodium. J. T. Dobbins.

*W. A. PERRY. Flotation of Metal Oxides from Aqueous Suspensions. F. K. Cameron.

R. H. WILLIAMS. The Extraction and Utilization of Nicotine from Tobacco Waste. R. W. Bost.

1939
R. C. HARRIS. The Action of Halogens on Certain Allyl Compounds. R. W. Bost.

J. H. LANGSTON. Some Derivatives of Thiosalicylic Acid. R. W. Bost.

W. L. MAULDIN. The Synthesis of gamma-Ethyl and gamma-n-Propyl Resorcinol. Alfred Russell.

*E. P. H. MEIBOHM. A Study of the Chain Photolysis of Acetaldehyde by the Rotating Sector Method. O. K. Rice.

*B. D. WEBB. Derivatives of 4,4'-Dihydroxydiphenyldimethylmethane. Alfred Russell.

1940
G. L. CHURCH. Reactions of Atomic Hydrogen. F. H. Edmister.

Y. J. DICKERT. Mixed Acetic Anhydrides in the Friedel-Crafts Reaction. J. W. Williams.

B. G. HAWKES. Some Derivatives of p-Thiophenetidin. R. W. Bost.

T. R. KIMBROUGH. The Inclusion of Four Rarer Elements in a Scheme of Qualitative Analysis Involving the Use of Organic Reagents. E. C. Markham.

LEE LEISERSON. The Addition of Molecular Oxygen to Cyclohexene. R. W. Bost.

F. T. LENSE, JR. The Application of Organic Compounds to Analytical Chemistry. J. T. Dobbins.

R. S. LEOPOLD. The Preparation of Mercury Derivatives of Some of the Acid Amides. J. W. Williams.

G. J. SHUGAR. The Synthesis of Some of the Polyhydroxy Chalcones and Anthocyanidins. Alfred Russell.

C. J. STARNES. The Preparations of Certain Derivatives of Thiophene. R. W. Bost.

---

* Master of Science.

CHEMISTRY

M.A.

1940   C. H. WITTEN. The Preparation of Aldehydes from Anilides. J. W. Williams.

1941   JOHN APPELDOORN. The Photolysis of Azomethane. O. K. Rice

HANNAH BOYLAN. A Revision of Several Semimicro Tests for the Anions. J. T. Dobbins.

MRS. WEN-HSIEN W. CHEN. Cellulose in Cotton and Certain Tree Growths. F. K. Cameron.

L. J. CONRAD. Para-Bromophenylisothiocyanate and Certain New Thiourethanes. R. W. Bost.

J. D. MARTONE. Para-Nitrophenylisothiocyanate and Certain New Thiourethanes. R. W. Bost.

E. L. POWELL. The Extraction and Clarification of Oil from Whole Cotton. F. K. Cameron.

1942   G. C. AID. The Action of 5,5-Dimethylcyclohexanedione-1,3 on Aldehydes. R. W. Bost.

J. D. FLEMING. The Characteristics of Cellulose Pulps from Whole Cotton and Its Components. F. K. Cameron.

M. L. HUCKABEE. The Dyeing Properties of Some Natural Coloring Matters. Alfred Russell.

*F. H. RUSSELL. Application of Organic Reagents in the Identification of Calcium and Strontium Ions. J. T. Dobbins.

E. N. STIREWALT. The Action of 2,2,4-Trimethylpentene on Naphthalene in the Presence of Aluminum Chloride. R. W. Bost.

J. M. WALLACE, JR. The Surface Activity of Certain Sodium Aryl Sulfonates. R. W. Bost.

1943   L. M. ADDISON. An Investigation of the Reaction between m-Dinitrobenzene and Potassium Cyanide in the Presence of Various Alcohols. Alfred Russell.

A. W. BAZEMORE. The Condensation of Butanedione-2,3 with Aromatic Aldehydes. R. W. Bost.

J. A. ESTES. A Search for Water Soluble Reagents for Nickel. J. T. Dobbins.

C. B. PARK. The Sulfonates of Certain Alkyl-Aryl Ethers. R. W. Bost.

1944   S. S. CODY. Synthetic Tanning Materials: Condensation Products of Polyhydric Phenols and Aromatic Aldehydes. Alfred Russell.

---
* Master of Science.

DISSERTATIONS AND THESES

M.A.

1944   F. McI. DEGGES. Some Derivatives of Beta-Naphthol. R. W. Bost.

C. R. VANNEMAN. The Synthesis of Polyesters of p-Hydroxybenzoic Acid with Certain Monosaccharides. Alfred Russell.

F. M. WRIGHT. A Study of Some Compounds of Phenoxathiin. Arthur Roe.

1945   *G. K. KING. Some Studies on 2,3-Dimethylquinoxaline. R. W. Bost.

D. M. ROESEL. Activity Coefficients of Hydrochloric Acid in Ethylene Glycol-Water Solutions. S. B. Knight.

DEPARTMENT OF CLASSICS

Ph.D.

1890   W. J. BATTLE. (No title available.)

1898   T. J. WILSON, JR. Genitive of Quality and Ablative of Quality in Latin.

1914   G. K. G. HENRY. The Characters of Terence.

1929   M. H. GRIFFIN. The Administration of the Roman Province of Cappadocia. G. A. Harrer.

E. P. WILLARD, JR. Seneca as a Source for Information on the Early Caesars. G. A. Harrer.

1931   P. M. CHEEK. Vergil's Treatment of the *Templum* in the *Aeneid*. Geo. Howe.

K. DE R. MEARES. Literary Patronage in the Silver Age of Latin Literature. G. A. Harrer.

1932   L. E. AUSTIN. A Study of the Characters in Cicero's Dialogues, Emphasizing the Principles of Character Selection. G. A. Harrer.

VAN C. ELLIOTT. Roman Senators in the Time of Hadrian and Antoninus Pius. G. A. Harrer.

LAURINE HAYNES. The Collation of a Manuscript of Cicero's *De officiis* in the Library of the University of North Carolina. G. A. Harrer.

E. B. JENKINS. Index of Terence. George Howe and G. A. Harrer.

M. J. SMITH. Fear of Eastern Influences in Roman Life as Expressed in Latin Literature of the Republic. George Howe.

---

* Master of Science.

CLASSICS

Ph.D.

1936	MARY DIGGS. Roman Literary Men in the *Noctes Atticae* of Aulus Gellius. G. A. Harrer.
	A. I. SUSKIN. The Arrangement of Material in Livy, Books 31-45. G. A. Harrer.
1938	B. W. DAVIS. The Administration of the Roman Province of Crete and Cyrenaica. G. A. Harrer.
1941	E. L. WAY. Seneca as a Source for Tacitus, Suetonius, and Dio. G. A. Harrer.
1943	B. T. MOSS. Sextus Aurelius Victor—*Liber de Caesaribus*: A Translation and Commentary (with Introduction and Notes). G. A. Harrer.
1945	F. B. NIMS. Cicero's Law-Court Cases. W. E. Caldwell.

M.A.

1883	H. H. WILLIAMS. (No title available.)
1889	W. J. BATTLE. (No title available.)
1890	ST. CLAIR HESTER. (No title available.)
1891	J. E. FORGARTIE. (No title available.)
1894	J. T. PUGH. Comparative Study of the Infinitive in the Satires of Horace and Persius.
1895	H. H. HORNE. Religion and Life.
1896	W. E. DARDEN. (No title available.)
	T. J. WILSON, JR. Grammar of the Scipio Epitaphs.
1897	D. J. CURRIE. (No title available.)
1899	M. P. KENDRICK. Nemesis Idea in Aeschylus: A Study in its Development from the Earliest Poetry of the Greeks.
1900	C. B. DENSON, JR. (No title available.)
1901	D. P. PARKER. Homer: His Real Work.
1902	M. C. BYNUM. Ideals and Ethics of Rome.
1904	W. S. BERNARD. Skopas: The Artist and Man.
	A. E. JONES. Individualism of the Terentian Types of the "Currens Servus."
1905	A. C. WHITEHEAD. The Character of Tiberius as Found in Tacitus.
1910	F. L. BLYTHE. Horace as a Critic of Public Morals.
1917	ELIZABETH BREAZEALE. (No title available.)
1920	M. G. PERRY. Development of the Atellan Farce. George Howe.

Dissertations and Theses

M.A.

1920 L. M. WARD. Episode of the Euryalus and Nisus in the Ninth *Aeneid*. George Howe.

1926 L. E. AUSTIN. Eumenii pro instaurandis scholis oratio: A Translation with Introduction and Notes. G. A. Harrer.

M. H. GRIFFIN. The Roman Governors of Cappadocia from Vespasian to Diocletian. G. A. Harrer.

J. W. HUFF. Mamertini Panegyricus Genethliacus Maximiano Augusto dictus. G. A. Harrer.

K. DE R. MEARES. The Gods of Italy in Virgil's Poetry. George Howe.

1927 J. M. GWYNN. The Personal Relations of Cicero and Caesar (50-49 B. C.). G. A. Harrer.

MRS. M. A. HONEYCUTT. Panegyricus Mamertini Maximiano Augusto dictus: A Translation with Introduction and Notes. G. A. Harrer.

E. B. JENKINS. The Role of Ascanius in the *Aeneid*. George Howe.

S. M. WERTZ. The Juno of the *Aeneid*. George Howe.

1928 P. M. CHEEK. Principles of Arrangement of Material in Tacitus' Major Historical Works. G. A. Harrer.

EVA GENTRY. Ovid's Correspondence with His Wife. George Howe.

LAURINE HAYNES. The Literary Works of Servius Sulpicus Rufus. G. A. Harrer.

F. E. UNDERHILL. Horace and the Early Latin Poets. George Howe.

1929 I. L. BARDEN. The Life and Literary Works of Marcus Caelius Rufus. G. A. Harrer.

VIRGINIA DEAN. Augustus in Contemporary Poetry. G. A. Harrer.

VAN C. ELLIOTT. A Military Diploma of 78 A. D. G. A. Harrer.

RUTH FLEMING. Gaius Trebatius Testa. G. A. Harrer.

M. S. LAWRENCE. Certain Questions of Composition in Ovid's *Heroides*. George Howe.

HORACE NIMS. The Legati of Caesar in Gaul. G. A. Harrer.

M.A.	
1930	S. J. BUSH. Marcus Aemilius Lepidus. G. A. Harrer.
	E. C. KENNEDY. The Reading of Pliny the Younger in the Literature of the Golden Age. George Howe.
	B. T. MOSS. The Structure of the Tenth *Aeneid*. George Howe.
	F. B. NIMS. Virgil's Use of Objects of Art in the *Aeneid*. George Howe.
	M. A. POWELL. The Followers of Aeneas. George Howe.
	HENRIETTA UNDERWOOD. Inscriptional and Palaeographical Evidence on the Addressees of Pliny's *Letters*. G. A. Harrer.
	E. L. WAY. Inscriptional and Literary Evidence on the Subjects of Statius' *Silvae*. G. A. Harrer.
1931	MARTHA BELL. Sketches of Individuals in the *Annals* and *Histories* of Tacitus. G. A. Harrer.
	R. L. RIGLEY. The Augustan Elegists in *Carmina Latina epigraphica*. George Howe.
1932	L. E. FORD. The Women of the *Aeneid*. George Howe.
	I. M. HIXSON. Ovid's Treatment of Medea. George Howe.
	W. J. HOGAN IV. Cicero's Use of Historical Characters in the Orations. G. A. Harrer.
	V. C. MARTIN. Certain Features of Catullus' Style in the First Sixty Poems. George Howe.
	E. R. SMITH. Index verborum *Coniurationis Catilinae* C. Sallusti Crispi. G. A. Harrer.
	A. I. SUSKIN. *De mirabilibus urbis Romae* by Magister Gregorius: A Translation, with Notes, Introduction and Word Study. G. A. Harrer.
1933	FRANCES STANSELL. The Character Anna in Virgil and Ovid. G. A. Harrer.
1934	L. B. PHILLIPS. Character Sketches in the *Catilina* and *Jugurtha*. G. A. Harrer.
	ELIZABETH WHITE. Seneca and Suetonius on the Lives of Caligula and Claudius. G. A. Harrer.
	M. C. WILLIAMS. Transitional Devices in Suetonius' *De vita Caesarum*. G. A. Harrer.

M.A.
1936 M. T. BERNARD. The Identification of the Persons Addressed in Books VI-IX of Pliny's *Letters*. G. A. Harrer.

B. W. DAVIS. A Study of the Personal and Political Relationships of Cicero and Pompey, 52-48 B. C. G. A. Harrer.

J. E. GODWIN. The Cultural Interests of Pliny the Younger. George Howe and G. A. Harrer.

1937 T. M. SIMKINS, JR. Claudii Mamertini Gratiarum actio Iuliano imperatori: A Translation, with Introduction and Notes. G. A. Harrer.

V. B. SIMKINS. Panegyricus Theodosio Augusto, by Latinius Pacatus Drepanius: A Translation with Introduction and Notes. G. A. Harrer and S. G. Sanders.

1938 ELOISE BAYNES. The Commentary of Asconius Pedianus on Cicero's *Pro Milone*. G. A. Harrer.

1939 L. E. BLAND. The Commentary of Asconius Pedianus on Cicero's *In Pisonem*. G. A. Harrer.

1941 J. B. OLIVER. New Inscriptions of the Period of Claudius and Nero. G. A. Harrer.

MARJORIE WHEATHERUP. *Scholia Bobiensia* on Cicero's *Pro Plancio*. G. A. Harrer.

1942 M. V. GILLIAM. The Commentary of Asconius Pedianus on Cicero's *In toga candida*. G. A. Harrer.

M. S. TANNER. Asconius' Commentary on Cicero's *Pro Cornelio*. G. A. Harrer.

DEPARTMENT OF COMPARATIVE LITERATURE
M.A.
1924 M. B. PENN. Comparative Study of the Similes of the *Divine Comedy* and the *Aeneid*. H. R. Huse.

1927 M. C. BLAND. French *Femmes de lettres* before 1600. U. T. Holmes.

J. W. POSEY. Byron and Escheverria. S. E. Leavitt.

M. L. RADOFF. Two Mediaevalists in the French Renaissance, Claude Fauchet and Étienne Pasquier. U. T. Holmes.

1930 B. F. CARPENTER. The Life and Writings of Maistre Wace, an Anglo-Norman Poet of the Twelfth Century. U. T. Holmes.

M.A.
1939   J. B. READ. A Study of the Christian Hebraists in Germany during the First Half of the Sixteenth Century, with Particular Reference to Sebastian Muenster. U. T. Holmes and W. P. Friederich.

1941   K. R. HAYES. The Italo-Celtic Theory. G. S. Lane.

1942   M. F. MUNCH. The Transmission of the Greek Alphabet to the Romans: A Survey of the Research. G. S. Lane.

1943   EDUARDO AMAYA-VALENCIA. The Tocharian Version of *The Lionmakers* and *The Painter and the Mechanical Girl*. G. S. Lane.

DEPARTMENT OF DRAMATIC ART

M.A.
1937   G. W. BERNHART. From Heaven Down: A Play of Domestic Relations. Samuel Selden.

F. M. DURHAM. Like Foolish Prophets: A Satirical Play of a University Reformer. F. H. Koch.

B. DuBOSE HAMER. Funeral Flowers for the Bride: A Comedy of Mountain People in Three Acts. F. H. Koch.

J. M. NIGGLI. Singing Valley: A Comedy of Mexican Village Life. Samuel Selden.

J. W. PARKER. Itching Heel: A Play of Negro Life in Eastern North Carolina. F. H. Koch.

WILLIAM PEERY. 13 Piccadilly Terrace: A Play of Byron, the Chameleon. F. H. Koch.

WALTER SPEARMAN. Free Indeed: A Play in Ten Scenes. F. H. Koch.

D. A. WATTERS. The Modern Approach to Stage Design as Exemplified in the Work of Three Scenic Interpreters of Eugene O'Neill. Samuel Selden.

1938   E. M. CLOUGH. Canned Health: A Modern Farce. Paul Green.

LYNETTE HELDMAN. Gird of the Wilderness. Paul Green.

LOIS LATHAM. A New Heart: A Mountain Play in Three Acts. Paul Green and F. H. Koch.

V. J. LEE, JR. The Last Pagan: A Chronicle Play of Julian the Postate, in Two Parts. F. H. Koch.

L. P. LEGGETTE. The Epigram in the Dramatic Works of Shaw and His Contemporaries, Pinero, Jones, and Wilde. R. B. Sharpe.

M.A.

1938   M. L. SCALES. A Study of Stage Decoration in America between the Years 1840 and 1882, as Described in Contemporary Documents. Samuel Selden.

VIVIAN VEACH. Growing Acres. Paul Green.

J. A. WALKER. Stage Lighting Apparatus in England and America during the Nineteenth Century. Samuel Selden.

1939   R. W. BAILEY. Heaven Ain't Far: A Play of Negro Life in Georgia. Paul Green.

ANNE BOWEN. Lady Gregory's Use of Folk-Lore in Her Plays. R. B. Sharpe and R. S. Boggs.

E. R. BOYLE. Southern Exposure: A Comedy in Three Acts. Paul Green.

H. J. BRABHAM. Some Technical Aspects of the Alternations of Comedy and Seriousness in Shaw and Shakespeare. R. B. Sharpe.

J. L. BROWN. Leave Them Alone. Paul Green.

E. P. CROW. Melissa: A Satiric Comedy. Paul Green.

M. A. DELANEY. Election: A Play of Texas County Politics. Samuel Selden.

R. L. GAULT. Goats: A Middle Western Folk Comedy. Paul Green.

L. N. JONES. "Swappin' Bill" Teeters: A Comedy of the Missouri Ozarks. Paul Green.

F. H. KOCH, JR. Smoky Mountain Road: A Comedy of the Carolina Highlands. Paul Green.

DOROTHY LEWIS. Hope for Justice: A Tragedy of Reform School Life. Paul Green.

K. P. LEWIS. Jed's Lamp: A Tragedy of the Backwoods of Alabama. Paul Green.

F. E. MEYER. Paisley Street: A Cross Section of the Depths of the City. Paul Green.

K. F. MORAN. The Stage Irishman. R. B. Sharpe and A. P. Hudson.

A. E. NOWELL. Yeats as a Poet Dramatist. R. B. Sharpe.

C. E. PASS. George Bernard Shaw and the Realistic Theatre. R. B. Sharpe.

G. M. PHARIS. Dark Harvest: A Tragedy of the Canadian Prairie. Paul Green.

M.A.
1939 L. A. SPARKS. Fair Lady, Whence?—A Comedy. Paul Green.

1940 M. E. ALLEN. Some Considerations of John Synge's Stage Business, Illustrated by a Prompt Scrip of Synge's "Riders to the Sea." R. B. Sharpe.

FLOYD CHILDS. Social Protest in the Plays of Sean O'Casey and Clifford Odets: A Comparison. R. B. Sharpe.

C. H. CRUM. De Promise Lan': A Negro Drama. Paul Green.

RHODA GILMAN. Man of Dreams: A Play of Frontier Heroism in Illinois, 1837. Paul Green.

W. I. LONG. Autumn Leaves: A Tragedy of Eastern North Carolina. Paul Green.

D. B. POPE. Boodle: A Comedy of the Gilded Age. Paul Green.

HOWARD RICHARDSON. Where There's a Will: A Comedy of Life in the French Alps. Paul Green.

F. G. WALSH. An Approach to the Critical Truth Concerning the Plays of Sean O'Casey. R. B. Sharpe.

C. H. WEBB. Torch in the Wind: A Saga Drama of Billy the Kid. Paul Green.

CLEMON WHITE. White Calendar: A Tragedy of Negro Life in West Texas. Paul Green.

1941 E. P. CARR. The Acting Theories of Nine Players Between 1845 and 1900. Samuel Selden.

F. W. GUESS. Kneel for the Dames: A Comedy of Southern Manners. Paul Green.

C. F. KAUFHOLZ. Scaldic Sonata: A Drama of Awakening. Paul Green.

MERLE MCKAY. The Great Republic: A Play in Three Acts. Paul Green.

SANFORD REECE. Eagle's Pinion: A Play in Two Acts with Prologue and Epilogue. Paul Green.

J. T. SALEK. George Bernard Shaw, Music Critic, 1890-1894. F. H. Koch.

F. F. SANDMEL. The Conception and the Creation: A Critical Evaluation of the Work of the Carolina Playmakers. R. B. Sharpe.

M.A.

1941

G. P. WILSON, JR. Grapes are Sometimes Sweet: A Comedy of Contemporary Life in Virginia. Paul Green.

L. H. WISMER. Fundamental Theories behind the Scenery of Six Independent Theatres Between 1887 and 1922. Samuel Selden.

1942

B. L. BOLCE. The Trend Toward Realism in Acting in France, Germany, and Russia from 1887 to 1914. Samuel Selden.

F. F. BUSBY. Proud to be Black: The Biography of a Negro. Paul Green.

VIRGINIA HAYES. The Emerging of the Artist-Director in the English Theatre. Samuel Selden.

F. J. HUNTER. People and Porcupine: A Play of Bad Manners. Paul Green.

EMILIE JOHNSON. Shaw and Money. R. B. Sharpe.

H. E. LOARING-CLARK. The Stage History of Marlowe's Doctor Faustus. R. B. Sharpe.

W. L. MANER, JR. Uncertain Death: A Domestic Comedy of the South. Paul Green.

J. P. NICKELL. Realism in the Dramatic Works of John Millington Synge. R. B. Sharpe.

HILMAR SALLEE. Come out of the Rain: A Realistic Play about Unrealistic People. Paul Green.

S. I. STEIN. Four on a Match. A Musical Comedy. Paul Green.

W. E. WOLFF. Legendary Materials in the Drama of the Irish Renaissance. R. B. Sharpe.

1943

ELIZABETH BLAIR. The Costuming of *Hamlet* from Shakespeare's Time to the Present. Samuel Selden.

K. O. HEIBERG-JURGENSEN. Down to the Sea: A Three Act Play. F. H. Koch.

M. A. SABBAGH. "Melody": A Biographical Drama in Three Acts. F. H. Koch.

L. E. TROTMAN. Storm over Salem: A Drama in Three Acts. F. H. Koch.

1944

T. A. AVERA. Invasion: A Three Act Play. F. H. Koch.

RUTH ONCLEY. A Tree on a Hill: A Play Based on the Early Years of the University of North Carolina. Samuel Selden.

ECONOMICS AND COMMERCE 37

M.A.
1945   MRS. C. J. MARLEY. Flora MacDonald, Preserver of Prince Charles. Samuel Selden.

E. K. SOLEM. The Dance as an Expressive Element in the Plays Produced in the United States from 1932-1944. Samuel Selden.

DEPARTMENT OF ECONOMICS AND COMMERCE

Ph.D.
1927   C. K. BROWN. A State Movement in Railroad Development: The Story of North Carolina's First Effort to Establish an East and West Trunk Line Railroad. C. T. Murchison.

1930   R. C. HON. Railway Efficiency Since 1920. M. S. Heath.

1932   H. L. MACON. A Fiscal History of North Carolina. 1776-1860. Clarence Heer.

1934   S. W. PRESTON. The Influence of Commodity Characteristics, Organizational Forms, and Institutional Environment on Price, as Shown in the Cases of Wheat, Rubber and Coal. C. T. Murchison and E. W. Zimmerman.

1936   F. H. ARNOLD. The Agricultural Adjustment Act as Applied to Cotton: An Example of Crop Control. E. W. Zimmerman.

H. M. DOUTY. The North Carolina Industrial Worker, 1880-1930. H. D. Wolf.

R. S. WINSLOW. A Study of Types of Approach Found in Recent American Economic Literature with Special Reference to the Organic and Pragmatic. M. S. Heath.

1937   E. H. ANDERSON. The Process of Internal Organization. G. T. Schwenning.

B. B. HOLDER. The Three Banks of the State of North Carolina, 1810-1872. J. B. Woosley.

J. B. McFERRIN, JR. Caldwell and Company: A Study in Southern Investment Banking. J. B. Woosley.

M. O. PHILLIPS. Tramp Shipping: Its Changing Position in World Trade. E. W. Zimmerman.

1939   F. H. BUNTING. Federal, State, and Local Relations in the Financing of Relief. Clarence Heer.

B. M. McGHEE. Industrial Development of North Georgia. M. S. Heath.

DISSERTATIONS AND THESES

Ph.D.

1939   F. S. WILDER. Some Regional Variations in Standards of Living. M. S. Heath.

1940   C. P. ANSON. A History of the Labor Movement in West Virginia. H. D. Wolf.

C. H. DONOVAN. The Readjustment of State and Local Fiscal Relations in North Carolina, 1929-1938. Wiley Kilpatrick.

McD. K. HORNE, JR. The Treatment of Seasonal Workers under the Mississippi Unemployment Compensation Law. H. D. Wolf.

O. T. MOUZON. The Social and Economic Implications of Recent Developments Within the Wood Pulp and Paper Industry in the South. E. W. Zimmerman.

1941   J. C. D. BLAINE. The Significance of Air Passenger Traffic on the Domestic Scheduled Airlines of the United States, 1935-1940. M. S. Heath.

C. E. KUHLMAN. Municipally Owned Electric Utilities in North Carolina. Clarence Heer.

FREDERIC MEYERS. The Economic Philosophy of Organized Labor in the United States during the Nineteenth Century. H. D. Wolf.

T. W. WOOD. The Contributions of Frederick W. Taylor to Scientific Personnel Management. G. T. Schwenning.

1942   BRANT BONNER. An Analysis of the Condition of Banks in the Southeast, 1920-1940. J. B. Woosley.

J. W. GUNTER. Factor Analysis of Price Variations. D. J. Cowden.

D. F. MARTIN, JR. An Historical and Analytical Approach to the Current Problems of the American Gum Naval Stores Industry. M. S. Heath.

J. T. MASTEN. The Financial Development of the Commonwealth and Southern Corporation. J. B. Woosley.

RODMAN SULLIVAN. The Inheritance Tax in Kentucky: Its Legal History and Operating Results as Indicated by an Analysis of Inheritance Tax Returns. Clarence Heer.

1944   W. H. JOUBERT. History of Railway Freight Rates in the South. M. S. Heath.

1945   E. M. DOUGLAS. An Analysis of the Retail Trading Area of Charlotte, North Carolina. R. S. Winslow.

M.A.

1909 T. W. DICKSON. Educational Influences of the English Merchant and Craft Guilds.

'1911 T. M. BROADFOOT. Some Rural Economic Problems of the United States.

C. C. FONVILLE. Conservation of the Forests of North Carolina.

SHINJIRO KITASAWA. Industrial Revolutions in England and Japan.

W. F. WARREN. (No title available.)

E. S. WELBORN. (No title available.)

1913 P. H. GWYN, JR. Social Insurance and the Progressive Party.

M. R. INGHRAM. Criticism of the General Property Tax as Administered by State and Local Government.

1914 W. S. COULTER. The State's Regulation of Railways in North Carolina.

T. W. FERGUSON. The Farmer and Cooperation in Wilkes County, North Carolina.

E. J. PERRY. Cooperation and the Work of the Farmer's Union in Wilson County, North Carolina.

R. H. SHUFORD. Cooperative Institutions Among the Farmers of Catawba County, North Carolina.

L. C. WILLIAMS. The Laborer of Carrboro, North Carolina.

1915 C. F. BENBOW. Utilization of North Carolina's Waste Lands.

B. B. HOLDER. Economic and Social Life of the Laborer in Winston-Salem, North Carolina.

C. M. MOORE. Study in Texas Economics: Farming in the Eastern Area of Excess Tenancy.

F. R. YODER. Study in North Carolina Economics: Economic Basis of the Rural Population of North Carolina.

1916 J. C. HARPER. Farm Loans and Interest Rates in North Carolina.

1917 F. F. ALLEN. Catawba County, North Carolina: Some of Its Economic Conditions and Problems.

E. C. BRICE. Study of Farm Tenacy in Northeast Texas.

DISSERTATIONS AND THESES

M.A.

1917 HARRIS COPENHAVER. An Industrial Survey of Winston-Salem, North Carolina.

B. F. EVANS. Financing the Public School System of Tennessee.

HIROSHI MOMIYAMA. The Problem of Japanese Factory Legislation.

E. A. WRIGHT. Zinc Industry in Eastern Tennessee.

1918 KIYOSHI NAGANO. Economic Interpretation of the Newspaper.

SEIJI SHIKI. Salesmanship: Its Principles and Practices.

1919 YASUSHIRO NAITO. China and the Great Powers (from the Economic Point of View). C. L. Raper.

*J. V. WHITFIELD. Production and Marketing of Coffee and Cocoa. C. L. Raper.

1920 KAZUE AIBARA. Agriculture in Japan. C. L. Raper.

SAICHIRO KITA. Interpretation of Agricultural Policy as Presented by a Japanese Economist, 1769-1850: The Economic Theories of Shinem Sato. C. L. Raper.

1921 B. W. SIPE. Some Practical Results of the Federal or Leitch Plan of Industrial Democracy. D. D. Carroll.

1923 C. K. BROWN. The 1922 Shopmen's Strike in the Light of a Changed Attitude Toward the Railroad Problem. C. T. Murchison.

J. G. ELDRIDGE. The Cooperative Marketing of Tobacco. C. T. Murchison.

A. G. GRIFFIN. The Financing of Highway Construction, with Particular Reference to North Carolina. C. P. Spruill, Jr.

S. A. MAUNEY. Cooperative Marketing of Cotton, with Special Reference to North Carolina. C. T. Murchison.

1924 *R. B. EUTSLER. History of the Cape Fear and Yadkin Valley Railway. T. B. Kibler.

M. G. PANGLE. Profits and Their Relation to the Business Cycle. C. T. Murchison.

1925 T. E. HINSON. Economic Development of Branch Banking. C. T. Murchison.

---

* Master of Science.

M.A.
1925   S. N. A. A. MUTNIAH. Some Economic Aspects of Jute Production and Trade with Special Reference to American Interests. C. T. Murchison.

G. E. NEWBY, JR. The Cotton Manufacturing Industry: New England and the South. W. J. Matherly.

*W. C. PRESNELL. The Peach Industry of North Carolina. C. T. Murchison.

C. G. REEVES. Current Economic Fallacies. C. T. Murchison.

1926   I. S. CLARK. Geographic Aspects of the Tobacco Industry: An Economic Study. Collier Cobb.

A. T. CUTLER. Rural Electrification: A Sketch of the Problems Involved in Bringing Electricity to the Farm, with Special Reference to North Carolina. D. M. Keezer.

M. O. PHILLIPS, JR. The Webb-Pomerine Law: A Critical Analysis of Its History, Operation, and Economic Significance. E. W. Zimmerman.

1928   R. M. LEE. The History of the Farmers' Federation Incorporated of Western North Carolina. C. T. Murchison.

*B. M. McGEE. Production Risks in the Peach Industry (with Special Reference to the Southern States). E. W. Zimmerman.

*C. B. SPARGER. Bus Accounting. C. T. Murchison.

*J. D. VANN, JR. Cost Accounting as an Aid to Management. C. T. Murchison.

1929   E. H. GRAVES. The Modern Wage Policy of the American Federation of Labor. C. T. Murchison.

1930   S. W. PRESTON. Some Economic Advantages of High Frequency Transmission Methods. C. T. Murchison.

WILLIAM WAY, JR. The Clinchfield Railroad. M. S. Heath.

1931   W. R. CURTIS. The World Demand for American Cotton. M. S. Heath.

A. M. HILLHOUSE. Brazilian Coffee Valorization. E. W. Zimmerman.

D. F. MARTIN, JR. The Naval Stores Industry in the United States. C. T. Murchison.

---

* Master of Science.

DISSERTATIONS AND THESES

M.A.

1931 *B. M. SINIAVSKY. The Cotton-Textile Institute, Inc., a Stabilizing Agency in the Cotton Textile Industry. G. T. Schwenning.

1932 *H. G. BRAINARD. Union-Management Cooperation in the Rochester Clothing Industry. G. T. Schwenning.

ROBIN HOOD. The Loray Mill Strike. H. D. Wolf.

McD. K. HORNE, JR. The Consolidated Printing of Weekly Newspapers. M. S. Heath.

L. G. PERRITT. Growth and Development of Electric Power in the Carolinas. C. T. Murchison.

1933 J. McC. AKERS. Finances of the City of Charlotte, North Carolina, 1917-1929. Clarence Heer.

*W. G. COLTRANE, JR. North Carolina Laws and Decisions Relating to Accounting. E. E. Peacock.

*L. J. FELTON. The First Year of the Reconstruction Finance Corporation. J. B. Woosley.

J. B. McFERRIN, JR. The Forces Making for the Demonetization of Silver since 1870, with Special Reference to the United States, the Latin Monetary Union, India, China, Japan, and Mexico. C. T. Murchison.

L. G. McNAIRY. The Effects of Changes in the National Banking Laws on the Relative Position of the National Banking System, 1900-1927. J. B. Woosley.

*J. S. MORRISON. An Analysis of Municipal Accounting Procedure, with Particular Reference to the Town of Chapel Hill. E. E. Peacock.

*HERMAN NOLEN. Modern Methods of Designing Retail Stores.. M. D. Taylor.

C. J. SHOHAN. Public Financing of Retail Stores, 1928-1930. J. B. Woosley.

1934 R. W. BARNETT. The Industrial Revolution: A Study in Comparisons and Contrasts, England of 1750 to 1800 and China of 1900 to 1934. E. W. Zimmerman.

J. H. McCORMACK. .Appalachian Coals, Incorporated: A Study of Its Organization, Legality and Functioning. M. S. Heath.

1936 J. J. OWENS. Labor Legislation in South Carolina. H. D. Wolf.

---

* Master of Science.

ECONOMICS AND COMMERCE

M.A.

1937 *R. C. Cox. A Standard Cost System for an Ice Cream Company. E. E. Peacock.

J. F. Fletcher. The Origin and Development of the Carolina Power and Light Company, 1881-1925. J. B. Woosley.

*A. G. Sadler. A Proposed System for Financing Student Activities in a Southern University. E. E. Peacock.

N. F. Yapar. Wastes in the Marketing of the Manufactured Products. M. D. Taylor.

1938 J. McC. Balch. A Post-War Survey of River Plate Trade Conditions as They Affect American Shipping Services. E. W. Zimmerman.

J. E. Hicks. The Monetary Theories of Alexander del Mar. E. M. Bernstein.

*W. W. Howell. Cost Accounting for a University Cafeteria. E. E. Peacock.

1939 *J. C. D. Blaine. Plant Location as a Problem in Industrial Management. G. T. Schwenning.

*R. W. Crutchfield. Accounting for Emergency Relief Expenditures. R. H. Sherrill.

E. M. Douglas. Protection Offered to Consumers by the North Carolina State Government. M. D. Taylor.

M. A. Eakins. The Problem of Union Structure in the American Labor Movement. H. D. Wolf.

E. H. Grosiak. An Analysis and Evaluation of Minimum Annual Wage-Payment Plans. G. T. Schwenning.

J. W. Gunter. The Measurement of the Cost of Living. H. D. Wolf and D. J. Cowden.

J. W. Kendrick. The Economics of Francis Walker. E. M. Bernstein.

Frederic Meyers. The Economic Opinions of the Knights of Labor. H. D. Wolf.

*F. McP. Sinclair. Illumination as an Industrial Management Problem. G. T. Schwenning.

1940 *C. C. Ballard. A Comparison of Some of the North Carolina Laws Relating to Corporations with Recognized Principles of Accounting and Finance. E. E. Peacock.

---

* Master of Science.

M.A.

1940
*J. B. HACKETT. An Analysis and Evaluation of Personnel Procedures Used in the Vocational Selection of Industrial Workers. G. T. Schwenning.

*F. M. HAWLEY, JR. Standard Cost System for a Medium Sized Furniture Plant, with Special Reference to Factory Costs. E. E. Peacock.

ROY F. HUTCHINSON. The Monetary Theories of J. Laurence Laughlin. E. M. Bernstein.

RAFAEL JIMENEZ-MACIAS. Labor Legislation in Venezuela. H. D. Wolf.

1941
J. A. ATKINS. The Demand for Transportation in China. D. H. Buchanan.

C. T. BAKER, JR. The Economics of the Frozen Food Locker Plant. M. S. Heath.

G. B. CORRIE. The Norfolk and Western and Its Eastern Coal Traffic. M. S. Heath.

ALEXANDER GUERRY, JR. The Advertising of Drug Products, with Particular Reference to the Effects of Recent Government Regulation. M. D. Taylor.

G. H. HOBART. The Economic Aspects of the Petroleum Policy of the Mexican Government. M. S. Heath.

1942
B. F. CURRY. The Development of Labor Legislation in the State of Florida. H. D. Wolf.

C. H. KREPS, JR. Some Theoretical Aspects of Wartime Price Control and Rationing. Clarence Heer.

M. L. WILLIAMS. The Development and Relative Importance of Occupational Privilege Taxes in North Carolina. Clarence Heer.

1943
A. V. ADLER. The National Defense Mediation Board: Its Creation, Activities, and Termination. H. D. Wolf.

M. L. COHNSTAEDT. Economic Factors in the Rise of Soybean Production in the United States. M. S. Heath.

T. T. HAMMOND. The Closed Shop Issue in Wartime Industrial Disputes. H. D. Wolf.

J. S. HENDERSON. Inter-Regional Differentials in Interest Rates. J. B. Woosley.

*L. G. LURCY. A Study of the Foreign Funds Control. J. B. Woosley.

---
* Master of Science.

M.A.
1943   M. L. WILLIAMSON. An Economic Study of the Peanut Industry in the United States. M. S. Heath.

1944   J. S. FLOYD. The Impact of National Banking Costs, 1921-1941. J. B. Woosley.

*S. M. HAMRICK. Simplified Income Tax Procedure for Individuals with Incomes of Five Thousand Dollars or Less. R. H. Sherrill.

1945   J. N. BEHRMAN. Proposals for International Exchange Stabilization, 1943-45. J. B. Woosley.

*MRS. F. B. HOUSTON. An Analysis of Retail Trade in North Carolina—1939. P. L. Brown.

DEPARTMENT OF EDUCATION

Ph.D.
1923   E. McK. HIGHSMITH. American State Normal School Curricula: Certain Current Practices and Tendencies Historically Interpreted. E. W. Knight.

1927   W. O. HAMPTON. How Principals Use Their Time. M. R. Trabue

1928   R. W. MORRISON. Some Inequalities of Education Opportunities in North Carolina Elementary Schools. M. R. Trabue.

1930   D. H. BRIGGS. The Influence of Certain Methods of Making the Assignment on the Study and Learning Process in the Social Sciences. A. M. Jordan.

W. E. DRAKE. Higher Education in North Carolina before 1860. E. W. Knight.

1931   R. R. HOLLINGSWORTH. The Influence of Reconstruction on Education in Georgia. E. W. Knight.

1933   F. W. GIRLINGHOUSE. Reconstruction and Education in Louisiana. E. W. Knight.

O. E. MICHIE. An Analysis of the Amount of Training Given Prospective High School Teachers in Certain Types of Teaching Activities and an Evaluation of These Activities for a Teacher-Training Program. W. J. McKee.

1935   E. C. HUNTER. An Analysis of Qualities Associated with Leadership among College Students. A. M. Jordan.

---

* Master of Science.

Ph.D.

1935 HERBERT KIMMEL. The Training of Teachers in North Carolina as a Function of the State. E. W. Knight.

J. H. A. WORKMAN. The Administrative Reorganization of North Carolina Public Schools. George Howard.

1936 H. P. SMITH. Some Limitations of the Education Theory of Thomas Jefferson. E. W. Knight.

S. H. THOMPSON. The Legislative Development of Public School Support in North Carolina. E. W. Knight.

1938 N. K. PYBURN. Antecedents of the North Carolina School Law of 1839. E. W. Knight.

F. C. SHEPARD. An Investigation of the Relation between Physiological and Personality Changes during Adolescence. A. M. Jordan.

1939 F. K. ELDER. Freedom in South Carolina as Shown by Church-State Relationships in Higher Education in South Carolina. E. W. Knight.

ALI KANI. The Reconstruction of Persian Education. E. W. Knight.

1940 W. T. GRUHN. An Investigation of the Relative Frequency of Curriculum and Related Practices Contributing to the Realization of the Basic Functions of the Junior High School. H. R. Douglass.

A. J. PARKHURST. A Comparison of the Scholastic and the Collegiate Records of Matriculants from Eleven-Year and Twelve-Year Schools. A. M. Jordan.

J. M. WESTBY. Values Accruing to Adults from Study in Literacy Classes in North Carolina, with an Appraisal of Resultant Learning Outcomes and Interests. H. R. Douglass.

1942 W. J. E. CRISSY. Physical Indices of Pubescence and Their Relation to Measured Aspects of Personal and Social Adjustment. A. M. Jordan.

1943 E. J. CARTER. The Educational Awakening in the South. E. W. Knight.

W. H. PLEMMONS. The Development of State Administration of Public Education in North Carolina. E. W. Knight.

1944 SIBYL HENRY. Children's Audiograms in Relation to Reading Attainment. A. M. Jordan.

EDUCATION

Ph.D.

1945   M. B. HOLMES. Graduate Work in the South. E. W. Knight.

M.A.

1896   J. A. MOORE. History of Common School Education in North Carolina.

1913   R. C. COX. Rural School Problems of North Carolina.

H. C. MILLER. Legal Status, Statistical Reports, and Suggested Needs of the State and Public High Schools of the South: A Comparative Study.

J. H. ROYSTER. Human Heredity.

1914   E. M. HIGHSMITH. An Inquiry into Student Government for Secondary Schools.

J. H. JOHNSTON. Social and Economic Survey of a Typical Rural District in North Carolina.

E. R. RANKIN. A Social Study of One Hundred Families at Cotton Mills in Gastonia, North Carolina.

H. E. TAYLOR. Vitalizing the Curriculum.

1915   S. H. DE VAULT. Uniformity versus Conformity in Education.

W. C. FURR. The Educated Man.

J. A. HIGHSMITH. An Educational Survey of Pender County, North Carolina, 1913-1914.

1916   J. R. MASTERSON. Intellectual Differences between the Caucasian and the Negro and Their Significance for Education.

1917   G. W. BRADSHAW. Variation and Unreliability of Teachers' Marks.

C. C. CARPENTER. (No title available.)

1918   L. L. LOHR, JR. Latin Form Test for Use in High School Classes.

M. E. MORRIS. Formation of Habit in the Masses.

W. M. UPCHURCH. Relation of Original Tendencies to School Work.

1919   E. L. DAUGHTRY. Study of the Pupils in Thirty-Three White Schools of Orange County. L. A. Williams.

C. M. FARMER. The Status of the Private Secondary Schools of North Carolina. L. A. Williams.

M.A.

1919

H. M. HOPKINS. Study in Comparison between the Scores of White and Negro Pupils in a Series of Standard Tests Given in the Elementary Grades of a Single School System in North Carolina. L. A. Williams.

J. R. WEAVER. Comparative Study of Eight Standard Methods of Testing Reading. L. A. Williams.

1920

J. C. PEEL. Study of Teachers' Salaries in North Carolina State Aided High Schools. L. A. Williams.

T. E. STORY. Efficiency of North Carolina Schools Based on Teacher Tenure. L. A. Williams.

1921

M. L. BACON. An Analysis of the Content of the American Histories Taught in North Carolina High Schools. L. A. Williams.

J. A. CAPPS. Methods and Content of French Course in Accredited High Schools of the South. L. A. Williams.

H. F. LATSHAW. Latin Form Test for High Schools. L. A. Williams.

1922

H. V. BAILEY. Development of the County Superintendency in North Carolina. E. W. Knight.

L. H. JOBE. Study of the Intelligence Levels of a Group of Cotton Mill Village School Children. L. A. Williams.

I. B. LEDBETTER. Status of the Public High Schools in Rowan County, North Carolina. L. A. Williams.

R. N. LEDFORD. Ante-Bellum Education in Georgia. E. W. Knight.

1923

R. A. DAVIS, JR. Study of the Academic Training and Experience of the Teachers in the Accredited Secondary Schools of North Carolina. N. W. Walker.

J. T. HATCHER. Compulsory School Attendance Laws and Practices in the South. E. W. Knight.

S. J. HUSKETH. A North Carolina Program of Community Recreation. E. W. Knight.

GENEVIEVE MACMILLAN. History of Higher Education of Women in the South. E. W. Knight.

G. B. ROBBINS. A Study of the Professional Training of Teachers in the Accredited Secondary Schools of North Carolina for the Year 1922-23. N. W. Walker.

M.A.

1923 S. H. THOMPSON. Public Education in Tennessee before 1860. E. W. Knight.

1924 D. H. BRIGGS. Influence of Reconstruction on Education in Tennessee. E. W. Knight.

C. R. HINSHAW. Public Education in Bertie County. E. W. Knight.

VERA MILLSAPS. Educational Theories and Influence of Archibald D. Murphey. E. W. Knight.

W. M. PICKENS. Development of Education in Rowan County. E. W. Knight.

ARTHUR RANES. Some Phases of North Carolina Education Prior to 1860. E. W. Knight.

L. R. SIDES. A Study of Examinations and Promotions in the Accredited Secondary Schools of North Carolina. N. W. Walker.

E. O. SMITHDEAL. Development of Education in Warren County. E. W. Knight.

R. W. WHITENER. Growth and Development of Education in Catawba County. E. W. Knight.

T. A. WHITENER. Guidance of College Freshmen: A Study of Some Special Factors. M. R. Trabue.

1925 NITA ANDREWS. Study of the Public Schools of Orange County. E. W. Knight.

F. M. ARROWOOD. Development of the Guilford County School System. E. W. Knight.

W. B. COVINGTON. History of Public School Finances in North Carolina. E. W. Knight.

W. O. HAMPTON. A Survey of the Sylva Public Schools. M. R. Trabue.

L. W. JARMAN. Survey of the Rocky Mount High School. E. R. Mosher.

R. F. MARSHBURN. Some Results of High School English Instruction in Warren County. M. R. Trabue.

H. D. PEGG. Study of Pupils' Abilities in English in Secondary Schools in Montgomery County, North Carolina, 1923. M. R. Trabue.

A. R. REEP. The Educational Influence of the Methodists in North Carolina. E. W. Knight.

H. C. RENEGAR. The Problems, Policies and the Achievements of Calvin Henderson Wiley. E. W. Knight.

DISSERTATIONS AND THESES

M.A.

1925
H. L. THOMAS. Public Education in Craven County. E. W. Knight.

C. H. WEATHERLY. Public Education in South Carolina prior to 1860. E. W. Knight.

C. L. WEATHERS. Public Teacher Training Agencies of North Carolina. E. W. Knight.

1926
RAY ARMSTRONG. The Mental Growth of Children Whose Parents Are Cotton Mill Operatives Compared with the Mental Growth of Children Whose Parents Follow Other Occupations. A. M. Jordan.

C. R. BIRD. Educational Finances of Jackson County in North Carolina. H. S. West.

E. J. CRAIG. Case Histories of Nine Retarded Students in the Hillsboro High School. M. R. Trabue.

W. G. CRAIG. A Survey of the Hillsboro Public Schools. M. R. Trabue.

O. K. GOODWIN. The Development of Secondary Education in Durham County. H. S. West.

S. G. HAWFIELD. The Development of Public High Schools in North Carolina. N. W. Walker.

A. M. MOSER. Administration of Public Education in Buncombe County, North Carolina. M. R. Trabue.

W. R. SCHAFF. The Growth and Development of Education in Caldwell County. E. W. Knight.

F. C. SHEPARD. Study of the Growth in Mental and Physical Abilities of the Children of the Chapel Hill Grammar School during a Period of Six Months. A. M. Jordan.

R. L. TREMAIN. The Development of the County Board of Education in North Carolina. E. W. Knight.

1927
J. P. ANDERSON. Learning and Retention of Latin Words and Phrases Studied with and without Attention to Derivation. A. M. Jordan.

J. O. BOWMAN. History of Academies and Private Schools in Wayne County. E. W. Knight.

E. T. BOYETTE. Growth and Development of Education in Johnston County. E. W. Knight.

J. L. CLARK. The Development of Public High Schools in Louisiana from 1900 to 1925. N. W. Walker.

EDUCATION 51

M.A.
1927

G. B. DIMMICK. Comparative Study of the Growth in Mental and Physical Abilities of the Mill and Non-Mill Children of the West Durham North Side School over a Period of Six Months. M. R. Trabue.

F. W. GIRLINGHOUSE. Development of Secondary Education in Louisiana from 1727 to 1900. N. W. Walker.

E. B. GOODWIN. The High Schools of Orange County. E. W. Knight.

N. H. GRAVES. Rivalry as an Incentive in the Learning of First Year Mathematics. M. R. Trabue.

HOMER HENRY. The Development of Public Education in Madison County. E. W. Knight.

A. C. HOLLAND. Vocational Information in the High School Curriculum as a Means of Vocational Guidance, Indicating Special Possibilities in English and Mathematics. M. R. Trabue.

R. W. MORRISON. The Validity of a Psychological Examination Administered to College Entrants. J. F. Dashiell.

C. H. PINNER. Some Evidences of the Need of a Vocational Guidance Program in North Carolina High Schools. M. R. Trabue.

D. P. WHITLEY. Study of the School Progress and Achievement of Children in High Point, North Carolina. M. R. Trabue.

L. L. WILLIAMS. A Comparative Study of Types of Rural White Elementary Schools in the One Hundred Counties of the State of North Carolina. M. R. Trabue.

1928

A. R. BULLOCK. An Educational Survey of the Placement of Pupils in the Elementary Grades of Salisbury City Schools. E. R. Mosher.

B. D. BUNN. The Growth and Development of Education in Harnett County. E. W. Knight.

G. C. BUSH. The Growth and Development of Education in Lenoir County. E. W. Knight.

CURTISS CRISSMAN. Some Present Practices in School Transportation in North Carolina. E. W. Knight.

LOUISE DAVIS. Growth and Development of Education in Greenwood County. E. W. Knight.

M.A.
1928
W. E. DRAKE. The History of Education in Tyrrell County. E. W. Knight.

S. McK. EDDLEMEN. Financing Extracurricular Activities. H. W. Odum.

H. M. FINCH. The Relationship Between the Age-Grade Status of High School Pupils and the Amount of Reading Material in Their Homes. M. R. Trabue.

R. W. HOLMES. The School Survey Movement in the United States Prior to 1860. E. W. Knight.

C. L. IVES. A Building Principal's Plan of Supervision. M. R. Trabue.

J. B. JONES. The Adaptability of the North Carolina Elementary School Curriculum to Boys as Compared with Girls. M. R. Trabue.

O. L. KISER. The Growth and Development of Education in Gaston County. E. W. Knight.

W. T. KNOX. A Health Program for a Rural Elementary School. M. R. Trabue.

C. R. McLAIN. The Growth and Development of Education in Iredell County. E. W. Knight.

G. E. METZ. The Relationship between Certain Social Factors and School Progress among High School Pupils in Charlotte, North Carolina. M. R. Trabue.

E. N. PEELER. The Status of the High Schools of Rowan County. M. R. Trabue.

P. B. POLLOCK. Public Education in Jones County. E. W. Knight.

R. T. RYLAND. Education in Pasquotank. E. W. Knight.

1929
W. E. ABERNETHY. A Survey of Educational Progress in Catawba County, 1923-1929. B. A. Stevens.

E. D. EDMONDS. Provisions for Kindergarten Training in North Carolina. M. R. Trabue.

G. H. HILL. The Development of a Junior High School Suitable to the Needs of a Small Community. E. R. Mosher.

M. A. HUGGINS. High School Libraries in North Carolina: A Study of Their Origin, Development, and Present Status. E. W. Knight.

EDUCATION

M.A.

1929   A. B. HURT. Educational Development of Ashe County. E. W. Knight.

G. P. LITTLE. Certain Techniques for the Elementary School Teacher to Use for Deriving Human Geography Principles. R. W. Tyler.

T. L. LOOPER. The Causes of Elimination of Pupils in the Elementary Schools of Gastonia, North Carolina. M. R. Trabue.

MRS. LINDA (SHUFORD) MCINTOSH. A Comparison of Two Methods of Teaching Problem-Solving in Arithmetic. M. R. Trabue.

J. E. SAWYER. Survey of the Pamlico County Schools. M. R. Trabue.

M. E. SMART. Provisions in the North Carolina Public Schools for the Mentally Handicapped Child. M. R. Trabue.

1930   MINNIE ATKINSON. Intercollegiate Sports and Physical Education: A Historical Study. W. E. Drake.

NORA BEUST. The Technique Employed in Formulating the American Library Association Graded List of Books for Children's General Reading (June, 1930). M. R. Trabue.

G. H. ELLMORE. The Junior College in American Education. E. W. Knight.

H. C. HUDSON. Baptist Education in South Carolina before 1860. E. W. Knight.

E. C. HUNTER. A Survey of the Academic Achievements of Pupils in the White Schools of Currituck County, 1929-1930. M. R. Trabue.

C. G. LAWRENCE. Education in Elbert County. E. W. Knight.

J. A. PARKER. An Investigation of the Progress in the Comprehension of French through Silent Reading. E. R. Mosher.

E. M. ROOME. A Study of the Principles of Education Underlying "Activity" or "Project" Teaching in Progressive Elementary Schools. M. R. Trabue.

CATHERINE SHERARD. The Development of Secondary, Industrial, and Higher Education of the Negro in Georgia. E. W. Knight.

1931   R. W. ADAMS. The Regulation of School Bus Operation with Respect to the Safety of the Children Transported. George Howard.

M.A.
1931

C. H. ADERHOLDT. An Analysis of Factors Contributory to Over-Ageness in Mecklenburg County. E. R. Mosher.

B. N. BARNES. A History of the Robeson County School System. E. W. Knight.

E. I. BAUGH. The Relation of the Training of the Rural School Teacher to Her Instructional Work and Classroom Problems. E. R. Mosher.

CLEMENTINE BRIDGES. The Relative Values of Various Criteria for Predicting Success in University French Courses I, II, and III. E. R. Mosher.

O. W. BUNDRICK. The Elementary School Principal of South Carolina and His Relationship to Instruction. M. R. Trabue.

H. A. CARROLL. North Carolina Public School Teachers' Retirement System. N. W. Walker.

F. M. COX. Development of Education in Randolph County. E. R. Mosher.

MRS. B. S. DARDEN. The Predictive Value of the North Carolina High School Senior Examinations in Mathematics and Reading. E. R. Mosher.

E. E. ENGLISH. The Relation of School Achievement Level and Socio-Economic Status of the Home to the Development of Character Traits. R. W. Morrison.

C. V. FERGUSON. Educational Growth in Alamance County. E. W. Knight.

C. A. FURR. A Suggested Vocational Agriculture Program for Rowan County. George Howard.

C. R. HUTCHINSON. The Organization of the Public Schools of Franklin Township, Rowan County, North Carolina. George Howard.

A. L. KISER. The Relative Values of Various Factors in Predicting Success in High School Freshman Mathematics. C. O. Mathews.

V. M. LOVE. The Value of the North Carolina High School Senior Examinations in English and Reading as a Prediction of the First Two College Grades in English. E. R. Mosher.

R. M. MCGIRT. The Development of Public Education in Scotland County. E. W. Knight.

M.A.
1931 C. E. McINTOSH. Factors that Condition the Scholastic Success or Failure of Freshmen in the School of Education, University of North Carolina. E. R. Mosher.

J. H. MOORE. A History of the Hertford County School System. E. W. Knight.

E. I. D. POOL. An Evaluation of Six Direct Programs of Character Education in the Public School. E. R. Mosher.

J. B. ROBERTSON. An Organization Plan for the Schools of Alamance County (White Rural Schools). George Howard.

H. H. SIMPSON. The History of Secondary Education in the Southern States before 1860. N. W. Walker.

O. A. TUTTLE. A Survey of Secondary Education in Johnston County. E. R. Mosher.

F. W. WEBSTER. A Study of Some Significant Differences in Certain Measures of School Efficiency in Supervised and Unsupervised Rural Schools in the Counties of North Carolina. George Howard.

MRS. F. P. WILSON. The Retarded Child, a Serious School Problem: Case Study of Twenty Retarded Children. A. M. Jordan.

E. M. YODER. Comparative Success of Junior College Students in Junior College and in Senior College. E. R. Mosher.

1932 M. B. BROOKS. An Integrated Unit Course in Fourth Grade Geography. M. J. McKee.

H. M. CHESTER. The Extent to Which the Teachers of the 1AA High Schools of North Carolina Continue Their Professional Training in Service. E. R. Mosher.

A. D. EARLY. The Most Common Errors in Multiplication in Algebra Made by Eighth Grade Pupils Who Are Studying Algebra for the First Time. R. W. Morrison.

J. S. FLEMING. A Study of Administrative Practices Applying to the Selection of Teachers in North Carolina Public Schools. George Howard.

L. H. FLOYD. Some Presbyterian Contributions to Education in North Carolina. E. W. Knight.

Dissertations and Theses

M.A.
1932
W. H. GARNER. Types of Errors and Inadequate Procedures Found in Subtraction of High School Algebra. R. W. Morrison.

A. G. GLENN. A Survey of Public Education in Watauga County, North Carolina. George Howard.

H. C. GREEN. Junior Colleges in North Carolina. E. R. Mosher.

R. C. HARRIS. The Development of the Rural Public Schools in Cabarrus County. E. W. Knight.

E. T. HINES. A Study of Failures in Freshman English at Virginia Polytechnic Institute. R. W. Morrison.

O. B. HOCUTT. The Conference for Education in the South: Its Work and Influence. E. W. Knight.

E. B. ISLEY. Cheating in the School Room and Some of Its Potential Causes. A. M. Jordan.

M. T. KWEI. Recent Education Tendencies in China. E. W. Knight.

W. W. MORGAN. Investigation of Causes of Failures in Grades Seven and Eight. A. M. Jordan.

H. E. STEPHENS. The Academy Movement in South Carolina to 1900. E. W. Knight.

J. W. STEWART. The Derivation of a Scale for Measuring General Science Information among High School Seniors. M. R. Trabue.

E. S. TEMPLE. An Analysis of Eighth Grade Subject Failures in the Moore County High Schools. E. R. Mosher.

H. E. WHITE. Methods of Conducting Teachers' Meetings. George Howard.

J. H. A. WORKMAN. A Study of the Present State School Organization in North Carolina in Its Relation to the Present Practices and a Proposed Plan for Its Reorganization. George Howard.

1933
C. M. ABERNETHY. A Survey of Public Education in Caldwell County, North Carolina. George Howard.

T. C. AMICK. The Development of the Curriculum in Mathematics in the Secondary Schools of the United States since 1890. N. W. Walker.

A. B. COLLINS. Historical Study of the Union County Schools. E. W. Knight.

EDUCATION

M.A.

1933   J. H. COWLES. A Study of Promotion Practices in the City Elementary Schools of North Carolina. George Howard.

A. B. JOHNSON. A Critical Study of the Marking System in the High Schools of Harnett County. E. W. Knight.

MRS. S. O. LIGON. Historical Survey of the Education of Orphan Children in North Carolina. E. W. Knight.

H. F. MCCURDY. A Study of the Extent and Nature of Teachers' Reading during a Summer School of the University of North Carolina Apart from the Required Reading of Classroom Assignments. W. J. McKee.

M. S. MENDENHALL. Relative Effect of Special Promotion and Repetition upon Progress in Achievement Tests. R. W. Morrison.

W. V. NIX. A Diagnostic and Remedial Study of the Causes of Irregular Attendance in Duplin County. George Howard.

E. Q. PROFFIT. An Investigation of the Background of Scientific Knowledge Passed by Children in Grades Four-Seven Inclusive in a Typical Rural County in Eastern North Carolina. C. E. Preston.

G. T. PROFFIT. A Study of the Academic Training and Experience of the Teachers in the Accredited Secondary Schools of North Carolina. George Howard.

M. A. SIMONS. Predicting College Grades in Schools of Education and Engineering. A. M. Jordan.

1934   N. L. CARROLL. The Relative Values of Certain Factors in Predicting Success in First Year Latin. R. W. Morrison.

A. W. FERREE. The History of Higher Education for Women in Virginia. E. W. Knight.

H. M. FLEMING. An Experimental Study of Two Methods of Teaching Reading to Beginners. W. J. McKee.

W. H. E. JOHNSON. Latin and Greek in Southern College Curricula from 1800 to 1865. E. W. Knight.

L. J. PERRY. A School Building Program for the Reidsville Public Schools. George Howard.

DISSERTATIONS AND THESES

M.A.

1934   N. B. RICHARDSON. Analysis of Pupil-Error in French Grammar. R. W. Morrison.

MARTHA TAYLOR. An Integrated Course of Study in Elementary Science for the Third Grade. W. J. McKee.

C. B. WILSON. Some Effects of Grade Repetition on Pupil Achievement. M. R. Trabue.

1935   E. S. CHRISTENBURY. A Comparative Study of the Activities Performed by Experienced Teachers and the Training Provided for Student Teachers in the Training School of Appalachian State Teachers College. R. W. Morrison.

C. W. DAVIS. Historical Background and Present Conditions in the Roanoke Rapids Junior-Senior High School, Roanoke Rapids, North Carolina. W. E. Drake.

G. C. GASKIN. Inequalities of School Support in the Schools of Lexington County. George Howard.

M. McC. MUSE. An Investigation in Classification of First Grade Children for Reading in the Statesville City Schools. George Howard.

W. G. PARKER. The Saint Pauls (North Carolina) Public Schools: A Survey. George Howard.

MRS. J. C. RICE. Some of the Educational and Social Gains and Losses to Children Who Start to School at Different Ages. W. J. McKee.

G. L. SAWYER. Some Aspects of the Relationship between Courses in Educational Psychology at Appalachian State Teachers' College and Teachers' Activities Performed by Graduates of the College. R. W. Morrison.

1936   C. R. ADAMS. A Comparison between the Candidates Who Passed and Those Who Failed the Personal Interview for the Position of Investigator in the Pennsylvania Emergency Relief Administration. A. M. Jordan.

O. I. FLEMING. The Use of Pictures in the Teaching of Written Composition in High School. P. C. Farrar.

M. H. INGLIS. Some Economic Influences on Education in the United States, with Special Reference to Labor and Capital. E. W. Knight.

M.A.

1936 P. G. DE S. KERSHAW. The Historical Development of Local Boards of Education in North Carolina and New Jersey. E. W. Knight.

M. S. LILES. An Integrated Unit Course in Fifth Grade Geography with Emphasis upon North Carolina. W. J. McKee.

R. F. LOWRY. Insuring Public School Property in North Carolina. George Howard.

M. B. SIMPSON. The Rental Text-Book System in North Carolina. George Howard.

M. H. SMITH. The Development of the Scientific Method of Thinking as an Aim of Chemistry Teaching in the Secondary Schools of the United States. C. E. Preston.

MRS. H. E. WELLS. The Influence of the Frontier on Education. E. W. Knight.

1937 NENA DE BERRY. A Diagnostic Study of the Reading Difficulties of a Group of Defective Readers. M. R. Trabue.

J. E. MORRIS. An Evaluation of Some Extracurricular Activities in North Carolina High Schools. R. W. Morrison.

N. W. SHELTON. An Investigation of Some of the Common Causes of Interests of Certain Sixth and Seventh Grade Pupils in the Social Studies. W. J. McKee.

L. B. TAYLOR. The Effect of Specific Training in the Skills and Technique of Reading Problems on Problem Solving Ability. R. W. Morrison.

1938 W. E. CONRAD, JR. Some Recent Trends in Higher Education. E. W. Knight.

H. McT. GILBERT. A Study of Reading Ability and Teachers' Marks. R. W. Morrison.

H. L. HAM, JR. A Study of Certain Aspects of Teacher Turnover in the Schools of North Carolina. R. W. Morrison.

W. N. REYNOLDS. The Status of the Teaching of Chemistry in the Public White High Schools of North Carolina. R. J. Maaske.

L. W. ROSS. The Influence of Southern College Presidents upon Secondary Education. E. W. Knight.

M.A.

1938 R. McI. UNGER. A Survey of the Organization and Administration of the Schools of Carroll County, Maryland. W. J. McKee.

1939 E. A. HOCKEMEYER. College Presidents: On Higher Education for Women. E. W. Knight.

F. L. LARSON. A Survey and Critical Study of the Summer Playgrounds of Greensboro, North Carolina (with Recommendations for Their Present and Future Development). W. J. McKee.

E. H. LEE. Trends in Education as Shown by Topics Discussed in the National Education Association. E. W. Knight.

E. C. SIPE. The Social Composition of Boards of Education in North Carolina. R. J. Maaske.

L. F. THOMASSON. Education in Swain County, North Carolina. E. W. Knight.

G. A. TRIPP. James Yadkin Joyner's Contributions to Education in North Carolina as State Superintendent. E. W. Knight.

R. S. WARREN. A Study of Typical Injuries Occuring in Physical Education and Athletics, Together with the Development of Methods for Their Prevention, Diagnosis and Treatment. O. K. Cornwell.

1940 S. H. ABELL. Some Aspects of Non-Promotion in Caswell County, North Carolina. R. W. Morrison.

E. M. ALLEN. A Study of the North Carolina High School Athletic Association. O. K. Cornwell.

A. E. BAUM. An Evaluation of the Curriculum Offerings in the High Schools of Dare County. J. M. Gwynn.

H. C. BEATTY. A Study of the Graduates of the Cliffside, North Carolina, High School, 1934-1939. R. W. Morrison.

N. G. BRYAN. The Status of the District Principal in North Carolina. R. J. Maaske.

L. S. CANNON. Supervisory Agencies Used by Principals of Certain Rural Consolidated Schools of North Carolina. W. J. McKee.

E. J. CARTER. A History of Mars Hill College. E. W. Knight.

M.A.
1940

A. M. S. CERNEY. Determination of Some of the Most Important Specific Objectives in Safety Education for the Elementary School, and Discovery of Certain Ones for Particular Emphasis in the Elm Street Elementary School of High Point, North Carolina. R. W. Morrison.

R. L. CROSBY. An Analysis of the Trends in Method of Teaching the Social Studies in High Schools, 1910-1940. R. J. Maaske.

T. B. FREEMAN. Views of American Schoolmen on the Social Studies in the *Yearbooks* of the National Education Association. E. W. Knight.

W. E. G. GATLING. A History of Public Education in Gates County. E. W. Knight.

J. S. GENTRY. A Survey of Certain Guidance Practices in North Carolina Secondary Schools, 1939-1940. R. W. Morrison.

L. C. GOODMAN. The Coordination of Health Education in the Public Schools of North Carolina. O. K. Cornwell.

J. R. HAWKINS. The Occupational Status of Graduates of Commercial Departments in Charlotte, North Carolina, High Schools. R. W. Morrison.

T. I. HINES. A Study of the Public Recreation Department in Winston-Salem. O. K. Cornwell.

J. M. HOUGH. A Critical Analysis of the Apex High School, Wake County, Apex, North Carolina. W. C. Ryan.

J. E. HUNEYCUTT. An Analysis of the Factors Related to Pupil Elimination in the Rutherfordton-Spindale High School. R. W. Morrison.

F. B. JOHNSTON. A Study of General Pupil Adjustment and Remedial Instruction in Two Fifth Grade Classes. R. W. Morrison and W. J. McKee.

G. N. KINCAID. An Analysis and Evaluation of North Carolina Student Mimeographed Newspapers and Magazines. W. J. McKee.

W. LE R. KISER. The Socio-Economic Status of Rural Boy High School Graduates. A. J. Parkhurst.

A. D. KORNEGAY. A Survey of the Diversified Occupations Programs in the Schools of the Southeastern States. H. R. Douglass and J. M. Gwynn.

M.A.
1940

J. R. McDonald. The Development of Principles and Plans for Distribution of Federal Aid to General Education. E. W. Knight.

C. M. Mercer. Mouth Health Education in the Elementary Schools of North Carolina: A Handbook for Teachers. O. K. Cornwell.

Mrs. G. R. Moore. A Study of Special Training in Study Reading in the Seventh Grade. R. W. Morrison.

E. W. Morgan. A Racial Comparison of Education in Robeson County (North Carolina). W. J. McKee and R. W. Morrison.

R. R. Morgan. A Study of the Withdrawals of Tri-High School, Caroleen, North Carolina, 1933-34 to 1937-38. R. W. Morrison.

C. E. Mullis. A Study of the Budget and Financial Records of the Charlotte Park and Recreation Commission. O. K. Cornwell.

W. H. Peacock. An Analysis of Student Handbooks of Junior High Schools in the United States. J. M. Gwynn.

J. le R. Pierce. The Physical Education Program for Boys in Grades Nine, Ten, and Eleven of the Class I AA White Public Schools in North Carolina, with Proposed Changes and Improvements. O. K. Cornwell.

A. D. Rabe. A Study of the Extent to Which an Unselected Group of School Teachers and Principals in North Carolina Subscribe to and Apply Certain Aims and Principles of Progressive Education to Disciplinary Problems and Practices. W. J. McKee.

W. R. Raynor. Educational Discriminations between Whites and Negroes in the South. E. W. Knight.

T. B. Sinclair. The Value of Certain Factors in Pupils' Elementary School Records for Predicting High School Success. W. J. McKee.

D. M. Snodderly. Teacher Absences and Provisions for Sick Leave in North Carolina Public Schools, 1939-40. J. M. Gwynn and R. J. Maaske.

J. A. Stanley. The Development of Secondary Education in Watauga County, North Carolina. E. W. Knight.

M.A.

1940 B. H. THARRINGTON. The Status of Organized Student Participation in School Management in North Carolina White High Schools. R. J. Maaske.

ELOISE WARD. What Some Educators Say about the Library as an Educational Aid. E. W. Knight.

M. M. WARD. The High School Newspaper in City Administrative Units in North Carolina. W. C. Ryan and G. B. Phillips.

G. T. WINDELL. A Critical Survey of the Spencer High School, Spencer, North Carolina. H. R. Douglass.

1941 L. B. ADCOX. A Suggested Program of Health and Physical Education for the Rowland Public School. O. K. Cornwell.

L. W. ANDERSON. A Study of the Robersonville Post-High School Youth for the Period 1937-38 to 1940-41 and In-School Youth during the 1940-41 Term. W. E. Rosenstengel.

G. H. ARNOLD. A Critical Survey of the Hugh Morson High School, Raleigh, North Carolina. W. C. Ryan.

C. L. BARNHARDT. Some Aspects of the Retardation Problem in Stanly County (North Carolina) Schools. R. W. Morrison.

MAE BLACKWELDER. A Study of Developments in Spelling, with Special Reference to an Investigation Carried On in the Asheboro Public Schools. W. C. Ryan.

F. L. BREWER. The Views of Educators Concerning the Hard of Hearing. E. W. Knight.

R. F. W. BRIMLEY. A Survey of the Practices and Needs in the Field of Elementary Science in North Carolina. W. C. Ryan.

V. M. BUNDY. Education in Bladen County, North Carolina. E. W. Knight.

E. M. BYNUM. An Analysis of the Voluntary Reading of the Sixth Grade Pupils of the Wilson City Schools, 1940. R. W. Morrison.

E. R. COWARD. Aims, Organization and Practices of Directed Teaching in the Laboratory Schools of Certain State Teachers Colleges. W. J. McKee.

P. N. DEAN. Posture as It Is Related to Personality. O. K. Cornwell.

DISSERTATIONS AND THESES

M.A.
1941

N. A. DEASON. Identifying and Meeting Some Special Needs of Problem Children Through Case Study and an Adjusted Program of Learning in a Third Grade. R. W. Morrison.

STEPHEN FOWLER. A Study of the Summer Camping Movement in Western North Carolina. O. K. Cornwell.

F. C. GODWIN. A Study of the Extent of Democratic Practices and Relationships among Principals and Teachers of Certain North Carolina Schools. W. C. Ryan.

L. E. HUNT. The Preparation of Certain Elementary School Principals of North Carolina for the Supervisory Responsibilities of Their Schools. W. J. McKee.

R. N. JEFFREY. The Relation of Nutrition to Physical Fitness in Athletics. O. K. Cornwell.

W. M. JENKINS. An Investigation of the Relative Efficiency of Adult and Student School Bus Drivers in North Carolina. J. M. Gwynn.

J. A. KISER. A Study of the Out-of-School Youth under Twenty-Six Years of Age in the Polkville School District, Polkville, North Carolina. R. W. Morrison.

C. C. LIPSCOMB. A Critical Survey of the Reidsville High School. R. W. Morrison.

ELISE MCGEHEE. Education in Certain English Literature of the Eighteenth Century. E. W. Knight.

C. F. MILNER. Audio-Visual Services through University Extension: A Comparative Study of the Organization and Available Film Resources in Six Selected Southern States, with Special Reference to Immediate Developments in North Carolina. W. C. Ryan.

MILDRED MOONEYHAN. The Value of Visual Aids in Teaching American History. W. J. McKee.

G. T. MYERS. A Study of the Graduates of Honea Path High School, South Carolina (1935-1939). W. C. Ryan.

T. L. PATRICK. School Lighting Practices of the District Schools of Rowan County, North Carolina. R. W. Morrison.

M.A.
1941   W. D. PAYNE. Curriculum Trends in the City High Schools of North Carolina. J. M. Gwynn.

D. B. PRUETTE. Editorial Treatment of Education in the North Carolina Press. E. W. Knight.

W. W. RABB. A Plan for a Program of Health and Physical Education for the Public High School at Lenoir, North Carolina. O. K. Cornwell.

B. B. REDMOND. A Study to Explore the Relationship between Ability, as Shown on Achievement Test Scores in Arithmetic Fundamentals, and the Grades Made in Eighth Grade Mathematics. W. C. Ryan.

C. G. SHREVE. The Development of Education to 1900 in Wilson, North Carolina. E. W. Knight.

T. H. SMITH. A Study of the Factors Operating to Cause Withdrawal from Summer High School, 1930-1940. J. M. Gwynn.

H. J. VERNON. Factors which Help to Determine the Vocational Placement of Adolescent Boys in Leaksville Township, North Carolina. W. J. McKee.

T. E. WALKER. The Place of Physical Education in Modern Education. O. K. Cornwell.

1942   W. J. BOGER. Status of Physical Education in the Elementary Schools of North Carolina. O. K. Cornwell.

S. S. BURNS. The Development of the Community School Idea. A. K. King.

M. S. CLARY. Progressive Education in Retrospect. E. W. Knight.

A. J. COOPER. A First-Grade Teacher Works with Parents. W. C. Ryan.

G. McN. COUNCILL. A Survey and Evaluation of Aims, Content, Methods, and Administration of the Teaching of Art in Certain Elementary Schools of North Carolina. W. J. McKee.

CLYDE DEANS. A Program in Health and Physical Education for Atlantic Christian College. O. K. Cornwell.

M. J. DE LOTTO. A Study of Athletic Accident Benefit Plans in High Schools. O. K. Cornwell.

J. F. DONNELLY. A History of the National Youth Administration in the Schools and Colleges of North Carolina. W. E. Rosenstengel.

M.A. 1942

R. V. EVERETT. In-Service Teacher Education Programs, with Special Implications for the University of North Carolina. W. C. Ryan.

T. R. EVERETT. Penderlea, an Experiment in Community Education. W. C. Ryan.

T. R. FINK. All-Year Schools. A. K. King.

MELEDIETH FRAZIER. Exploring and Identifying Some Integration Needs of Fifteen to Eighteen Year Olds. W. C. Ryan.

H. C. GADDY. An Exploratory Study of the Social Status, Opinions, and Practices of Selected District School Committeemen in North Carolina. G. B. Phillips and A. K. King.

J. M. GARBER. The Development of Health and Physical Education in Virginia since 1920. W. C. Ryan.

R. R. GINNINGS. An Investigation of a Special Group of Girls (National Youth Administration) as to When, Where, and Why They Dropped Out of School. W. D. Perry.

F. T. HARDY. The Development of Teaching Procedures in Track and Field Events for the Secondary School Program of Physical Education. O. K. Cornwell.

J. S. JOHNSON. A Study of Personality Traits of Retarded Students and Techniques for Improving Them. J. M. Gwynn.

MINNIE JOHNSTON. A Study of Some Aspects of Growth and Development in a High School English Class. W. C. Ryan.

E. C. LONGEST. A Program of Health and Physical Education and Community Recreation for Elizabeth City, North Carolina. O. K. Cornwell.

C. W. MCCARTHA. Comparative Achievements of the Seventh Grade Pupils from the Mill Homes and from the Non-Mill Homes of Gastonia Junior High School, Gastonia, North Carolina. W. E. Rosenstengel.

J. G. MCCRACKEN. A Survey of the Elizabeth City High School, Elizabeth City, North Carolina. W. E. Rosenstengel.

L. R. MEDLIN. An Investigation in the Educational Opportunities for Crippled Children in North Carolina. W. E. Rosenstengel.

M.A.

1942 S. A. NEAL. A Plan of Budget and Finance in Health and Physical Education for Eight Denominational Colleges in North Carolina. O. K. Cornwell.

E. P. PEARCE, JR. Some Major Issues in American Education as Revealed in the Resolutions of the National Education Association, 1857-1941. E. W. Knight.

J. W. PUCKETT. Evaluation of the Seriousness of Certain Behavior Traits of Pupils. W. J. McKee.

ANGELIKA RECKENDORF. The Preparation of Teachers in Fine and Industrial Arts in the South, Especially in North Carolina. W. C. Ryan.

E. B. RUTH. North Carolina State Parks System—Present Status and Plans for Future Development. O. K. Cornwell.

N. A. STALLINGS. Health Instruction in the Secondary Schols of North Carolina. O. K. Cornwell.

H. L. SWAIN. Editorial Views of the Religious Press on Education in North Carolina, 1869-1940. E. W. Knight.

L. D. WELLONS. Historical Development of the Raleigh Public Schools. E. W. Knight.

R. H. WOOD. A Health and Physical Education Program Geared to Meet the Needs of the Junior High School Boy. O. K. Cornwell.

1943 LE R. M. ADCOCK. A Critical Analysis of the Cerro Gordo High School, Cerro Gordo, North Carolina. W. E. Rosenstengel.

MRS. E. L. BARNETTE. An Experiment in Socialization in an Eighth Grade. R. W. Morrison.

E. G. BROOKES. A Course of Study for the Teaching of Journalism for Reynolds High School, Winston-Salem, North Carolina. W. E. Rosenstengel.

H. D. BROWNING, JR. A Survey of Public Education in Columbus County, North Carolina. G. B. Phillips.

H. E. COBLE. A Study of the Views of Some High School Seniors on Good Teachers and Good Teaching. J. M. Gwynn.

R. C. FLURRY. A Collection of Original Stories for Children. W. C. Ryan.

M.A.
1943

M. S. B. FONVILLE. Pre-Plans for a Course in General Social Studies on the Junior High School Level. A. K. King.

R. A. FORD. Business English in the Commercial Curriculum. W. C. Ryan.

E. J. GRIFFIN. Beginning Group Golf Instruction for College Women with Specific Reference to the Motion Picture as a Visual Aid. O. K. Cornwell.

W. B. HARRILL. Probable Effects of the Removal of Diseased Tonsils on Pupils' School Achievement and Attendance. W. J. McKee.

H. C. HOUSE, JR. Study of National Youth Administration Recreation in North Carolina. O. K. Cornwell.

G. W. JORDAN. A History of Wake County (North Carolina) Schools. E. W. Knight.

RACHEL LEE. A Study of the Health Status and Health Resources of Children in a Small Rural School. R. W. Morrison.

T. H. LINGERFELDT. Curriculum Trends in the II A High Schools of North Carolina. J. M. Gwynn.

D. L. LOFLIN. A Study of Guidance in the Elementary School. R. W. Morrison.

A. L. MCDONALD. An Exploratory Study in Health Education. R. W. Morrison.

L. S. MCDONALD. A Study of Commencement Activities with Special Emphasis on Graduation Purposes and Practices of One Hundred Public White High Schools of North Carolina. G. B. Phillips.

M. A. MCLEOD. Some Problems of Truancy in Durham Public Schools. W. C. Ryan.

S. C. MURPHY. The Development of Public School Music in the United States, with Some Views of Public Educators on the Subject. E. W. Knight.

N. B. NORMAN. A Teachers' Guide in Community Study. R. W. Morrison.

K. G. PHILLIPS. The Annual Reports of the Superintendent of Schools. W. E. Rosenstengel.

ANTONIO PITHON-PINTO. Education in Brazil. E. W. Knight.

M.A.
1943 M. A. PUCKETT. A Suggested Course of Study for the Elementary Teacher in the Field of Health and Physical Education to be Used by the Teacher Training Institute in North Carolina. O. K. Cornwell.

MRS. M. B. RICKS. Higher Education in the South Today: Views of Some Contemporary Southern Educators. E. W. Knight.

E. S. SIMPSON. History of Education in Sampson County, North Carolina. E. W. Knight.

F. S. SMITH, JR. An Administrative Plan of Vocational Education for Raleigh, North Carolina. W. E. Rosenstengel.

MRS. H. E. STRICKLAND. Developing and Evaluating a Program of Health Education in a Rural School. R. W. Morrison.

S. C. WEBB. Diagnosis and Remedial Measures of Achievement for Certain First Grade Pupils of the Shelby Public Schools. W. J. McKee.

M. S. WEEKS. Physical Education as a Contributing Factor in the Education of Secondary School Girls. O. K. Cornwell.

J. R. WELLS. The Status of the Public School Cafeteria in North Carolina. W. E. Rosenstengel.

R. L. WIGGINS. The Status and Development of Science Teaching in the Elementary Schools of Stanly County (North Carolina) in Grades 1—8. G. B. Phillips.

1944 KATHERINE AUSTIN. Community Resources Used in Teaching Health. W. C. Ryan.

A. L. BROWNE. Coordinating the High School and Community for a Vocational Program. W. E. Rosenstengel.

MRS. I. O. BYRD. A Study of the Fundamental Principles in Planning a Health and Physical Education Program for the Elementary Schools of North Carolina. O. K. Cornwell.

R. McK. CARTER. A Study of Juvenile Delinquency among White Children from Twelve to Sixteen Years of Age in High Point, North Carolina, from 1939 through 1943. W. C. Ryan.

J. C. COLLEY. A Plan for Consolidation of Negro Schools of Rockingham County, North Carolina. W. E. Rosenstengel.

M.A.
1944

A. M. DANIEL. Changing Concepts of Geography Teaching. W. C. Ryan.

J. D. HALES, JR. Extracurricular Activities in Walkertown High School. W. E. Rosenstengel.

W. W. HARTSELL. A Study of the Extent and Character of Safety Education in the Elementary Schools of North Carolina. R. W. Morrison.

A. W. HONEYCUTT. An Evaluation of the Chapel Hill High School. A. K. King.

A. D. HUFFINES. A Survey of the School Buildings of Caldwell County, North Carolina. W. E. Rosenstengel.

R. A. LEE. An Exploratory Study of Reading Readiness. J. S. Tippett.

J. L. MACGREGOR. School-Community Relations in Tarboro, North Carolina. W. C. Ryan.

R. B. McLAIN. Federal Government Activities Pertaining to Recreation. O. K. Cornwell.

FLOSSIE MARTIN. Resources in Winston-Salem Available for the Enrichment of Problems in a Health-centered Biology Course. C. E. Preston.

MAVIS MITCHELL. A Physical Education Program for Queens College. O. K. Cornwell.

REX MITCHELL. A Survey of the School Lunch Program in Chatham County, North Carolina. W. E. Rosenstengel.

MRS. G. S. MORGAN. The Study of Thirty-Four Grade Children in Wartime. R. W. Morrison.

O. L. NORMENT. Promotional Policies and Pupil Progress in Elementary Schools. W. E. Rosenstengel.

C. L. PHILLIPS. The Development of the Guidance Program at Central Junior High School, Greensboro, North Carolina. W. E. Rosenstengel.

M. Q. PLUMBLEE. Twelve Years of the Life of Anderson High School, Caswell County, North Carolina, 1931-43. W. C. Ryan.

N. R. SMITH. The Development of Consumer Education in the High School. J. M. Gwynn.

E. L. WETHERELL. A Guidance Program for Girls in High Schools of the Larger Cities. W. C. Ryan.

M.A.
1945

A. E. ANDERSON. Trends in the Teaching of Mathematics in Secondary Schools since 1923 as Determined by an Analysis of Certain Reports and Yearbooks. H. F. Munch.

A. H. BETTS. A Study of Failure or Unsatisfactory Work in a Seventh Grade. R. W. Morrison.

J. H. BOHLINGER. The Development of Compulsory School Attendance in Kentucky. W. C. Ryan.

BETTY BRIDGFORTH. Do Comic Magazines Have Educational Values? J. M. Gwynn.

MRS. M. P. ERTEL. An Investigation and Evaluation of the Activities of the Social Dean of Girls in the Junior Colleges in North Carolina. W. E. Rosenstengel.

C. L. FARTHING. Duties of School Principals in North Carolina. W. E. Rosenstengel.

M. F. GARBEE. Mexico in the Elementary Schools of the United States: A Study of the Ways of Developing Inter-American Relationships. W. C. Ryan.

KATHERINE GASTON. Job Techniques for High School Pupils: A Teaching Guide. W. E. Rosenstengel.

A. N. GRAVES. Educational Trends and Potentialities in Nigeria. W. C. Ryan.

J. P. GREGORY, JR. A Handbook for North Carolina School Boards. W. E. Rosenstengel.

T. T. HAMMACK. A Study of the Development of Visual Education in the State of Virginia from 1928 to 1944. W. E. Rosenstengel.

L. B. INGRAM. A Study of the Kind of Teachers' Methods of Securing, and Values of Pupil Participation in Community, Whole School, and Classroom Activities. J. S. Tippett.

C. R. JOYNER. Principles and Practices of Extracurricular Activities in a Limited Number of Schools. G. B. Phillips.

G. H. KING. Studies in Promotional Policies for First Grade. J. S. Tippett.

M. L. LEONARD. An Introduction to Counseling in Camps For Girls. O. K. Cornwell.

C. C. LINDLEY. The School Sites of the Burlington City Schools. W. E. Rosenstengel.

M.A. 1945

Mrs. H. L. Macon. Developments of the Idea and the Practice of Education for Democracy, 1893-1943. A. K. King.

J. B. McDuffie. Student Participation in Cooperative School Government. W. E. Rosenstengel.

H. E. McSwain. Enriching Individual and Group Living through Science in the First Grade. J. S. Tippett.

L. L. B. Miller. A Controlled-Elective Squad Leader Program for Health and Physical Education Teachers. O. K. Cornwell.

M. J. Montgomery. Applying Personnel Work in College. W. C. Ryan.

Mrs. L. H. Morrison. Inventorying the Recreational Needs of Rural Youth. R. W. Morrison.

M. E. Moseley. A Guidance Program in a Seventh Grade. R. W. Morrison.

*C. M. Neale. A Program for Guidance in the Donora (Pennsylvania) Junior High School. W. C. Ryan.

Mrs. R. C. Porter. A Study of Some Mental Hygiene Aspects of Truancy. W. C. Ryan.

J. R. Sawyer. A Study of the Development and Present Conditions of the State School for the Blind, Raleigh, North Carolina. W. E. Rosenstengel.

N. L. Sitterson. An Investigation to Identify Progressive Practices in the Elementary School. J. S. Tippett.

G. B. Teachey. Educational Opportunities for Negroes in the Public High Schools of Sampson County, North Carolina. W. E. Rosenstengel.

W. F. Veasey. Pupil Progress in Lee County Schools. W. E. Rosenstengel.

C. E. Wike. A Study of the Function of School Boards in the Program of Public Education. G. B. Phillips.

C. C. Williams. A Study of Seventh Grade Pupils Enrolled in Patton School, Canton, North Carolina: A Case Study. W. E. Rosenstengel.

---

* Master of Science in Personnel Administration.

SCHOOL OF ENGINEERING

M.S.

1915 J. W. McIver. Design of Distribution System for the University Power Plant.

M. N. Oates. (No title available.)

E. Y. Keelser. Inventory and Appraisal of the Overhead System, University Power Plant, Chapel Hill, North Carolina.

1923 R. J. Morton. Capillary Moisture in Highway Sub-Grades. G. M. Braune.

1924 L. B. Aull, Jr. (with J. G. Wardlaw, Jr.) Report on Experiments Conducted at the University of North Carolina in Co-operation with the North Carolina State Highway Commission, with a View to Determining the Vertical Pressure of Earth Fills on Conduits, Pipes, Culverts, etc., Together with a Resumé of Past Experiments, and an Attempt to Interpret the Results of the Present Series of Investigations. P. H. Daggett.

J. G. Wardlaw, Jr. (See L. B. Aull, Jr., directly above.)

1926 Harry Cantey, Jr. (with H. McC. Holmes, Jr.) Vertical Earth Pressures on Culvert Pipes. G. M. Braune.

H. Mc. Holmes, Jr. (See Harry Cantey, Jr., directly above.)

J. B. Padgett. Design of a Two-hinged, Spandrel Braced Steel Arch, 200 Feet Span, 25 Feet Clear Rise at the Crown, 31 Feet Total Rise, and a 20 Feet Clear Roadway, for Heavy Highway Traffic. T. F. Hickerson.

1927 W. McK. Franklin. (with W. C. Johnson.) Experiments to Determine Earth Pressure on Culvert Pipes. H. F. Janda.

W. C. Johnson. (See W. McK. Franklin directly above.)

R. McC. Trimble. Studies on Segregation and Analysis of Filter Sand Used in Water Purification. H. F. Janda.

1928 F. M. Bell. Studies on North Carolina Rainfall: I. Distribution of Annual Rainfall. Thorndike Saville.

A. A. Cory. Multiplex Radio Communication. P. H. Daggett.

M.S.

1928
E. G. DOBBINS. (with H. A. Schmitt.) A Comparison of Laboratory and Field Data Relative to Pressure on Culvert Pipe. H. F. Janda.

H. A. SCHMIDT. (See E. G. Dobbins directly above.)

T. B. SMILEY. A Study of Local Interference in Radio Receiving Sets. P. H. Daggett.

A. M. WORTH. Studies on the Treatment of Combined Textile Wastes and Domestic Sewage. H. G. Baity.

1930
T. B. BENNETT, JR. Electric Arc Welding. T. F. Hickerson.

J. R. MARTINEZ-PONTE. Breves consideraciónes preliminares al saneamiento antipalúdico. Thorndike Saville.

FRED MERRYFIELD. (with A. B. Uzzle, Jr.) The Effect of Pre-Chlorination of Sewage upon Stream Quality. H. G. Baity.

T. P. NOE, JR. A Critical Study of the Methods of Elasticity Applied to Statically Indeterminate Structures. T. F. Hickerson.

A. B. UZZLE, JR. (See Fred Merryfield above.)

1931
ADOLPHUS MITCHELL. A New Method for the Analysis of Stresses in Building Frames Caused by Vertical Loads. T. F. Hickerson.

J. B. PITTANA. A Study of Temperature Variations in Spheres with External Temperatures Suddenly and Cyclically Applied. N. P. Bailey.

R. F. STAINBACK. A Stable Direct-Current Amplifier as First Developed for Oscillographically Recording Temperature Variations in Thermocouples. J. E. Lear.

1932
A. C. BOYAZIS. A Program for a Federal Bureau of Sanitary Engineering for Greece: II. Rural Communities and Public Instructions. Thorndike Saville.

M. S. CAMPBELL. Studies on the Treatment of Industrial Wastes and the Effect of Waste Sulfite Liquor on Sewage Sludge Digestion. H. G. Baity.

C. L. FLORAS. A Program for a Federal Bureau of Sanitary Engineering for Greece: I. Municipalities. Thorndike Saville.

SCHOOL OF ENGINEERING

M.S.

1932 F. P. HUNSICKER. Thermal Stresses in Materials During the Transient Period of Heat Flow. N. P. Bailey.

F. A. MARCH. A Sanitation Program for the Near East Foundation. Thorndike Saville.

T. M. RIDDICK. A Comparative Study of the Effects of Lime and Ammonia in Reaction Control of Separate Domestic Sewage Sludge Digestion. H. G. Baity.

J. D. WATSON. An Investigation of the Flow-Duration Characteristics of North Carolina Streams. Thorndike Saville.

1933 H. F. CHRISCO. Studies in the Treatment of Textile Wastes. A. McL. White.

A. R. HOLLETT. Studies on the Operation and Control of a Separate Sludge Digestion Treatment Plant. H. G. Baity.

1934 EDWARD BRENNER. The Effect of Tank Diameter on the Power of Simple Paddle Agitators. A. McL. White.

COLIN CARMICHAEL. Heat Transfer from Internal Combustion Engine Cylinders. N. P. Bailey.

C. E. FELTNER. Sedimentation Studies on Coagulated Water in an Experimental Water Purification Plant. G. P. Edwards.

W. M. MCKINNEY. Load Coefficients for Beams of Variable Sections. T. F. Hickerson.

A. C. PRAZERES. Grease and Fats in Sludge Digestion. G. P. Edwards.

1935 TSU-YUAN KOO. A Study of Behavior and Efficiency of Rapid Sand Filtration. J. C. Geyer.

J. R. MARVIN. The Calculation of Third-Harmonic Currents in Three-Phase Transformer Networks. W. J. Miller.

E. W. WINKLER. Operation of Three-Phase Induction Motors on Unbalanced Voltages. W. J. Miller.

1936 L. C. HSIANG. Chemical Treatment of Rapid Sand Filter Bed for Cleaning Sand and Breaking up Mud Balls. J. C. Geyer.

J. A. MACLEAN. A New Measure of the Performance of Internal Combustion Engines. Colin Carmichael.

M.S.

1936   E. L. MIDGETT. The Design and Calibration of a Six-Inch Throat Wind Tunnel. N. P. Bailey.

1937   W. L. BLANKENBURG. An Investigation of a Rigid Frame Bridge of Variable Moment of Inertia. T. F. Hickerson.

DEPARTMENT OF ENGLISH

Ph.D.

1888   S. B. WEEKS. The Maid of France: Schiller *versus* Shakespeare.

1905   L. R. WILSON. Chaucer's Relative Constructions.

1907   E. E. RANDOLPH. The *-ing* Words in English, with Special Reference to the Present Participle.

1914   H. W. STARR. Reflections of English Movements for Reform in the Popular Literature of the Fifteenth Century.

1919   J. S. MOFFATT. Tennyson, Spenser, and the Renaissance. Edwin Greenlaw.

1923   E. S. LINDSEY. Music of the Songs in the Elizabethan Drama. Edwin Greenlaw.

1924   IRENE DILLARD. A History of Literature in South Carolina. Norman Foerster.

A. C. HOWELL. Sir Thomas Browne and Seventeenth Century Thought. Edwin Greenlaw.

H. B. MOCK. Influence of Ovid on Spenser. Edwin Greenlaw.

1925   J. M. ARIAIL. Some Immediate English Influences, *Faerie Queene*, Books I-III. Edwin Greenlaw.

A. T. JOHNSON. The Supernatural in Epic. Edwin Greenlaw.

W. D. MACMILLAN III. Planché's Extravaganzas. Edwin Greenlaw.

F. T. THOMPSON. Emerson's Debt to Coleridge, Carlyle, and Wordsworth. Norman Foerster.

1926   R. R. POTTER. Some Aspects of the Supernatural in English Comedy from the Origins to the Closing of the Theatres in 1642. J. F. Royster.

W. W. STOUT. The Progress of Linguistic Science before 1700. J. F. Royster.

L. B. WRIGHT. Vaudeville Elements in English Drama from the Origins until the Closing of the Theatres in 1642. J. F. Royster.

Ph.D.
1927 R. P. McCLAMROCH. The Gothic Drama: A Study of That Part of English Drama between the Years 1780 and 1820 Which Owed Its Existence to the Gothic Novel. H. M. Jones.

1928 R. W. ADAMS. Henry Thoreau's Literary Theory and Criticism. Norman Foerster.

J. W. HARRIS, JR. The Glorification of American Types in American Literature from 1775 to 1825. H. M. Jones.

H. A. POCHMANN. The Influence of the German Tale on the Short Stories of Irving, Hawthorne, and Poe. H. M. Jones.

G. C. SPIVEY. Elizabethans in Victorian Poetic Drama. J. M. Booker.

AGNES STOUT. Reflections of Current Social Conditions in Milton's Major Poetry. G. C. Taylor.

1929 A. W. KELLEY. Music and Literature in the American Romantic Movement: A Study of the Knowledge of, Use of, and Ideas Relating to the Art of Music in Emerson, Hawthorne, Longfellow, Poe, Thoreau, Lowell, Whitman, and Lanier. Norman Foerster.

K. E. WILSON. Old English Poetic Traditions and Conventions in Layamon's *Brut*. J. F. Royster.

1930 M. M. BRASHEAR. Formative Influences in the Mind and Writings of Mark Twain. H. M. Jones.

A. P. HUDSON. Folk-Songs of Mississippi and Their Background: A Study, with Texts. G. C. Taylor.

H. A. STEVENSON. Herbal Lore as Reflected in the Works of the Major Elizabethan Poets and Dramatists. G. C. Taylor.

W. F. TAYLOR. Economic Unrest in American Fiction, 1880-1901. H. M. Jones.

1931 H. K. RUSSELL. Certain Doctrines of Natural and Moral Philosophy as an Approach to the Study of Elizabethan Drama, with an Appendix Containing Illustrative Material from the Plays of Ben Jonson. G. C. Taylor.

E. P. VANDIVER. The Parasite in the Elizabethan Drama. G. C. Taylor.

1932 L. B. HURLEY. The American Novel 1830-1850: Its Reflection of Contemporary Religious Conditions, with a Bibliography of Fiction. G. L. Paine.

Ph.D.

1932   A. I. LADU. Political Ideas of New England Transcendentalism as Represented by Five Typical Transcendentalists. G. L. Paine.

W. H. SHINE. Carlyle's Intellectual Development during His Scottish Period, 1795-1834. J. M. Booker.

1933   W. R. ABBOTT. Studies in the Influence of Du Bartas in England, 1584-1641. G. C. Taylor.

S. J. McCOY. The Language and Linguistic Interests of Sir Thomas Elyot, with Incidental Chapters on His Cultural Background and His Relations to His Contemporaries and Successors. E. E. Ericson.

M. M. PARLETT. George Eliot and the English Literary Periodical. J. M. Booker.

T. B. STROUP. Type-Characters in the Serious Drama of the Restoration, with Special Attention to the Plays of Devenant, Dryden, Lee, and Otway. Dougald MacMillan.

1934   J. O. BAILEY. Scientific Fiction in English, 1817-1914: A Study of Trends and Forms. J. M. Booker.

F. P. CAUBLE, JR. William Wirt and His Friends: A Study in Southern Culture, 1772-1834. G. L. Paine.

J. S. DAVENPORT. The Ode in American Literature. G. L. Paine.

G. F. SENSABAUGH. John Ford: An Historical and Interpretative Study, with Special Reference to Burton's *Anatomy of Melancholy* and to the Court of Henrietta Maria. G. C. Taylor.

M. P. WELLS. Pantomime and Spectacle on the London Stage, 1714-1761. Dougald MacMillan.

V. C. WHITE. Symbolism in Herman Melville's Writings. G. L. Paine.

1935   S. F. JENKINS. The Treatment of Tyranny in Elizabethan English History Plays. G. C. Taylor.

A. L. WILLIAMS. The Influence of the Genesis Commentary on the Genesis Material of Sir Walter Raleigh and Sir Thomas Browne. G. C. Taylor.

1936   G. A. CARDWELL, JR. Charleston Periodicals, 1795-1860: A Study in Literary Influences, with a Descriptive Check-List of Seventy-Five Magazines. G. L. Paine.

Ph.D.
1936   E. H. Cox. Certain Middle English Poetic Survivals in the Religious and Semi-religious Poetry of the Sixteenth Century. G. C. Taylor.

LOUISE LANHAM. The Poetry of William Cowper in Its Relation to the English Evangelical Movement. R. P. Bond.

A. J. MAHLER. Risible Devices and Their Employment in Victorian Literature. J. M. Booker.

H. E. SPIVEY. The *Knickerbocker Magazine*, 1833-1865: A Study of Its History, Contents and Significance. G. L. Paine.

1937   J. E. CONGLETON. The Neo-Classic Theory of Pastoral Poetry in England. R. P. Bond.

W. J. OLIVE. Burlesque in Elizabethan Drama. G. C. Taylor.

H. T. SWEDENBERG, JR. The Neo-Classic Theory of the Epic in England. R. P. Bond.

1938   M. H. ELIASON. A Study of Some Relations between Literature and History in the Third Estate of the Fourteenth Century: Chaucer, *Piers the Plowman*, and the English Mystery Cycles. G. R. Coffman.

G. F. HORNER. A History of American Humor to 1765. G. L. Paine.

J. W. MCCAIN, JR. Certain Aspects of John Heywood's Vocabulary in Relation to His Cultural Interests. E. E. Ericson.

C. L. PITTMAN. A Study of Changes in Wordsworth's Conception of the Relationship of Poetry and Science. A. P. Hudson.

M. S. SHOCKLEY. A History of the Theatre in Richmond, Virginia, 1819-1838. G. L. Paine.

1939   K. G. PFEIFFER. Periodical Criticism of Walter Savage Landor by His English and American Contemporaries. A. P. Hudson.

M. C. RANDOLPH. The Neo-Classic Theory of the Formal Verse Satire in England, 1700-1750. Dougald MacMillan and R. P. Bond.

1940   G. G. GRUBB. Charles Dickens, Journalist. J. M. Booker.

A. D. B. LANGSTON. Tudor Books of Consolation. G. C. Taylor.

Ph.D.

1940   W. F. McNEIR. Elements of English Medieval Romance in the Plays of Robert Greene. G. R. Coffman.

D. J. RULFS. The Lesser Elizabethan Playwrights on the London Stage from 1776 to 1833. Dougald MacMillan.

J. H. SVENDSEN. Milton's Use of Natural Science, with Special Reference to Certain Encyclopedias of Science in English. G. C. Taylor.

1941   G. H. DAGGETT. Whitman's Poetic Theory. G. L. Paine.

G. H. FOSTER. British History on the London Stage, 1660-1760. Dougald MacMillan.

E. C. MORGAN. The Public Career of Joseph Addison. R. P. Bond.

A. C. MORRIS. Folksongs of Florida and Their Cultural Background. A. P. Hudson.

H. W. SAMS. The Background of Bishop Joseph Butler's Idea of Conscience. Dougald MacMillan.

J. B. WILSON. Activities of the New England Transcendentalists in the Dissemination of Culture. Raymond Adams.

1942   E. H. HARTSELL. Wordsworth's Ideas of Duty and Recompense as Related to His Interest in Vocations. A. P. Hudson.

N. H. HENRY. Milton's Puritanism: A Study of the Theological Implications of His Thoughts. G. C. Taylor and A. C. Howell.

JAMES HOWELL. The Rogue in English Comedy to 1642. G. C. Taylor.

B. D. KIMPEL. Herman Melville's Thought after 1851. G. L. Paine.

R. M. LUMIANSKY. A Modern English Version of the Old English Dialogues of Gregory. E. E. Ericson.

L. R. C. YOFFIE. Creation, the Angels, and the Fall of Man in Milton's "Paradise Lost," and "Paradise Regained," and in the Works of Sir Richard Blackmore. G. C. Taylor.

1943   R. W. ACHURCH. The Literary and Historical Relations of the *Tatler* to Defoe's *Review* and the *London Gazette*. R. P. Bond.

M. L. GRIFFIN. The Relations with the South of Six Major Northern Writers, 1830-1861. G. L. Paine.

Ph.D.

1943 E. S. MILLER. Medieval Biblical and Ritualistic Elements in the English Drama, 1497-1562. G. R. Coffman.

W. W. PEERY. The Comedies of Nathan Field. R. B. Sharpe.

1944 MRS. M. T. KURZ. Health Books of Renaissance England. G. C. Taylor.

B. G. LUMPKIN. Diversity in the Characters Portrayed in Southern Regional Short Stories of the Nineteenth Century. G. L. Paine.

1945 R. C. ELLISON. Early Alabama Publications: A Study in Literary Interests, with a Checklist of Alabama Imprints, 1807-1870. Raymond Adams.

J. G. HARRISON. American Newspaper Journalism as Described in American Novels of the Nineteenth Century. Raymond Adams.

D. W. ROBERTSON, JR. A Study of Certain Aspects of the Cultural Tradition of "Handlying Synne." G. R. Coffman.

R. M. WALLACE. Henry Fielding's Narrative Method: Its Historical and Biographical Origin. Dougald MacMillan.

M.A.

1886 E. P. MANGUM. (No title available.)

1887 S. B. TURRENTINE. (No title available.)

S. B. WEEKS. The Chester Mysteries.

1895 J. M. OLDHAM. The Interpretation of Nature in the English Poets, with Special Reference to Wordsworth.

M. A. YOUNT. The Transition from the Classical to the Romantic School of English Poetry.

1896 G. S. WILLS. William Cullen Bryant as a Poet.

1897 T. T. CANDLER. The Struggle for Italian Unity and Its Reflection in Mrs. Browning's Poetry.

1899 W. J. HORNEY. Poetic Interpretation of Nature: Chaucer and Wordsworth Compared.

1900 C. C. BROWN. The Wicliffite Version and Its Influence upon the English Bible Diction.

THOMAS HUME, JR. Treatment of Roman Subjects by Shakespeare and Pierre Corneille.

F. M. OSBORNE. The Nature of Moral Authority.

M.A.

1901 A. R. BERKELEY. Civic Ideal in English Poetry.

B. B. LANE. The Novel and the Drama.

1902 JACOB WARSHAW. (No title available.)

L. R. WILSON. Works of Lyly and Greene and the Pastoral Comedy of Shakespeare.

1903 J. K. ROSS. Gothic Romances, with a Special Comparison of Horace Walpole and Mrs. Radcliffe.

1904 A. L. COX. The Eulogy.

J. B. HUFF. Relation of the Shakespearean Drama to the English Romantic Movement of the Eighteenth Century.

1905 M. C. S. PELTON. The Novel and the Drama as Literary Vehicles.

M. T. PLYLER. David in the English Drama.

1906 J. T. COBB. Some Ethical Relations of the Gothic Romance.

J. M. GRAINGER. Syntactical Studies in the King James Version.

1907 G. M. McKIE. Review of Milton's Satan.

FRANK McLEAN. A Study of the Pronouns of the Authorized Version of the Bible.

1908 W. F. BRYAN. Sidney Lanier's Poems: A Study in Style and Content.

1909 D. L. CLARKE. The Evolution of the Soliloquy.

R. S. FAIRES. Philosophy of Tennyson's *Idylls of the King*.

CLAUDE HOWARD. The Dramatic Monologue.

H. H. HUGHES. Character Description in Dickens.

O. W. JONES. Scott as a Romantic Poet.

O. P. RHYNE. Conjunction and Participle Groups in English.

ADOLF VERMONT. John Selden, Humanist.

B. E. WASHBURN. The Uncle Remus Stories.

G. T. WHITLEY. Development of the American Short Story.

1911 W. P. BIVENS. Use of the Negative in Ben Jonson and Beaumont and Fletcher.

L. A. BROWN. The Personal Essays of Robert Louis Stevenson.

M.A.

1911 A. C. LINEBERGER. A Middle English Poem on Confession.

R. W. MCCULLOCH. Relation of George Eliot to Mrs. Gaskell.

MAUDE PRITCHARD. Keats's Treatment of Medieval Subjects.

1912 J. N. DAILY. The *Atlantic Monthly* as a Factor in American Literature.

1913 F. W. MORRISON. (No title available.)

1915 J. L. EASON. Browning's Interpretation of Leading Renaissance Ideas.

A. A. MCKAY. Studies in the Influence of Robin Hood on English Literature.

BALDWIN MAXWELL. Studies in the English Drama, 1790-1815.

R. E. PARKER. Archaisms in Spenser.

D. L. SECKINGER. Political Ideas of Shakespeare.

1916 EDGAR LONG. Studies in the Fairy Lore of Michael Drayton.

1917 P. H. EPPS. Studies in English Classicism in the Seventeenth Century.

J. A. HOLMES. Influence of Virgil's *Georgics* on Eighteenth Century English Nature Poetry.

R. L. LASLEY. Literary Cult of Friendship in the English Renaissance.

J. S. MOFFATT. Tennyson, Spenser, and the Renaissance.

1918 M. R. DOUGHTON. Theory of Translation in the Sixteenth and Seventeenth Centuries.

1919 M. S. SPARROW. Symbolism and Allegory in the Writings of Nathaniel Hawthorne. Edwin Greenlaw.

1920 J. B. DAVIS. (No title available.)

CLEMENT EATON. Spiritual Kinship of Plato and Emerson. Edwin Greenlaw.

W. D. MACMILLAN III. Certain Recent Dramatizations of Ancient Irish Legends. J. M. Booker.

FRANCES WOMBLE. Studies in the Criticism of University Education as Reflected in Elizabethan Literature. Edwin Greenlaw.

M.A.

1921
R. W. ADAMS. A Study of the Chief Literary Magazines of the South during the Years 1865 to 1880. Edwin Greenlaw.

J. L. AYCOCK. Ideal Commonwealth in the Renaissance Period. Edwin Greenlaw.

MARIE CLEGG. English Theories of the Epic between 1650 and 1725. Edwin Greenlaw.

A. P. ELLIOTT. Studies in Feminism in the *Spectator* and *Tatler*. Edwin Greenlaw.

S. L. LATSHAW. Status of the Acted Drama in the Colleges and Universities of the United States.

E. S. LINDSEY. Relation of Spenser to Sidney. Edwin Greenlaw.

L. P. REID. Washington Irving's Interpretation of America. Edwin Greenlaw.

C. G. SMITH. Studies in the Theory of Translation in the Elizabethan Period. Edwin Greenlaw.

J. F. SPAINHOUR, JR. Study of the Ideal Commonwealth in Modern Prose Fiction. H. M. Dargan.

1922
J. W. DANIELS. Development, Trend, and Aims of Contemporary Middle Western Literature in the United States. Norman Foerster.

T. H. HAMILTON. Chapters toward a History of American Opera Librettos. Edwin Greenlaw.

H. C. HEFFNER. Mysticism in Spenser's "Fowre Hymnes." Edwin Greenlaw.

W. F. MCCANLESS. The Auxiliary Use of "Get." J. F. Royster.

R. P. MCCLAMROCH. Attitude of the Restoration towards James Shirley. T. S. Graves.

M. J. SPRUILL. Masque Elements in Spenser's *Faerie Queene*. Edwin Greenlaw.

W. W. STOUT. Platonic Ideas in Bacon. Edwin Greenlaw.

1923
W. H. ATKINSON, JR. Satire in the Recent American Novel, 1913-1922. Addison Hibbard.

SYBIL BARRINGTON. Edmund Spenser's Letter to Sir Walter Raleigh: A Letter Prefixed to the *Faerie Queene*, Edited with Introduction and Notes. Edwin Greenlaw.

M. C. GORHAM. *Jean Christophe* and the English *Genius* Novel. Edwin Greenlaw.

M.A.
1923   C. B. MILLICAN. Antiquarianism in Edmund Spenser. Edwin Greenlaw.

H. B. MOCK. Influence of Ovid on Spenser. Edwin Greenlaw.

VIVIAN MONK. Narrative Types in the *Tatler* and *Spectator*. H. M. Dargan.

G. B. PORTER. Benedetto Croce as a Literary Critic. Norman Foerster.

F. T. THOMPSON. Influence of Wordsworth upon Emerson. Norman Foerster.

1924   J. M. ARIAIL. Some Immediate English Influences upon Spenser's *Faerie Queene*. Edwin Greenlaw.

KANSAS BYERS. The Arthurian Legend in American Literature. Norman Foerster.

C. F. HARD. Studies in Deloney's Prose. Edwin Greenlaw.

R. C. HARRELL. Medieval Echoes in Hawthorne. Addison Hibbard.

A. W. KELLEY. Walt Whitman's Knowledge and Use of the Art of Music. Norman Foerster.

T. A. LITTLE. Bunyan's Indebtedness to His Times. Edwin Greenlaw.

H. M. REAVES. Origin of Francis Bacon's Theories of the Method and the Purpose of Science. Edwin Greenlaw.

C. McK. SUTTON. Milton's Attitude toward Educational Theories of the Seventeenth Century. Edwin Greenlaw.

E. P. WILLARD, JR. Study in the Influence of Horace on Herrick's *Hesperides*. Edwin Greenlaw.

S. H. WILLIS. Treatment of Nature in Hawthorne. Norman Foerster.

K. E. WILSON. Satire in Poe's Works. Addison Hibbard.

L. B. WRIGHT. Vaudeville Elements in English Drama Before Shakespeare. T. S. Graves.

1925   S. L. DUNCAN. Fame in the English Renaissance. Edwin Greenlaw.

P. L. ELLIOTT. Plutarch's Idea of Poetry and Fine Art as Related to Renaissance Criticism. Edwin Greenlaw.

M.A.

1925
C. F. GADDY. James Russell Lowell's Knowledge and Use of Classical Mythology. Norman Foerster.

A. O. HARMON. Hawthorne's Reading. Norman Foerster.

R. L. HEFFNER. Spenser and the British Sea-Power. Edwin Greenlaw.

J. C. McGALLIARD. Classical and Romantic Elements in Walter Savage Landor. Norman Foerster.

JESSIE McKEE. Elements of Transcendentalism in the Writings of Herman Melville. Addison Hibbard.

A. C. SESSUMS. Studies in Samuel Daniel. Edwin Greenlaw.

W. H. SHINE. The Influence of Keats on Rossetti. J. M. Booker.

G. C. SPIVEY. Elizabethanisms in Swinburne's Tragedies. Edwin Greenlaw.

E. S. TRABUE. The English Fair and Its Theatricals. Edwin Greenlaw.

W. S. WEBB. Studies in the Renaissance Fable with Special Reference to Spenser. Edwin Greenlaw.

1926
D. R. HODGIN. Henry Arthur Jones: Dramatist of the Middle Class. H. M. Jones.

J. W. McCAIN. The Origin, Development, and Uses of the Dramatic Prologue and Epilogue from the Greek Down to 1700, with Special Attention to Their Significance during the Restoration. H. M. Jones.

R. C. PETTIGREW. The Influence of Wordsworth on Timrod. Addison Hibbard.

L. McD. PRINCE. Milton's Synthesis of Material in *Paradise Lost*. G. C. Taylor.

L. S. SHINE. Types of Humanity in Wordsworth's Poetry. Norman Foerster.

C. E. SNODDY. Milton and the English University in the Seventeenth Century. Addison Hibbard.

1927
J. O. BAILEY. Scientific Novel of H. G. Wells. H. M. Jones.

W. R. BOURNE. The Theatre in the *Gentleman's Magazine*, 1731-1776. R. A. Law.

L. M. COBB. Traditional Ballads and Songs of Eastern North Carolina. Addison Hibbard.

M.A.
1927　M. H. ELIASON. The Significance of the Distressed Mother in the Eighteenth Century Drama. H. M. Jones.

A. S. JENKINS. The Jealous Husband in the Plays of Chapman, Jonson, Heywood, and Shakespeare from 1597-1611. G. C. Taylor.

A. I. LADU. Conception of the Ego in the Writings of Ralph Waldo Emerson and Walt Whitman. Norman Foerster.

LOUISE LANHAM. Hymnic Elements in Milton's Poetry. A. C. Howell.

H. A. RANKIN, JR. Scientific References in Dryden's Works. H. M. Jones.

C. H. SCHWENNING. Promotion Literature in the American Colonies. G. L. Paine.

T. B. STROUP. Conventional Elements in Raleigh's *Discoverie of Guiana*. W. F. Thrall.

LILY WINN. Gypsies in English Literature, 1700-1825. G. L. Paine.

1928　B. B. ARMFIELD. The Chivalric Vocabulary in the Middle English Romances of the Latter Half of the Fourteenth Century. J. F. Royster.

MARGARET CHREITZBERG. Prevailing Types of Women in English Drama from Its Beginning to 1640. G. C. Taylor.

O. M. CLAYTON. Contemporary People in Shakespeare's Plays. G. C. Taylor.

V. M. FENLEY. Structural and Verbal Repetitions in Chaucer. J. F. Royster.

M. A. MOORE, JR. Sir Isaac Newton in Early Eighteenth Century Poetry (from the Publication of the *Principia* in 1687 to the Death of Pope in 1744). H. M. Jones.

W. A. OLSEN. Francis Bacon's Ideas on the Aim of Learning. G. C. Taylor.

H. K. RUSSELL. An Inquiry into the Nature of Comic Effect. G. R. Coffman.

E. P. VANDIVER, JR. The Parasite in English Drama from Its Beginnings Up to and Including Ben Jonson. G. C. Taylor.

M.A.

1928
W. L. WILSON. A Problem in Byron's Prosody: What Does Rime-Variation in Byron's Fourstress Iambic Tales Show of His Artistic Power and Growth? H. M. Jones.

1929
F. M. ALEXANDER. The Reflection of Courtesy-Book Subjects in Shakespeare's Comedies with Subject Indices to *The Courtier*, *The Galateo*, and *Civile Conversation*. G. C. Taylor.

A. Y. BOWIE. English Periodicals, 1750-1760. Dougald MacMillan.

A. D. BUTLER. The Bible in Thomas Hardy. J. M. Booker.

K. J. CARMICHAEL. Herman Melville's Literary Reputation. G. L. Paine.

ELIZABETH CHESLEY. The Pirate as a Literary Figure in the Nineteenth Century English Novel. H. M. Jones.

ELSIE CREW. Learned Women in England from 1760-1830. H. M. Jones.

E. B. ELMORE. Traditionality of Chaucer Note-Making. J. F. Royster.

COLLIE GARNER. The Relation of More's *Utopia* and Bacon's *New Atlantis* to the Advancement of Learning in Their Times. A. C. Howell.

K. A. JENKINS. Browning's Criminals. J. M. Booker.

F. M. KINARD. The Machiavellian Villain on the Elizabethan Stage. A. C. Howell.

C. Y. McDANIEL. Washington Irving's Interest in the Drama. G. L. Paine.

V. M. McDANIEL. Rousseauistic Traits in Wordsworth's Poetry Prior to 1805. Norman Foerster.

M. K. MONROE. The Country Clergy in English Prose Fiction, 1740-1830. H. M. Jones.

W. J. OLIVE. Shakespeare in Relation to Literary Satire and Burlesque in Elizabethan Drama. G. C. Taylor.

A. M. OSBORNE. The Contribution of Shakespearean Actors to Shakespearean Criticism. G. C. Taylor.

T. B. PEET. The Roaring Forties of the London Stage; or, Melodrama from 1840 to 1850. Dougald MacMillan.

M.A.
1929 M. E. RIESS. Essay-Types in Shakespeare's Drama. A. C. Howell.

E. M. SNIDER. The Change in Wordsworth's Thought in 1805. Norman Foerster.

H. E. SPIVEY. A Critical Bibliography for the Years 1917 to 1922 of Representative American Authors. G .L. Paine.

1930 F. E. AHNER. Courtesy-Book Subjects and Ideas in the Plays of James Shirley. H. S. V. Jones.

J. E. CARVER. Byron and Shakespeare. H. M. Jones.

E. R. COKER. Parental and Filial Relations in Shakespeare's Plays. G. C. Taylor.

M. J. HILL. Sydney Smith as a Literary Critic. H. M. Jones.

S. F. JENKINS. Figurative References to Nature in Shakespeare's Three Earliest Comedies, His Earliest Tragedy, His Earliest Chronicle History Play, and in *Titus Andronicus* and *Henry VI*. H. S. V. Jones.

J. A. McLEOD. The Southern Highlands in Prose Fiction. G. L. Paine.

J. B. McMILLAN. Thomas Hardy's Views on Sex. J. M. Booker.

DOROTHY MUMFORD. The Idea of Progress in Ralph Waldo Emerson. Norman Foerster.

S. E. SCOTT. Stoicism in the Poetry of Wordsworth. Norman Foerster.

G. F. SENSABAUGH. The Element of Wonder in American Romanticism. Norman Foerster.

LUCILE TURNER. Anticipations in the Renaissance of the Quarrel between the Ancients and the Moderns. W. F. Thrall.

R. M. WALLACE. William Cobbett, the Poor Man's Friend. H. M. Jones.

A. L. WILLIAMS. Christopher Marlowe and the Raleigh Circle. G. C. Taylor.

1931 C. R. BANNER. Lessons to Youth in Tudor Drama to 1580. G. R. Coffman.

A. W. BRADDY. Rest for My Soul: A Play in Three Acts. F. H. Koch.

H. J. CROSSEN. The Treatment of Death in the History Plays of Shakespeare. G. C. Taylor.

M.A.
1931

L. A. EGLESTON. Sidney Lanier as a Critic and Interpreter of American Life. G. L. Paine.

F. S. ELLIOTT. Emerson as a Lecturer. G. L. Paine.

V. P. GEIGER. The Trend in Poetic Taste from 1557 to 1602 as Revealed in the Elizabethan Anthologies. G. C. Taylor.

LELIA HAMPTON. Studies in Beaumont and Fletcher's Theories of Kingship. G. C. Taylor.

JAMES HOWELL. The Rogue in Non-dramatic English Literature to Robert Greene, Preliminary to a Study of the Rogue in Elizabethan Comedy. G. C. Taylor.

E. S. MACKAY. The English Political Traveller in the Age of Elizabeth. A. C. Howell.

E. C. MORGAN. The Politics of Joseph Addison. R. P. Bond.

ELISABETH MURPHY. The Heroines in the Novels of Jane Austen. Dougald MacMillan.

E. H. PHILLIPS. A Study of Some Epic Aspects of the *Ludus Coventriae*. G. R. Coffman.

C. E. REYNOLDS. The Bible in the Life and English Works of George Herbert. L. B. Wright.

MRS. C. P. SARTAIN. Realistic Characterization of the Minor Figures in Shakespeare's Chronicle Plays. G. C. Taylor.

M. P. WELLS. The Plays of George Colman the Younger: A Critical and Historical Study. Dougald MacMillan.

1932

GENEVA ANDERSON. A Collection of Ballads and Songs from East Tennessee. A. P. Hudson.

I. P. BROOKS. The Philosophical Background of Pope's *Essay on Man*. Dougald MacMillan.

D. A. BROWN. Satire in the Works of George Crabbe before *The Borough*. R. P. Bond.

W. J. CHANDLER. Thoreau's Walden Experiment as an Example of American Transcendental Economic Protest. Raymond Adams.

K. D. COATES. Hugh Swinton Legaré, Literary Critic. G. L. Paine.

R. M. FAULKNER. Jacobean Art Songs. A. C. Howell.

M.A.
1932
- BERNICE FREEMAN. Shakespeare's Changing Technique in Staging *Love's Labors Lost*, *Twelfth Night*, and *The Tempest*. R. B. Sharpe.
- M. J. HAGOOD. The Early Demand for a Native Amercan Literature, from the Revolution to 1825. G. L. Paine.
- A. E. LILLY. Solitude and Retirement in English Poetry, 1700-1751. Dougald MacMillan.
- W. F. MCNEIR. Dramatic Values in the Passion Groups of the Corpus Christi Cycles. G. R. Coffman.
- W. B. MCQUEEN, JR. The Literary Background of Colonal William Byrd. G. L. Paine.
- C. L. PITTMAN. Byron and the Counter-Revolution. A. P. Hudson.
- FRANCES ROBERTS. The Supernatural in Scott. A. P. Hudson.
- J. W. SCOTT. Notable Aspects of Satire in the Towneley Cycle. G. R. Coffman.
- K. K. SMITH. A Study of the Women Characters in Smollett's Novels. Dougald MacMillan.
- H. S. SPIERS. The Pastoral Elegy in English Literature. A. C. Howell.
- M. B. THOMAS. The Humanitarian Interests of Henry Fielding as Manifested in His Writings. Dougald MacMillan.
- M. A. TUFTS. The Characteristic Importance of Solitude in Hawthorne's Life and Works. G. L. Paine.
- D. M. UNANGST. *The Atlantic Monthly*, 1857-1881. G. L. Paine and Raymond Adams.
- DEAN A. WARD. Characterization in the Novels of Herman Melville Previous to, and Including, *Moby Dick*. Raymond Adams.
- R. B. WILSON. Ælfric, Abbot of Eynsham: A Translation of Ælfric's *Homilies*, with an Introductory Chapter on Ælfric's Relation to Old English Culture. E. E. Ericson.
- H. E. WORMELL. Some Aspects of the Early Biographies of Spenser and Milton. G. C. Taylor.

1933
- H. E. COLEMAN. Edward Fitzgerald's Translations and Their Influence upon His Philosophy. J. M. Booker.

M.A.
1933

O. U. DOWNS. The "Original" Dramatic Works of David Garrick. Dougald MacMillan.

KATHERINE HARBIN. Studies in the Poetry of Walter De La Mare. H. M. Jones.

N. H. HENRY. Milton's Latin Secretaryship. A. C. Howell.

LOIS JOHNSON. A Study of Willa Cather's Novels of the Middle West. Raymond Adams.

C. B. KESTLER. The Influence of Goethe upon Matthew Arnold. J. M. Booker.

P. G. LONG. An Anatomy of "Wit." R. P. Bond.

W. L. MOSES. The Meretrix of English Renaissance Drama. G. C. Taylor.

E. W. ROBERTS. The Social Poetry of Elizabeth Barrett Browning. J. M. Booker.

W. W. SILLIMAN, JR. Keats's Use of Tropes Based upon Classical Mythology. A. P. Hudson.

K. B. SMITH. Charles Lamb's Criticism of His Contemporaries. A. P. Hudson.

R. G. WALSER. Anti-Catholicism in the Gothic Novel. A. P. Hudson.

D. D. WICKENS. Nineteenth Century Utopias as Reflections of Social Issues. J. M. Booker.

1934

H. A. ANDERSON. Gothic Elements in the Novels of Charlotte, Emily, and Anne Brontë. H. K. Russell.

FRANK ARMFIELD. Influences of Gautier and Baudelaire upon Swinburne. J. M. Booker.

C. I. HILDEBRAND. Medieval Romance Motifs in the Drama of the Renaissance. R. B. Sharpe.

M. M. HORNE. A Study of the Development of Americanism in James Russell Lowell. Raymond Adams.

F. L. JONES. The Literary Reputation of Thomas Chatterton. Dougald MacMillan.

J. M. MCDILL. A Study of Milton's Synonyms for the Major Characters in *Paradise Lost*, with Special References to Sylvester's *Du Bartas' Divine Weeks*, Caedmon's *Genesis*, and the *Bible*. G. C. Taylor.

K. M. MCMILLAN. Addison *vs.* Pope. R. P. Bond.

M.A.
1934   M. W. McNeer. The Boy as a Character in American Fiction by Standard Authors from Cooper to Mark Twain. Raymond Adams.

Vida Miller. Terminology of Supernatural Beings in Chapman, Daniel, Drayton, Marlowe, and Spenser. W. F. Thrall.

W. L. Raddatz. Aspects of Characterization as Observed in Some Selected Moralities (Including Moral "Interludes") That Are Broadly Theological, Secular, or Humanistic, and Controversial in Tendency. G. R. Coffman.

C. E. Swor. The Influence of Latin on the Poetry of Thomas Gray. R. P. Bond.

1935   C. E. Abernethy. Courtesy-Book Subjects and Ideas in the Comedies of John Lyly. R. B. Sharpe.

L. Y. Bryant. The Pocahontas Theme in American Literature. G. L. Paine.

Marjorie Craig. Survivals of the Chivalric Tournament in Southern Life and Literature. A. P. Hudson.

R. C. Elliott. Character Writing and Its Influence on the Drama of Ben Jonson. R. B. Sharpe.

E. H. Hartsell. Wordsworth's Problem of Loss and Recompense. A. P. Hudson.

R. D. Hume. Edward Alleyn, Elizabethan Actor. R. B. Sharpe.

M. D. Jones. The Record of Milton's Disillusionment as Found in His Writings. G. C. Taylor.

Mrs. L. H. McCain. Linguistic History and Semantic Values of Representative Words in the "Prologue" of the *Canterbury Tales*. E. E. Ericson.

Rosamond McCanless. Shakespeare's Use of the Unfaithful Wife Motif. R. B. Sharpe and G. C. Taylor.

O. E. Newell. This Cunning Cardinal. R. B. Sharpe.

N. C. North. A Study of William Byrd's *Journal*, His *Secret History*, and His *History of the Dividing Line*. G. L. Paine.

S. L. Royall. James Russell Lowell and *The Boston Miscellany*. Raymond Adams.

J. K. Svendsen. Milton's Use of Personal Epithet. G. C. Taylor.

M.A.

1935 A. W. TERRY. Constance Fenimore Woolson as a Local Color Writer. Raymond Adams.

ALTON WILLIAMS. Water: A Play of Pioneer Settlement in California. F. H. Koch.

1936 S. M. BRETT. Mr. Samuel Pepys, Esq.: His Reading as Revealed in the *Diary*. A. C. Howell.

G. W. CHANDLER, JR. The History and Present Status of Folk-Song Scholarship in the South. A. P. Hudson.

J. L. COULTER, JR. Byron's Ethical, Religious, and Political Principles, as Revealed in His Judgment of Men. A. P. Hudson.

E. M. DANIEL. Plowed Ground: A Play of Pioneer Health Work in Rural North Carolina. Samuel Selden.

L. M. DAVEY. A Study of the Realistic Elements in the Novels of Thomas Deloney. A. C. Howell.

C. D. DELONG. A Comparison of the Influence of Virgil on Milton and Spenser. G. C. Taylor.

WILBUR DORSETT. Pillar of Fire: A Negro Drama in Three Acts. F. H. Koch.

K. M. KRAHENBUHL. The Influence of Inigo Jones on Ben Jonson's Masques. R. B. Sharpe.

A. H. C. PENNEKAMP. The Treatment of the Negro in the Literary Magazines of the South During the Reconstruction Period from 1865 to 1880. Raymond Adams.

M. T. SPIERS. An Analysis of the Themes and Technique of the *Spectator*. R. P. Bond.

MERCEDES STEELY. The Folk-Songs of Ebenezer Community. A. P. Hudson.

1937 M. E. BITTING. Contempt of the World in the Poetry of John Milton: A Study in Milton's Changing Personal and Artistic Emphases. G. C. Taylor.

ELROY DUPUIS. A Comparison of Certain Aspects of Revolutionary Thought as Found in the Writings of Thomas Paine and Jean-Jacques Rousseau. G. L. Paine.

MANNING HAWTHORNE. The Youth of Hawthorne. G. L. Paine.

M.A.
1937 M. S. MILLS. Imagery in Chaucer and Dryden: A Comparative Study of the Images in Chaucer's "Knight's Tale," "Wife of Bath's Tale," and "Non's Priest's Tale," and in Dryden's Versions of Those Stories. G. R. Coffman.

C. A. P. MOORE. Cosmological Ideas in the Poetry of Edmund Spenser. G. C. Taylor.

W. A. MURPHY. The Literary Relations of Poe with Bryant, Hawthorne, and Lowell. G. L. Paine.

D. W. ROBERTSON, JR. A Preliminary Survey of the Controversy over Aristotle's Doctrine of Tragic Catharsis. G. R. Coffman and H. K. Russell.

N. V. ROSE. Milton's Nature Images: A Study of Their Sources, Their Uses, and Their Characteristic Qualities. G. C. Taylor.

J. E. THORPE, JR. John Keats as a Literary Critic. A. P. Hudson.

1938 J. M. ALLEY. Topical Allusions in the Savoy Operas. Dougald MacMillan.

W. B. BEZANSON. A Study of Thomas Morton's *New English Canaan*. G. L. Paine.

CLYDE DEANS. The Function of the Songs in Elizabethan Pastoral Romances. W. F. Thrall.

M. E. DICHMANN. Linguistic Interests in the *Gentleman's Magazine*, 1731-1800. E. E. Ericson.

ARABELLA GORE. The History of the Interpretation of Shylock in English and American Literary Criticism, 1796 to 1935. G. C. Taylor.

E. S. LANE. Byron and the Fine Arts: Music, Architecture, Painting, and Sculpture. A. P. Hudson.

J. A. MORRIS. The Stories of William Gilmore Simms. G. L. Paine.

M. M. PETTIGREW. A Study of Edwin Arlington Robinson's Arthurian Poems. G. L. Paine.

1939 M. T. ALLEN. Destinal Forces in the Narrative Pattern of the *Canterbury Tales*. G. R. Coffman.

WILLIAM BRACY. Jaques: A Study in Shakespearean Criticism. G. C. Taylor.

JESS BYRD. The Comedies of Mrs. Susanna Centlivre: A Critical Study. Dougald MacMillan.

C. LA C. CRANE, JR. The Decline in the Literary Reputation of Bret Harte. Raymond Adams.

M.A.

1939
E. V. DEANS, JR. Sir Thomas Browne's Botanical Learning as Illustrated in His Writings. A. C. Howell.

E. L. EDWARDS. The Evolution of the Tragic Flaw, with Special Reference to Shakespeare's Chronicle History Plays. G. C. Taylor.

W. P. HUDSON. The Literary Theory and Critical Practice of William Cullen Bryant. Raymond Adams.

N. T. JOOST, JR. A Study of the *Free-Thinker*, 1718-1719. R. P. Bond.

J. B. LEWIS. North Carolina English as Reflected in Old Documents. E. E. Ericson.

R. H. LINTON. The Code of Arms in Spenser's *Faerie Queene*. W. S. Wells.

D. A. MACDOWELL. The History of the Interpretation of Lady Macbeth in English and American Literary Criticism, 1747-1939. G. C. Taylor.

J. T. MCCULLEN, JR. The Use of Madness in Shakespearean Tragedy for Characterization and for Protection in Satire. G. C. Taylor.

S. W. SEWELL. The Relation of *The Merry Wives of Windsor* to Jonson's *Every Man in His Humour*. G. C. Taylor.

L. DE L. WALLACE. The Duke of Buckingham's *The Rehearsal*: A Collation of the First and Third Quartos, with Notes on the Text. Dougald MacMillan.

E. T-C. WANG. The Beginning of Chinese Studies in the English-Speaking World. E. E. Ericson.

H. F. WITTMEYER. The Spirit of Man in the Writings of Joseph Conrad. J. M. Booker.

1940
N. B. BOOKER. William Blake's *Annotations to Sir Joshua Reynolds' Discourses*. A. P. Hudson.

WAYNE BOWMAN. The Comedies of Mrs. Aphra Behn. Dougald MacMillan.

F. C. CROWE. Keats' Interest in Things Italian and Its Influence on His Poems and Letters. A. P. Hudson.

M. C. DOUGLAS. An Examination of the Structure of *A Week on the Concord and Merrimack Rivers*, by Henry David Thoreau. Raymond Adams.

M.A. 1940

M. H. FRAZER. Scott's Treatment of Folk-Song Material in His Scottish Novels. A. P. Hudson.

L. L. HAYNES. Nomenclature of Grammatical Terms in Ælfric's Translation of the Latin Grammar. E. E. Ericson.

ANNABELLE HOLLOWELL. Shakespeare's Use of Comic Materials in Tragedy: A Survey of Criticism. T. B. Stroup.

S. E. INMAN. Chaucer in America. Raymond Adams.

A. W. JOHNSON. A Critical Biography of Corra Harris. G. L. Paine.

M. L. JOHNSON. The Relation of Gay's Fable to the Moral Verse of Swift, Young, and Pope. Dougald MacMillan.

J. P. MACBRYDE. The Highwayman in Non-dramatic English Literature, 1560-1728. A. C. Howell.

JANE MCKEE. The Literary Reputation of Daniel De Foe as a Novelist, 1719-1935. R. P. Bond.

VIRGINIA MARY. French Invasion and English Literature, 1793-1805. A. P. Hudson.

D. B. Moss. Some Aspects of Chaucer's Literary Reputation in England from 1400 to 1600. G. R. Coffman.

R. S. OSBORNE. Whittier's Religion as It Is Expressed in His Poetry. G. L. Paine.

LAWRENCE PATTEN. Poe's Treatment of Terror in Fiction. G. L. Paine and Raymond Adams.

M. L. PETTIS. Medicine in the Poetry of John Donne. G. C. Taylor.

J. S. REYNOLDS. The Similes in Book I of *Paradise Lost* Compared with Those in Book I of the *Faerie Queene*. G. C. Taylor.

J. N. SMITH. Sir Thomas Wyatt: A Study in His Literary Reputation over Four Hundred Years. W. S. Wells.

DOROTHY STANSELL. The Lost Words of Ælfric. E. E. Ericson.

E. L. WALTERS. Some Social Criticism Expressed in Herman Melville's Shorter Narrative Works. G. L. Paine.

M.A.

1940

M. M. WYNN. Wordsworth as a Poet of the City. A. P. Hudson.

1941

MARGARET DUCKETT. A Study of Racial Intolerance as a Phase of Social Criticism in the Writings of Bret Harte. Raymond Adams.

J. H. GARDNER. The Literary Reputation of John Wilmot, Earl of Rochester. A. C. Howell.

F. T. GERARD, JR. A Study of the Imagery of the Poetry of Thomas Chatterton. L. C. Hartley.

E. C. GLASGOW. Verse Satire of the Restoration: A Study of Methods and Devices. A. C. Howell.

E. H. GOOLD, JR. Philip Freneau's Humanitarian Interests. G. L. Paine.

ARCHIBALD HENDERSON, JR. The Influence of William Hazlitt on John Keats. A. P. Hudson.

E. F. HENING. The Role of Woman in Coteries of the Renaissance. R. B. Sharpe.

M. M. HINES. Literary and Philosophical Aspects of the Theme of Good and Evil in Milton's Poetry. G. C. Taylor.

C. W. JONES. Reason *versus* Passion in Shakespeare's Comedies. G. C. Taylor.

J. S. LAYTON. Emerson's Theory of Tragedy. Raymond Adams.

L. M. MORTON. Shakespeare's Attitude toward History. R. B. Sharpe.

R. J. SKINNER. American Letters to Children. Raymond Adams.

D. H. SLICER. The Heritage of the Soliloquy of Classical and of Native English Comedy in the Plays of John Lyly. G. R. Coffman.

1942

H. M. ANDERSON. Henry James's Estimate of Women Novelists. Raymond Adams.

J. L. CURTIS. The Dialect Writing of Charles Egbert Craddock in the Light of the Author's Background. E. E. Ericson.

ANN DAWSON. Changing Conceptions of Isabella. G. C. Taylor.

C. D. ECHOLS. The Curse in Shakespeare's Plays. G. C. Taylor.

M. N. GALLMAN. A Critical Biography of Virginia Frazer Boyle. Guy Cardwell and Raymond Adams.

M.A.
1942　L. C. Goss. The Influence of Marcus Aurelius upon Matthew Arnold. J. M. Booker.

M. H. Osborne. Studies in Spenser's Use of Theory of Kinds. W. S. Wells.

C. J. Pace. The Interest in Learning in Shakespeare's Plays. G. C. Taylor.

H. C. Pritchard. A Study of Repetition as an Architechtonic Device in *Paradise Lost*. W. S. Wells.

J. G. Rice. The Jacobin Character as a Type in the Pre-Romantic Novel. W. S. Wells and A. P. Hudson.

R. R. Richardson, Jr. A Study of the *Free-Holder*. R. P. Bond.

Louise Tapp. Switzerland in the English Romanticists. A. P. Hudson.

C. A. Wegelin. Frontier Features in Mark Twain's Attitude toward Europe. Raymond Adams.

1943　M. H. Butler. Robert Southey's Interest in Ballads and Romances. A. P. Hudson.

W. J. Dukes. Shakespeare Criticism and *Richard II*. G. C. Taylor.

L. de S. Duls. The Middle English *Bestiary*: A General Study of the Bestiaries, with Emphasis upon the Middle English Version and a Modernization of the Middle English Text. E. E. Ericson.

M. J. Earp. The Domestic Life of the Wordsworths. A. P. Hudson.

L. A. Marsh. The Critical and Poetic Theories of Nathaniel Hawthorne. Raymond Adams.

Mrs. L. G. Mizell. The Women in Lyly's Plays with Reference to Selected Aspects of Contemporary Relationships and to High Comedy. G. R. Coffman.

M. B. Talmage. The Epic in American Literature. Raymond Adams.

1944　E. K. Beach. Hazlitt on Byron. A. P. Hudson.

N. L. Clark. Thoreau's Theory of Nature as a Teacher, Compared with Wordsworth's. Raymond Adams.

M. V. Cubine. The Religious History of Samuel Taylor Coleridge to 1807. A. P. Hudson.

J. C. Disque. The Literary Criticism of A. Bronson Alcott. Raymond Adams.

M.A.

1944

J. E. FARRIOR. The Use of Historical Characters by William Gilmore Simms in His Romances of the Revolution. G. L. Paine.

PASCHAL JARRATT. A Study of Death in English Renaissance Tragedy. R. B. Sharpe.

KATHERINE LACKEY. Shakespeare's Political Philosophy. G. C. Taylor.

MRS. G. G. LILLY. The English Critics on the *Shepheardes Calendar* to the Time of Pope. W. S. Wells.

D. D. PAIGE. The Art of War in the Jacobean Drama, 1603-1625. Hardin Craig.

F. G. PRITCHETT. The History and Interpretation of Cordelia in English and American Literary Criticism, 1710 to 1940. G. C. Taylor.

M. A. SEELYE. Nature in *King Lear* as a Basis for the Unity of Action. G. C. Taylor.

R. H. SELF. Dorothy Wordsworth as a Reader and Critic. A. P. Hudson.

D. R. SHARPE. William Dean Howells's Theory of Realism in Prose Fiction. G. L. Paine.

S. M. SIEBER. The Epigram in the Restoration Comedy of Manners. R. B. Sharpe.

M. O. THOMAS. A Study of the Criticism of Iago. G. C. Taylor.

E. C. WALKER. Some Characteristics of "Barbara Allen" in America. A. P. Hudson.

MRS. F. P. WOODARD. Adverse Comments on the West by Reputable Authors between 1830 and 1860. Raymond Adams.

1945

S. I. DAVIS. The Doctrine of Necessity in the Early Philosophical Periods of Coleridge and Shelley. A. P. Hudson.

W. E. EDMUNDS. The History of the Criticism of the Character of Richard III. G. C. Taylor.

H. A. ELLIS, JR. The Phonology of Sam Slick. E. E. Ericson.

MRS. B. K. GEROW. Critical and Scholarly Interest in Chaucer (1775-1850). E. E. Ericson.

P. M. GRIFFITH. Michel-Guillaume Jean de Crevecoeur as an Observer and Critic of Colonial America. G. L. Paine.

M.A.
1945   M. L. HAMMER. The Saviour as Protagonist in the *Ludus Coventriae*. G. R. Coffman.

C. M. HANIFORD. The Treatment of the Creoles in the Fiction of George Washington Cable, Grace Elizabeth King, and Kate Chopin. G. L. Paine.

LILA HERMANN. The Literary and Personal Relations of Herman Melville and Nathaniel Hawthorne. Raymond Adams.

I. R. HOWELL. A Critical Biography of Ruth McEnery Stuart. Raymond Adams.

CATHERINE NICHOLSON. The History of the Criticism of the Character of Othello. G. C. Taylor.

MRS. G. E. WEEKS. Wordsworth's, Coleridge's and Southey's Interest in the Iberian Peninsula. A. P. Hudson.

A. A. WHIPPLE. Hamlin Garland's Ideas of Middle Age as Seen in the Characters of His Books. Raymond Adams.

DEPARTMENT OF GEOLOGY AND GEOGRAPHY

Ph.D.
1926   G. R. MACCARTHY. The Colors Produced by Iron in Minerals and in the Sediments. Collier Cobb.

1927   W. B. COBB. A Comparison of the Development of Soils from the Acid and Basic Crystalline Rocks of Piedmont North Carolina. Collier Cobb.

1932   M. E. NORBURN. The Influence of the Physiographic Features of Western North Carolina on the Settlement and Development of the Region. Collier Cobb.

1938   R. A. EDWARDS. Yorktown and Duplin Ostracoda of North Carolina and Virginia. J. W. Huddle.

H. W. STRALEY III. Some Geomagnetic Traverses in the Appalachian Mountains. W. F. Prouty and L. D. Burling.

W. A. WHITE. The Mineralogy of Desert Sands. W. F. Prouty.

1940   D. DE L. JETER. The Geo-economic Potentialities of the North Carolina Kaolin Deposits. W. F. Prouty.

1941   R. O. BLOOMER. Geology of the Blue Ridge in the Buena Vista Quadrangle, Virginia. J. W. Huddle.

Ph.D.

1941   J. R. CLAIR. Stratigraphy, Structure, and Economic Geology of the Belton Area, Cass County, Missouri. W. F. Prouty.

1942   J. H. WATKINS. Origin of the Phosphate Deposits of the Southeastern States. W. F. Prouty.

1944   J. C. McCAMPBELL. Further Geomagnetic Evidences as to the Origin of the Carolina Bays. W. F. Prouty.

1945   C. T. PHILLIPS. Durham: A Geographic Study. S. T. Emory.

M.A.

1896   *J. E. MATTOCKS. (No title available.)

1908   *R. T. ALLEN. The Triassic Rocks of the Wadesboro Area.

*HUBERT HILL. Origin of Soil Through the Disintegration of Rocks.

*L. G. SOUTHARD. Soil Series and Soil Adaptation to the Chapel Hill, North Carolina, Region.

1912   H. R. RAY. Origin and Treatment of Soils.

1913   W. B. COBB. Geology in Relations to Soil Types and Soil Fertility in the Chapel Hill, North Carolina, Region.

1915   A. R. BROWNSON. Stratigraphy of the Triassic in Eastern North Carolina.

H. D. LAMBERT. The Soils of the Chapel Hill Region and Their Adaptation to Crops.

E. O. RANDOLPH. Study of the Physiography of the Isle of the Palms.

1916   M. J. DAVIS. Geology as Related to Plant Growth, with Especial Reference to the Chapel Hill Area.

W. L. GOLDSTON, JR. Soils of the University Station Area.

1917   C. N. DOBBINS. Soil Survey of the Chapel Hill Triassic Area.

1920   H. T. DAVIS. Notes to Accompany Map of the Triassic Contacts of East Chapel Hill, North Carolina. Collier Cobb.

H. E. MARSH. Geology of Triassic Area Southeast of Chapel Hill, North Carolina. Collier Cobb.

J. L. STUCKEY. Notes on the Triassic East of Chapel Hill, North Carolina. Collier Cobb.

---

* Master of Science.

GEOLOGY AND GEOGRAPHY 103

M.A.
1921 J. S. BABB. The Conglomerates of the Jones' Ford Quadrangle. Collier Cobb.

W. H. BUTT. Igneous Rocks of the Jones' Ford Quadrangle. Collier Cobb.

S. B. LEE. Soils of the Jones' Ford Quadrangle. W. F. Prouty.

1922 H. S. BOYCE. Geology of the Burhenglen Knob Quadrangle. W. F. Prouty.

B. E. LOHR. Geology and Soils of the Burhenglen Knob Quadrangle. W. F. Prouty.

J. B. MILLER. Flint-like Slates of the Jones' Ford Quadrangle. Collier Cobb.

1923 H. C. AMICK. Geology of Booker Creek Quadrangle. W. F. Prouty.

C. H. WALKER. Comparative Study of the Newark of North Carolina and New England. W. F. Prouty.

1924 H. J. BRYSON. Stratigraphy of Deep River Coals. W. F. Prouty.

T. E. POWELL, JR. The Geology of the St. Mark's Quadrangle. W. F. Prouty.

G. R. MACCARTHY. The Laccolith: A Theoretical and Experimental Study. W. F. Prouty.

1926 *J. C. BYNUM. The Climate of North Carolina and Some Other Influences Affecting the Textile Industry within the State. Collier Cobb.

*C. S. JOHNSTON. The Orientation of Mineral Particles During Rock Flowage: A Theoretical and Experimental Study. W. F. Prouty.

*C. E. MILLER. Certain Problems Connected with the Mineralogical Analysis of Kaolin Clays and the Introduction of a New Method of Mechanical Analysis. W. F. Prouty.

*R. G. SASSCER. Microscopic Study of Sediments. W. F. Prouty.

1927 R. D. SHEARER. A Cross Section through the Triassic Basin. W. F. Prouty.

M. M. WEBSTER. The Weathering of Soil Minerals. Collier Cobb.

1928 *I. L. MARTIN. A Petrographic and Micro-paleontological Study of Some Marls of Eastern North Carolina. W. F. Prouty.

---

* Master of Science.

M.A.

1928   M. D. SLAVENS. Clays in Industry in Ohio. Collier Cobb.

H. T. THOMPSON. A Study of the Physiographic History of Swamp Lands in Relation to Their Drainage. Collier Cobb.

1930   *T. L. KESLER. Geology of the Catawba Mountain (Virginia) Area. W. F. Prouty.

1931   *W. T. HOLLAND. A Geophysical and Geological Survey of the Northern Part of the Deep River Triassic Basin. Collier Cobb.

1932   K. R. BYERLY. A Study of the Physical Characteristics of Leading American Ocean Ports with Reference to Their Hinterlands. Collier Cobb.

C. S. MAURICE. An Investigation of a Residual Clay for Use as a Filler in Rubber or Other Compounds. W. F. Prouty.

W. A. WHITE. A Petrographic Examination of Some Atlantic Coastal Sands. G. R. MacCarthy.

1935   J. W. SMITH. Geographical Aspects of World Cotton. S. T. Emory.

1937   N. E. GREENE. Some Upper Cretaceous Foraminifera of North Carolina. J. W. Huddle.

R. W. HORNBECK. Topographic and Geological Mapping of a Part of the Morgan Creek Basin. W. F. Prouty.

P. M. LE BARON. Geology of the White Belt, Portis Gold Mine Property of Franklin County, North Carolina. W. F. Prouty.

*J. H. WATKINS. Origin of the Phosphates of South Carolina. W. F. Prouty.

1938   W. M. LAIRD. The Stratigraphy and Structure of the Martinsburg Formation near Harrisburg, Pennsylvania. W. F. Prouty.

1939   *H. E. VITZ. Some Cretaceous Ostracodes from North and South Carolina. J. W. Huddle.

1940   R. J. MARTIN. The Geology of the Thicketty Creek Area, South Carolina. W. F. Prouty.

1942   O. S. CLARK. Henderson County. S. T. Emory.

---

* Master of Science.

DEPARTMENT OF GERMANIC LANGUAGES

Ph.D.

1936   F. E. COENEN. The Men-Characters in the Dramas of Franz Grillparzer. A. E. Zucker.

1938   L. S. THOMPSON. Wilhelm Waiblinger's Interpretation of Italy. Richard Jente.

1940   M. L. HUTH. Das Sprichwort bei Moscherosch. Richard Jente.

1942   J. C. CORNETTE, JR. Proverbs and Proverbial Expressions in the German Works of Martin Luther. Richard Jente.

1943   R. B. NANCE. Friedrich Hebbel's Criticism of Dramatic Authors and Their Work. K. J. Brown.

1945   G. W. RADIMERSKY. Verfall und Erhaltung als Menschengestaltende Elemente bei Gustav Frenssen. Richard Jente.

M.A.

1899   K. C. AHERN. Genesis of Goethe's Mephistopheles.

1930   L. J. BELL. Novalis' Conception of the Golden Age. W. D. Toy.

1931   R. S. COLLINS. Hebbel and Tragic Guilt. K. J. Brown.

1937   R. E. BACKENSTOSS, JR. Figures of Speech in Heinrich von Kleist's *Der zerbrochene Krug*: An Investigation into Kleist's Style. A. E. Zucker.

       J. F. COOK. A Diplomatic Edition and Translation of a Moravian Travel Diary of the Year 1750 by Michael Singer. A. E. Zucker.

1938   N. M. KORFF. Paul Ernsts "Demetrios" im Rahmen der deutschen Demetrius-Dramen. Richard Jente.

1939   V. S. REDFERN. Metaphor and Simile in "Storm and Stress" Drama. Richard Jente.

1940   A. W. BEERBAUM. Land und Leute in Timm Krögers Novellen. Richard Jente.

       A. L. LANCASTER. The Words for "Man, Warrior, Hero, Prince," in the Poetic Edda. G. S. Lane.

       C. H. MUELLER. An Investigation of the *Schwabenspiegel*, with Particular Reference to the Legal Terminology. G. S. Lane.

       R. B. NANCE. Faulty Rimes in Schiller's Poetry. Richard Jente.

---

* Master of Science.

M.A.

1942   M. F. MUNCH. The Transmission of the Greek Alphabet to the Romans: A Survey of the Research. G. S. Lane.

         NELSON VAN DE LUYSTER. Emigration to America as Reflected in the German Novel of the Nineteenth Century, Especially in the Fiction of Bitzius, Laube, Gutzkow, Auerbach, Freytag, Storm, Keller, Spielhagen, Heyse, and Raabe. Richard Jente.

*DEPARTMENT OF HISTORY AND POLITICAL SCIENCE

Ph.D.

1926   F. C. ANSCOMBE. The Contribution of the Quakers to the Reconstruction of the South. J. G. de R. Hamilton.

1927   F. M. GREEN. Constitutional Development in the South Atlantic States, 1776-1860: A Study in the Evolution of Democracy. J. G. de R. Hamilton.

         W. S. JENKINS. The Political Theories of the Slave-Holder. W. W. Pierson.

         G. G. JOHNSON. Social Conditions in North Carolina, 1800-1860. R. D. W. Connor.

         C. C. NORTON. The Democratic Party in Ante-Bellum North Carolina, 1835-1850. R. D. W. Connor.

1928   A. L. BRAMLETT. North Carolina's Western Lands. R. D. W. Connor.

         J. A. PADGETT. The History of the Enactment and Operation of the Federal Election Laws. W. W. Pierson.

1929   J. W. PATTON. The Brownlow Regime in Tennessee. J. G. de R. Hamilton.

         H. T. SHANKS. The Secession Movement in Virginia. J. G. de R. Hamilton.

1930   C. B. ALEXANDER. An Abstract of the Public Career of Richard Caswell. R. D. W. Connor.

         C. H. PEGG. The First Republican Uprising in France. M. B. Garrett.

         C. B. ROBSON. The Influence of German Thought on Political Theory in the United States in the Nineteenth Century: An Introductory Study. W. W. Pierson.

---

* Until 1935 History and Political Science were combined in one department under the name of the Department of History and Government. Work completed in Political Science after this date is listed under Political Science.

HISTORY AND POLITICAL SCIENCE

Ph.D.
1930   S. D. SMITH. The Negro in Congress, 1870-1901. J. G. de R. Hamilton.

1931   MARY WATTERS. The History of the Church in Venezuela, 1810-1930. W. W. Pierson.

1932   D. J. WHITENER. History of the Temperance Movement in North Carolina, 1715-1908. R. D. W. Connor.

1933   H. D. PEGG. The Whig Party in North Carolina, 1834-1861. R. D. W. Connor.

C. N. SISSON. The Creation, Organization, and Mobilization of the Army of the French Revolution, October 1, 1789 to April 20, 1792. M. B. Garrett.

M. L. SKAGGS. North Carolina Boundary Disputes Involving Her Southern Line. H. M. Wagstaff.

1935   D. A. LOCKMILLER. The Second United States Intervention in Cuba, 1906-1909. W. W. Pierson.

CHANDLER SHAW. A Study of Perugia in Prehistoric and Etruscan Times. W. E. Caldwell.

1936   W. A. BROWN. Attempts at Reconciliation between Great Britain and Her American Colonies. H. T. Lefler.

M. E. EDWARDS. Decius: A Study of the Roman Empire in the Middle of the Third Century. W. E. Caldwell.

L. F. LONDON. The Public Career of George Edmund Badger. A. R. Newsome.

1937   C. E. CAUTHEN. Secession and Civil War in South Carolina. F. M. Green.

J. C. SITTERSON. The Secession Movement in North Carolina, 1847-1861. A. R. Newsome.

J. H. WOLFE. Jeffersonian Democracy in South Carolina. J. G. de R. Hamilton.

C. V. WOODWARD. The Political and Literary Career of Thomas E. Watson. H. K. Beale.

1939   M. B. POUND. The Public Career of Benjamin Hawkins. F. M. Green.

J. B. SELLERS. History of the Prohibition Movement in Alabama. F. M. Green.

Ph.D.

1940
J. M. GRIMES, JR. The Life of Caracalla. W. E. Caldwell.

A. B. KEITH. Three North Carolina Blount Brothers in Business and Politics, 1783-1812. A. R. Newsome.

E. G. MCPHERSON. The History of Reporting the Debates and Proceedings of Congress. H. T. Lefler.

M. S. MENDENHALL. A History of Agriculture in South Carolina, 1790 to 1860: An Economic and Social Study. H. T. Lefler.

PAUL MURRAY. The Whig Party in Georgia, 1825-1853. F. M. Green.

R. W. PATRICK. Jefferson Davis and His Cabinet. F. M. Green.

V. L. WHARTON. The Negro in Mississippi, 1865-1890. F. M. Green.

1941
W. E. CHACE. The Descent on Democracy: A Study of American Democracy as Observed by British Travellers, 1815-1860. F. M. Green.

C. B. CLARK. Politics in Maryland during the Civil War. F. M. Green.

E. A. HAMMOND. The Medical Profession in England in the Late Middle Ages. J. C. Russell.

1942
S. W. MARTIN. The Territorial Period of Florida, 1819-1845. F. M. Green.

W. L. MURRAY. The International Control of the Slave Trade from 1885 to 1937. M. B. Garrett.

OSCAR SVARLIEN. International Control of the Traffic in Women: A Study of International Organization. M. B. Garrett.

1943
J. C. BONNER. Agricultural Reform in the Georgia Piedmont, 1820-1860. F. M. Green.

A. F. MEISEN. Thomas Jefferson, War Governor of Virginia. A. R. Newsome.

1945
S. C. DESKINS. The Presidential Election of 1928 in North Carolina. A. R. Newsome.

A. S. LINK. The South and the Democratic Campaign of 1910-1912. F. M. Green.

M.A.

1898
R. H. GRAVES. The Puritan and Cavalier of 1640.

1900
S. W. STOCKARD. The History of Alamance.

M.A.

1902	J. F. DUNCAN. History of the Louisiana Territory.
1905	W. P. JACOCKS. Federal Operations in Eastern North Carolina during the Civil War.
	J. H. VAUGHAN. Downfall of Royal Government in North Carolina.
	I. C. WRIGHT. North Carolina's Rejection and Adoption of the Federal Constitution.
1907	B. L. WHITAKER. The Provincial Council and the Committees of Safety in North Carolina.
1910	P. G. GUNTER. Comparison of Jeffersonian and Jacksonian Democracy.
1912	E. V. PATTERSON. Attempts to Secure a Compromise in 1861.
1913	T. E. MCMILLAN. The Press in Early American Politics. (1789-1809).
1914	K. B. BAILEY. The Campaign of 1912.
	R. C. GLENN. Relation of North Carolina to the Confederacy.
	J. L. ORR. Military Government in the South during 1865-66.
	L. W. PEARSON. The Presidential Campaign of 1864.
1915	J. N. HALL. The Cartoon in American Politics.
1916	SELDEN GOODE, JR. (No title available.)
1920	R. H. TAYLOR. The Free Negro in North Carolina. J. G. de R. Hamilton.
1921	E. M. CLEGG. David Caldwell: A Study in Early County and State History. J. G. de R. Hamilton.
	K. C. FRAZIER. Political Theories of Alexander Hamilton. W. W. Pierson.
	L. D. MARTIN. Recent Diplomatic Relations Between the United States and Nicaragua. W. W. Pierson.
1922	C. R. EDNEY. Political Theories of John C. Calhoun. W. W. Pierson.
	F. M. GREEN. Presidential Campaign and Election of 1832. J. G. de R. Hamilton.
	T. C. TAYLOR. Notes on Taxation in North Carolina, with Special Emphasis on the General Property Tax. R. D. W. Connor.
	M. H. WOLFF. Limitations of Armaments. J. R. Flournoy.

M.A.

1923
V. V. ADERHOLT. Political Theories of Elisha Mulford. W. W. Pierson.

C. B. ALEXANDER. Woodrow Wilson's Political Ideas. W. W. Pierson.

J. W. COKER. Political Theory of John C. Hurd. W. W. Pierson.

C. J. MOSS. Origin and Development of the General Assembly in Colonial North Carolina. R. D. W. Connor.

J. C. SPRUILL. Political Ideas of Orestes A. Brownson. W. W. Pierson.

D. J. WHITENER. Rise of the Standing Committee System in Congress. J. G. de R. Hamilton.

1924
F. C. ANSCOMBE. The Work of the Baltimore Association: The Quakers and Reconstruction in North Carolina. J. G. de R. Hamilton.

1925
WALKER BARNETTE. The Beginning of Party Organizations in North Carolina: A Documentary History of the Campaign of 1836. R. D. W. Connor.

W. P. BRANDON. Van Buren and the Establishment of the Independent Treasury. A. R. Newsome.

I. N. CARR. The Relation of the United States with Panama since 1903. F. B. Simkins.

W. S. JENKINS. The Internal Organization of National Political Parties. J. G. de R. Hamilton.

E. G. McPHERON. Edward Moseley: A Study in North Carolina Politics. R. D. W. Connor.

J. W. PATTON. Early Applications of the Principles of Extra-Territoriality in China. K. C. Frazier.

C. P. POWELL. Political Theories in Colonial North Carolina. R. D. W. Connor.

1926
O. M. BROWN. The Roman Religion and Cicero. W. E. Caldwell.

S. C. DESKINS. The Boundary Dispute between the Carolinas. R. D. W. Connor.

R. M. LYON. John C. Calhoun and Internal Improvements. A. R. Newsome.

E. S. MOSHER. The Political Theories of Religious Toleration, 1776-1835. W. W. Pierson.

J. M. SAUNDERS. The Political Theories of Thomas Paine. W. W. Pierson.

M.A.

1926
A. M. SNIDER. A Study of the Economic Conditions in Rome during the Revolution. W. E. Caldwell.

CORNELIA WEARN. Social Conditions in North Carolina in the 18th Century. R. D. W. Connor.

1927
H. P. NAYLOR. Political Theories of John Marshall. W. W. Pierson.

C. H. PEGG. A History of the Italian Republic, 1802-1805. C. P. Higby.

N. O. SAPPINGTON. The Cisalpine Republic. C. P. Higby.

1928
S. H. ASKEW. The Guarantee Clause of the Constitution since 1870. W. W. Pierson.

G. L. DICKSON. The Early Career of John C. Calhoun. H. M. Wagstaff.

M. E. EDWARDS. The Doctrine of the Separation of Powers and the Relations of the Judicial and Legislative Departments in North Carolina. E. J. Woodhouse.

K. M. WOLFF. The Conflict between Congress and the Executive over the Control of the Administrative Service, 1789-1837. W. W. Pierson.

1929
J. B. FORDHAM. Political Ideas of James Iredell. W. W. Pierson.

J. B. HARRISON. France on the Eve of the Reign of Terror. M. B. Garrett.

E. M. HOLDER. Community Life in Wachovia, 1752-1780. R. D. W. Connor.

T. H. LEATH. The Know Nothing Party in North Carolina. R. D. W. Connor.

C. K. MADDRY. The North Carolina Constitution of 1776. R. D. W. Connor.

H. McC. OWL. The Eastern Band of Cherokee Indians before and after Removal. R. D. W. Connor.

M. L. SKAGGS. The Condition of the Roman Senate from Tiberius Gracchus to Sulla. W. E. Caldwell.

W. E. UZZELL. History of Tobacco in North Carolina before the Civil War. F. P. Graham.

1930
R. W. ACHURCH. The Colonial Policy of the French Legislative Assembly. M. B. Garrett.

RUTH BLACKWELDER. The Attitude of North Carolina Moravians toward the American Revolution. R. D. W. Connor.

M.A.

1930

E. C. COUCH. The Political Theories of Francis Lieber. W. W. Pierson.

R. S. FUNDERBURK. South Carolina in the House of Representatives, 1825-1837. J. G. de R. Hamilton.

MINNIE HOLLOWELL. The Doctrines and Practices of the Anabaptists of the Sixteenth Century and Their Attitude toward Religious Tolerance. M. B. Garrett.

CHANDLER SHAW. Anthropological Observations of Tacitus. W. E. Caldwell.

A. S. SMITH. Anglo-German Relations in the Far East, 1895-1900. M. B. Garrett.

GUSTIE YARBROUGH. The Rise and Decline of the Anti-Masonic Party. F. M. Green.

1931

H. M. BUCK. Non-noble Women in Western Europe in the Middle Age. L. C. MacKinney.

ELIZABETH CALDWELL. Reconstruction in Yazoo County, Mississippi. J. G. de R. Hamilton.

J. B. DEYTON. History of the Toe River Valley to 1865. C. C. Crittenden.

M. R. DICKSON. Political Ideas of American Socialists. W. W. Pierson.

M. E. EDWARDS. The Elder Pliny as an Historian. L. C. MacKinney.

W. McK. GRUBBS. The Diplomatic Aspects of the Bering Sea Controversy through the Arbitration of Paris, 1893. K. C. Frazer.

M. E. HIGHT. The Council in Royal North Carolina. R. D. W. Connor.

J. A. LANG. The Movement for a National University, 1787-1829. F. M. Green.

G. F. TAYLOR. Calvinism of the Sixteenth Century Compared with Lutheranism and Zwinglianism. M. B. Garrett.

V. L. WHARTON. The Movement in the United States for the Annexation of Cuba, 1789-1861. F. M. Green.

1932

I. W. BARBER, JR. The Ocean-borne Commerce of Port Roanoke, 1771-1776. C. C. Crittenden.

T. C. BRYAN. The Robert J. Walker Tariff Act of 1846. F. M. Green.

M.A.
1932 R. E. BYRD. The History of the Force Bill of 1890 and Its Effect upon State Constitutions. W. W. Pierson.

V. K. DIXON. The Contest in Congress and in Court over the Reed Parliamentary Rules. W. W. Pierson and W. S. Jenkins.

E. E. ERICSON. Anson Burlingame as United States Congressman and Minister to China. J. F. Rippy.

ELIZABETH FERGUSON. A Critical Study of the Rioting in Paris during the Month of July, 1789. M. B. Garrett.

W. D. HARRIS. The Movement for Constitutional Change in North Carolina, 1868-1876. E. J. Woodhouse.

M. M. HICKS. The Vicomte de Mirabeau. M. B. Garrett.

E. H. HUNNICUTT. The Consulados of Caracas and Havana: A Comparative Study. W. W. Pierson.

M. F. JUSTICE. The History of the Relations of the Ptolemaic Dynasty of Egypt with the Roman Republic. W. E. Caldwell.

J. M. McNEIL. The American Policy of Non-Recognition toward the Russian Soviet Government. C. B. Robson.

E. F. POLHILL. The Movement for and the Adoption of the Grandfather Clause in Alabama. W. W. Pierson.

J. C. SITTERSON. The Sugar Industry in the Old South. F. M. Green.

KATHERINE SMEDLEY. The Northern Teacher on the South Carolina Sea Islands. J. G. de R. Hamilton.

J. H. WOLFE. The South Carolina Constitutional Convention of 1865. J. G. de R. Hamilton.

1933 L. W. CURRIE. The Organization and Method of the League of Nations in Reference to the Problem of International Communications and Transit. K. C. Frazer.

J. S. FRAZER. The Second Venezuelan Crisis and the Question of the Forcible Recovery of Public Debts. W. W. Pierson.

J. L. GODFREY. Reforms in Criminal Procedure during the French Revolution, 1789-1792. M. B. Garrett.

DISSERTATIONS AND THESES

M.A.

1933

J. M. GRIMES, JR. Literary Evidences of Graeco-Roman Relations before 264 B. C. W. E. Caldwell.

R. F. JOHNSTONE. The United States and the Panama Congress of 1826. F. M. Green.

L. F. LONDON. Sectionalism in the Colony of North Carolina. C. C. Crittenden.

E. F. MCCULLOUGH. The Federal Revolution and the Constitution of 1864 in Venezuela. W. W. Pierson.

S. W. TURLINGTON. Steam Navigation in North Carolina Prior to 1860. F. M. Green.

J. C. WILSON. Some Political Aspects of the Revolution in Georgia, 1763-1776. F. M. Green.

1934

R. M. ALBRIGHT. The Development of the Powers and Duties of the Governor of North Carolina under the Constitution of 1868. R. D. W. Connor and E. J. Woodhouse.

W. A. BROWN. Attempts at Reconciliation between Great Britain and Her Colonies, 1774-1779. R. D. W. Connor.

S. M. CARTER. The Ballinger-Pinchot Controversy. W. W. Pierson.

RACHEL CORDLE. The Decline of the Knights of Labor, with Special Reference to the Haymarket Riot. W. W. Pierson.

F. R. DWELLE. Medicine in Merovingian and Carolingian Gaul. L. C. MacKinney.

W. H. GEHRKE. The German Element in Rowan and Cabarrus Counties, North Carolina. R. D. W. Connor and H. M. Wagstaff.

E. K. GRAHAM. The *De Universo* of Hrabanus Maurus: A Medieval Encyclopedia. L. C. MacKinney.

R. G. MCAULIFFE. The Commerce of Royal Georgia. C. C. Crittenden.

M. C. MCCULLOUGH. The Work of Dorothea Lynde Dix for the Insane, 1841-1861. F. M. Green.

G. C. NORMAN. The Legislative History of the Act Abolishing Alien Contract-Labor. W. W. Pierson.

R. W. PATRICK. British Prisoners of War in the American Revolution. R. D. W. Connor.

E. E. PFAFF. The Committee of General Security: Its Genesis. M. B. Garrett.

M.A.
1934 PAULINE ROGERS. Qualifications for Suffrage and Eligibility in the Constitution of 1791. M. B. Garrett.

D. L. SCHNEIDER. Social Life in the First Continental Congress. R. D. W. Connor.

1935 W. E. BOONE. Land Value Taxation in Great Britain from 1909 to 1933. H. M. Wagstaff.

A. T. EDELMAN. The View of Justice Holmes Regarding the Functions of the Courts in Cases Involving Labor Problems. C. B. Robson.

G. K. GORDON. Theodore Roosevelt and the Algeciras Conference. W. W. Pierson.

C. C. HUSKINS. Transcontinental Railroad Surveys. F. M. Green.

D. M. LACY. The Beginnings of Industrialism in North Carolina, 1865-1900. R. D. W. Connor and C. C. Crittenden.

STUART NOBLIN. George William Curtis and Edwin Lawrence Godkin as Reform Leaders in the United States, 1865-1900. W. W. Pierson.

ESTELLE POPPER. The First National Bank as an Issue in Federalist Politics, 1791-1801. A. R. Newsome.

J. W. WEBSTER. Parliamentary Practice in the Constituent Assembly (May 5—Dec. 31, 1789). M. B. Garrett.

1936 J. A. McGEACHY, JR. Intellectual Interests of the Roman Nobility as Portrayed in the Works of Q. Aurelius Symmachus. W. E. Caldwell and L. C. MacKinney.

P. B. SCHROEDER. Manchuko and the American Policy of Non-Recognition. M. B. Garrett.

1937 W. B. AYCOCK. Tobacco Regulation in Colonial Virginia. H. T. Lefler.

J. R. CALDWELL, JR. Lotteries in North Carolina. A. R. Newsome.

R. W. CARROLL. Benjamin Franklin: Colonial Agent to Great Britain, 1757-1762. H. T. Lefler.

E. W. CASON. L'Abbé Grégoire in the Committee of Public Instruction of the National Convention. C. H. Pegg.

DISSERTATIONS AND THESES

M.A.
1937

M. C. CHAPMAN. Indian Relations in Colonial North Carolina, 1584-1754. H. T. Lefler.

E. H. GIBSON III. Hospices and Hospitals in France in the Early Middle Ages. L. C. MacKinney.

W. H. KAMPSCHMIDT. Lycurgus, the Eminent Statesman and Financial Adviser of the Athenian Commonwealth. W. E. Caldwell and J. C. Russell.

J. A. KARLIN. The French Annexation of Avignon and the Comtat Venaissin in 1791. M. B. Garrett.

M. B. McPHERSON. The Administration of Governor Sir Francis Nicholson in Virginia. H. T. Lefler.

J. W. RABUN. Georgia and the Creek Indians. A. R. Newsome.

W. L. RHYNE. Joseph Chamberlain and South Africa to the Outbreak of the Boer War in 1899. H. M. Wagstaff.

DOROTHY SEAY. A Georgia Planter and His Plantations, 1837-1861. F. M. Green.

A. B. STEWART. A Critique of *Uncle Tom's Cabin*. A. R. Newsom.

P. J. WEAVER. The Gubernatorial Election of 1896 in North Carolina. H. K. Beale.

1938

SOLOMAN BREIBART. The South Carolina Constitutional Convention of 1868. F. M. Green.

KATHERINE CHATHAM. Plantation Slavery in Middle Florida. F. M. Green.

CORNELIA ESTABROOK. The Trial of King Louis XVI. M. B. Garrett and C. H. Pegg.

E. A. HAMMOND. The Medical Profession in Thirteenth Century England. J. C. Russell.

P. A. REID. Gubernatorial Campaigns and the Administrations of David S. Reid, 1848-1854. A. R. Newsome.

R. B. STARLING. The Plank Road Movement in North Carolina. A. R. Newsome.

W. G. WHICHARD. The Rider Legislation of the Hayes Administration. W. W. Pierson.

1939

H. S. ANDRUS. Church Building Activities in Early Medieval Germany. L. C. MacKinney.

L. A. BROWN. Western Sanitary Commission. F. M. Green.

M.A.

1939
A. LE R. DUCKETT. The Trial and Execution of Marie Antoinette. M. B. Garrett.

W. O. FOSTER. The Life of Montford Stokes. A. R. Newsome.

A. G. GREENE. Conscription in Ireland during the World War. H. M. Wagstaff.

A. M. HOLMAN. Diplomatic Relations of the United States with Russia from the March Revolution to the Treaty of Brest-Litovsk. H. K. Beale.

J. M. JUSTICE. The Work of "The Society for the Propagation of the Gospel in Foreign Parts" in North Carolina. H. T. Lefler.

E. M. LANDER, JR. The Attitude of Andrew Jackson toward the Second Bank of the United States. A. R. Newsome.

A. H. McLEOD, JR. Jean-Sylvain Bailly as First Mayor of Paris. M. B. Garrett.

R. F. McNEILL. The First Fifteen Months of Governor Daniel Lindsey Russell's Administration. H. K. Beale.

T. F. NORFLETT, JR. Missionary Societies of the Church of England, 1800-1825. H. M. Wagstaff.

J. W. WILLIAMS. Emigration from North Carolina, 1789-1860. A. R. Newsome.

1940
W. H. BROWN. America in Her Quest for Mesopotamian Oil, 1920-1924. H. K. Beale.

W. F. BURTON, JR. The Issue of *ad valorem* Taxation in Ante-Bellum North Carolina. A. R. Newsome.

B. G. CRABTREE. Attitude of the French Chamber of Deputies toward the Adjustment of the American Spoliation Claims against France, 1833-1836. M. B. Garrett.

H. H. CUNNINGHAM. Edward Alfred Pollard: Historian and Critic of the Confederacy. F. M. Green.

M. W. EVANS. Crimes and Punishments in Colonial North Carolina. H. T. Lefler.

CAROLINE KEELER. A Study of Some Examples of Civil Disobedience in the United States since 1865. H. K. Beale.

M. E. MASSEY. Refugee Life during the Civil War. F. M. Green.

M.A.

1940

H. F. MEARS. Cordova during Roman and Visigothic Times. W. E. Caldwell and L. C. MacKinney.

K. T. PFAFF. The Kingdom of Westphalia, 1807-1813. M. B. Garrett.

I. P. SCHILLER. A Political Philosophy of John Taylor, of Caroline: A Study in Jeffersonian Agrarianism. A. R. Newsome.

A. E. TAYLOR. The Convict Lease System in Georgia, 1866-1908. F. M. Green.

C. W. TURNER. The Louisa Railroad (1836-1850). A. R. Newsome.

B. H. WALL. Charles Pettigrew: A Study of an Early North Carolina Religious Leader and Planter. F. M. Green.

E. A. WEST. The Controversy in Congress over the Abolition Petitions from 1830 to 1844. A. R. Newsome.

1941

M. F. DUPUY. Conditions in the Highlands of Scotland, 1745-1800. M. B. Garrett.

J. L. HODGES. The "First French Republic" of 1791. M. B. Garrett.

H. D. WILKIN. The Promotion of Agriculture in North Carolina, 1810-1860. A. R. Newsome.

M. C. WYCHE. The War in North Carolina. H. T. Lefler.

1942

J. F. BARNWELL. John Barnwell, Carolina Imperialist. H. T. Lefler.

M. H. DUNNING. The Role of the French Parliament during the February Revolution of 1848. M. B. Garrett.

E. D. JOHNSON. The War of the Regulation: Its Place in History. H. T. Lefler.

A. S. LINK. The Wilson Movement in the South: A Study in Political Liberalism. F. M. Green.

H. S. McKAY. Convict Leasing in North Carolina, 1870-1934. F. M. Green.

JOHN PERIAN. Winston Churchill's Attitude toward Hitler's Germany, 1933-1939. C. H. Pegg.

B. M. TOMBERLIN. William Richardson Davie. H. T. Lefler.

M.A.

1942   H. J. ZIMMERMAN. The Formative Years of the North Carolina Board of Health, 1877-1893. F. M. Green.

1943   M. F. BOWDITCH. The North Carolina Railroad Commission, 1891-1899. F. M. Green.

R. McC. DANIEL. William Porcher Miles, Champion of Southern Interests. F. M. Green.

M. D. JOHNSON. The Problem of Slavery in the Federal Convention of 1787. A. R. Newsome.

G. V. KING. The Blair Educational Bill With Special Reference to Southern Attitudes. F. M. Green.

R. M. LANGDON. Alexander McLeod and the Caroline Affair. A. R. Newsome.

H. C. McFADYEN. The Administration of Jonathan Worth. A. R. Newsome.

W. P. ROBERTS. James Dunwoody Bulloch and the Confederate Navy. F. M. Green.

M. L. THORNTON. Public Printing in North Carolina from 1749 to 1815. A. R. Newsome.

EVELYN UNDERWOOD. The Struggle for White Supremacy and the Grandfather Clause in North Carolina. F. M. Green.

E. W. YATES. The Public Career of Alexander Martin. A. R. Newsome.

1944   J. B. BONE. Rebecca Latimer Felton, Social Reformer and Feminist Leader. F. M. Green.

H. A. ESTEVE ABRIL. The Controversy in Sixteenth Century Spain concerning the Legal and Social Status of the Indian. W. W. Pierson.

ELEANOR TAPP. The Public Career of James Mathews Griggs. F. M. Green.

1945   F. W. ASHLEY. Origin of the Republican Attack on the Federal Judiciary, 1798-1801. A. R. Newsome.

W. M. BAGBY. The Democratic and Republican National Conventions of 1920: A Study of Political Reaction. A. R. Newsome.

M. S. R. CUNNINGHAM. Gabriel Johnston, Governor of North Carolina, 1734-1752. H. T. Lefler.

W. B. GRIER. North Carolina Baptists and the Negro, 1727-1877. F. M. Green.

M.A.
1945 M. F. GYLES. A Preliminary Survey of the Commercial Relations of Egypt during the Saite Period. W. E. Caldwell.

DEPARTMENT OF MATHEMATICS

Ph.D.
1901 ARCHIBALD HENDERSON. Cone of the Normals and an Allied Cone for Central Surfaces of the Second Degree.

1933 G. W. NICHOLSON. The Generalized Form of the Lorentz Transformation. Archibald Henderson.

1936 E. A. CAMERON. On Loci Associated with Certain Osculants of a Plane Curve. J. W. Lasley, Jr.

1939 R. C. BLACKWELL. Cubic Having R-Point Contact with a Plane Curve. J. W. Lasley, Jr.

H. M. NAHIKIAN. Conditions That a Matrix B be Expressible as a Polynomial in a Set of Partial Idempotent and Nilpotent Elements of a Matrix A, and Applications to the Solution of Matric Equations. E. T. Browne.

H. V. PARK. Conditions on Two Singular Matrices A and B Such That AB and BA May Have the Same Reduced Characteristic Function. E. T. Browne.

C. L. SEEBECK, JR. Vectors Associated with a Curve in a Riemann N-Space. B. A. Hoyle.

1941 C. H. FRICK. The Development of Formulas for Columns with Varying Moment of Inertia and End Conditions. T. F. Hickerson.

1945 C. L. CARROLL, JR. Normal Simple Lie Algebras of Type D and Order 28 over a Field of Characteristic Zero. Nathan Jacobson.

M.A.
1898 J. K. HAIR. Maximum Stresses in a Through Pratt Truss for Wheel-Loads.

1899 ARCHIBALD HENDERSON. Theory of the Generating Lines of an Hyperloid of One Sheet.

1903 G. P. STEVENS. Mathematics and Progress.

1904 M. H. STACY. Brief Study of the Nebular Hypothesis.

1907 T. F. HICKERSON. The Transition Curve: A Field Method.

MATHEMATICS

M.A.

1908 — *W. T. McGowan. Construction of Eight Circles Touching Three Given Circles.

1909 — J. W. Speas. Stresses in a Through Pratt Truss by Comparative Methods.

1911 — J. M. Costner, Jr. Design for a Reinforced Concrete Railway Arch Bridge.

J. W. Lasley. Design of a Highway Bridge.

1912 — T. R. Eagles. Singular Solution of Differential Equations.

W. W. Rankin. The Cubic Equation.

J. E. Wood. Design of an Engineering and Physics Building for the University of North Carolina.

1914 — J. B. Scarborough. Equilibrium Conditions for the Motion of a Motor Cycle on the Motor Drome.

1916 — H. W. Collins. A Design for a High Masonry Dam.

1920 — J. B. Linker. Calculation of Symmetric Functions. Archibald Henderson.

1922 — M. A. Hill, Jr. Eugenio Beltrami's Contribution to the Theory of Surfaces. Archibald Henderson.

1923 — F. H. Eaton. The Role of Cross Ratio in Projective Geometry. J. W. Lasley, Jr.

1924 — C. H. Benson. Some Constructions Used in Projective Geometry. J. W. Lasley, Jr.

G. S. Bruton. Applications of Projective Geometry to Elementary Mathematics. J. W. Lasley, Jr.

W. V. Parker. Fundamental Properties of Symmetric and Skew-symmetric Determinants and Matrices. E. T. Browne.

1925 — J. R. Abernathy. Notes in Differential Geometry on the Pseudosphere and Its Geodesics. Archibald Henderson.

C. C. Edwards. The Development of Some Fundamental Principles of Mechanics. A. W. Hobbs.

V. A. Hoyle. Algebraic Properties of Resultants. E. T. Browne.

1926 — *L. E. Bush. Some Metric Properties of Conics. J. W. Lasley, Jr.

1927 — R. C. Blackwell. Geometry of the Triangle. A. W. Hobbs.

---

* Master of Science.

M.A.

1927 A. T. CURLEE. Elliptic Integrals and Their Relation to Elliptic Functions. A. W. Hobbs.

Z. T. FORTESCUE, JR. Some Properties of Discriminants. E. T. Browne.

L. L. GARNER. A Comparison of the Properties of Indices in the Solution of Congruences with the Properties of Natural Logarithms. E. T. Browne.

C. W. HOOK. A Comparison from the Pedagogical Point of View of Solutions in Radicals of the General Quartic Equation. E. T. Browne.

E. S. ROGERS. Desargues and His Contribution to Projective Geometry. J. W. Lasley, Jr.

HERBERT SCHOLZ, JR. The Historical Development of Conic Sections. A. W. Hobbs.

1928 R. C. BULLOCK. Some Properties of Orthogonal Matrices and Their Application to Elementary Mathematics. E. T. Browne.

DAN HALL. A Criterion for Examining the Roots of an Algebraic Equation. E. T. Browne.

M. W. HOOK. Some Problems of Euclidean Geometry Treated Projectively. J. W. Lasley, Jr.

C. R. ROGERS. The Tschirnhausen Transformations. A. W. Hobbs.

V. M. SCHAIBLE. Parametric Representation of Curves. J. W. Lasley, Jr.

M. A. THOMPSON. The Icosahedron Studied from the Viewpoint of Analytic Geometry. J. W. Lasley, Jr.

F. T. WILLIAMS. Some Applications of Mathematics to the Problem of Fluid Motion. A. W. Hobbs.

1929 E. A. CAMERON. The Role of the Absolute in Geometry. J. W. Lasley, Jr.

J. A. L. SAUNDERS. Methods of Interchanging Point and Line Equations of Plane Curves. J. W. Lasley, Jr.

1930 M. J. BRUTON. Study of Lorentz Transformation. Archibald Henderson.

E. C. COKER, JR. Dimensionality in Projective Geometry. J. W. Lasley, Jr.

H. L. DILLIN. Infinite Series. E. L. Mackie.

M.A.

1930   R. L. GARRETT. Reduction of Quadratic Forms to Canonical Form. E. T. Browne.

J. A. L. SAUNDERS. Methods of Interchanging Point and Line Equations of Plane Curves. J. W. Lasley, Jr.

*J. J. SLADE, JR. The Coordinates of Geometry. J. W. Lasley, Jr.

G. R. TROTT. Some Properties of Functional Determinants and Their Application to Elementary Mathematics. E. T. Browne.

MRS. L. C. WILSON. Various Types of the Equations of Curves with Application to Elliptic Motion. A. S. Winsor.

1931   LOUISE ADAMS. Methods of Finding the Differential Equation Whose Envelope Is Four Straight Lines. Archibald Henderson.

F. M. ANGE. Circles Connected with a Triangle. Archibald Henderson.

1932   C. A. DENSON. On the Classification of Non-singular Correlations. J. W. Lasley, Jr.

*J. D. LINKER. Fundamental Properties of the Characteristic Equation of a Matrix. E. T. Browne.

D. M. SEWARD. Plane Coordinate Systems as Special Cases of Homogeneous Projective Coordinates. J. W. Lasley, Jr.

I. J. STEPHENSON. Systems of Two Conics and Steiner's Quartic Surface. A. W. Hobbs.

1933   H. B. HERBERT. Geometric Conditions That De-ermine a Conic. J. W. Lasley, Jr.

H. V. PARK. Analytical Criteria for Geometrical Conditions. J. W. Lasley, Jr.

S. G. ROTH. The Method of Abridged Notation. J. W. Lasley, Jr.

J. G. WALL. Existence Theorems and Certain Applications for Ordinary Differential Equations. E. L. Mackie.

W. R. WALL. Elementary Invariants. J. W. Lasley, Jr.

1934   F. M. JAMES. Determination of Asymptotes. J. W. Lasley, Jr.

---

* Master of Science.

DISSERTATIONS AND THESES

M.A.

1934 R. E. MARSHALL. Properties of Algebraic Equations All of Whose Roots Are Real. E. T. Browne.

H. M. NAHIKIAN. Application of the Analytic Triangle to Higher Plane Curves. J. W. Lasley, Jr.

B. J. PETTIS. An Introduction to Periodic Decimal Fractions and Their Properties. E. T. Browne.

J. P. TORIAN. A Problem in Inversion. A. S. Winsor.

G. A. YORK. Various Methods of Determining the Upper Limits of the Real Roots of Algebraic Equations. E. T. Browne.

1935 H. B. HOYLE, JR. On Conformal Mapping. E. L. Mackie.

1936 M. C. BELL. The Solution of Pell's Equation. E. T. Browne.

T. H. LEE. Normal Matrices. E. T. Browne.

J. L. MCDANIEL. Some Properties of Longchamps' Circle. A. S. Winsor.

C. C. WILLIAMS. On Certain Methods of Approximation for Plane Curves. J. W. Lasley, Jr.

1937 C. P. BROOKS. Historical Development of the Cross Ratio Concept. J. W. Lasley, Jr.

C. L. CARROLL, JR. The Role of the Imaginary in Projective Geometery. J. W. Lasley, Jr.

ELIZABETH JOHNSON. Certain Riemann Surfaces. E. L. Mackie.

R. E. SMITH. Applications of the Moving Trihedral. J. W. Lasley, Jr.

1938 J. V. HOWELL. Geometric Solutions of the Biquadratic Equation. Archibald Henderson.

J. F. MUNCH. Fermat's Last Theorem for the Case $n=3$. E. T. Browne.

1939 E. S. ASHCRAFT. The Historical Development of the Basic Theorems of Applied Mechanics. T. F. Hickerson.

ROBERT HOOKE. Operational Analysis. E. L. Mackie.

C. H. LITTLE, JR. Harmonic Polygons. A. S. Winsor.

F. E. PEARSALL. A Proof that e and Π Are Transcendental Numbers. A. S. Winsor.

A. J. WILLIAMS. Some Projective Concepts in Metric Differential Geometry. J. W. Lasley, Jr.

MATHEMATICS

M.A.

1940 JOSEPHINE BARNETT. The Trisection of Angles: A Technical Study with Historical Introduction. Archibald Henderson.

G. K. CLARK. An Analysis of a Mathematics Placement Test and the Mathematical Theory in the Factorial Method of Analysis. R. J. Wherry and M. A. Hill.

C. L. DAVIS. An Introduction to the Theory of Sampling with Applications. M. A. Hill.

NESTORE DI COSTANZO. On Some Relations between Projective Geometry and Theory of Equations. J. W. Lasley, Jr.

E. L. JENKINS. An Introduction to the Theory of Correlation, with Applications. M. A. Hill.

J. O. REYNOLDS. The Algebra of Homogenous Linear Equations in Projective Geometry. J. W. Lasley, Jr.

1941 A. B. CORRY. A Study in Quaternions with Special Reference to Rotations in Space. E. T. Browne.

MARGUERITE HUTCHINSON. Some Constructions and Properties of the Center of Curvature of the Conic Sections. E. A. Cameron and V. A. Hoyle.

ANNE MEWBORNE. Metric-projective Properties of Quadric Surfaces. E. T. Browne.

G. E. NICHOLSON, JR. Certain Number Theoretic Functions and Some of Their Properties. E. T. Browne.

M. McC. TEMPLETON. Special Modifications of Geometric Figures by Projection. J. W. Lasley, Jr.

C. B. TOXEY. Certain Special Methods of Integration. E. L. Mackie.

1942 B. C. HORNE, JR. Confocal Quadric Surfaces. E. T. Browne.

JACK NEELY. Some Applications of Modern Higher Algebra to the Study of Analytic Geometry of Space. E. T. Browne.

1944 C. M. SMITH. A Critical Study of Vector Analysis. T. F. Hickerson.

IRWIN STONER. The Lemma of Schwarz: Its Generalization and Applications. A. T. Brauer.

L. P. WALKER. Certain Fundamental Properties of Skew Symmetric Matrices and Determinants. E. T. Browne.

M.A.
1945   GERTRUDE EHRLICH. The Irreducibility of Polynomials Which Take Certain Values for Integral Arguments. A. T. Brauer.

DEPARTMENT OF MUSIC

Ph.D.
1939   P. S. HANSEN. The Life and Works of Dominico Phinot (C.1510—C.1555). Glen Haydon.

M.A.
1938   K. I. KENNARD. The Beginnings of the Violincello Sonata in Italy. Glen Haydon.

1940   D. P. BENNETT. A Study in Fiddle Tunes from Western North Carolina. J. P. Schinhan.

1941   N. C. SMITH. A Study of the Problem of Expressiveness as Exemplified in Certain of the Choral-orchestral Works of Johannes Brahms: A Style-critical Study. Glen Haydon.

1942   JOSEPHINE ANDOE. The Clavier Suites of Kindermann, Pachelbel, Johann Krieger, Kuhnau, and Franz Murschhauser: A Style-critical Study. Glen Haydon.

1944   L. G. SCHMEISSER. A Study of the Development Section of the Sonata-Form as Exemplified by Beethoven's Piano Sonatas. Glen Haydon.

SCHOOL OF PHARMACY

M.S.
1938   *W. R. LLOYD. A Phytochemical Study of *Kalmia angustifolia*. M. L. Jacobs.

*H. D. ROTH. The Preliminary Examination of *Chrysopsis graminifolia*, with Particular Reference to the Water-soluble Constituents. H. M. Burlage.

1940   *E. P. RIGSBY. A Phytochemical Study of *Impatiens biflora*. M. L. Jacobs.

1944   *J. P. LA ROCCA. The Assay of Nux Vomica Preparations by Chromatographic Methods. H. M. Burlage.

---

* Master of Science.

DEPARTMENT OF PHILOSOPHY

Ph.D.

1924   A. F. LIDDELL. The Logical Relationship of the Philosophy of Hegel to the Philosophies of Spinoza and Kant. H. H. Williams.

1931   P. A. CARMICHAEL. The Nature of Freedom. H. H. Williams.

1937   C. J. BURWELL. The Relation of Hegelian Epistemology to the Development of Individuality. H. H. Williams.

M.A.

1892   W. M. COLEMAN. (No title available.)

1895   M. H. YOUNT. Future of Popular Government.

1904   W. J. GORDON. Study of *The World and the Individual*—Royce: A Statement of His Doctrine and a Short Criticism.

1906   O. B. ROSS. Review and Criticism of Royce's Conception of Reality as Developed in *The World and the Individual*.

1908   F. M. HAWLEY. The Authority of Religion.

L. R. HOFFMAN. Dogma in Religion.

1910   YUTAKA MINAKUCHI. Two Interpretations of Life: Personal and Institutional or *Sachlich*.

J. T. REECE. The Two Interpretations of Life—the Personal and the *Sachlich*.

1914   M. T. SPEARS. Meaning of Law.

1915   W. R. PARKER. The Institution and Its Part in Life.

1917   R. F. BROWN. Search for Reality.

1920   H. G. WEST. Logic of the Newspaper. H. H. Williams.

1931   O. H. CHAMBERLAIN. A Study of John Dewey's Logical Reconstruction. H. H. Williams.

J. M. CHEEK. The Religion of Ancient India: A Study in the Logic of Civilization. H. H. Williams.

C. A. MADDRY. Kant's Conception of Causality: An Interpretation. S. A. Emery.

1932   M. H. WILLIAMS. A Logical Classification of Certain Philosophies of History. H. H. Williams.

1933   A. E. WALKER. What Is Education? H. H. Williams.

1935   C. J. BURWELL. A Study of the Process of the Hegelian Dialectic. H. H. Williams.

DISSERTATIONS AND THESES

M.A.

1935   WHITFIELD COBB, JR. The Logical Development of the Conception of God in Relation to Values. H. H. Williams.

J. A. ROSS. The Logic of the Spiritual Process. H. H. Williams.

1938   J. W. C. GROTYOHANN. The Disparity between Form and Content in the Contemporary Drama with Reference to Aristotle's "Poetics." G. F. Thomas.

DEPARTMENT OF PHYSICS

Ph.D.

1930   M. L. BRAUN. Current, Frequency, and Pressure Relationships for the Initiation and Maintenance of the Electrodeless Glow Discharge in Gases. Otto Stuhlman, Jr.

J. F. DAUGHERTY. The Infra-Red Absorption Spectra of Benzene and Its Halogen Derivatives. E. K. Plyler.

O. P. HART. Intensity Variation of Arc and Spark Lines in the Electrodeless Discharge of Mercury. Otto Stuhlman, Jr.

1935   C. J. CRAVEN. The Infra-Red Absorption of Aqueous Solutions of Various Copper Salts from 0.6μ to 6.2μ. E. K. Plyler.

WALTER GORDY. The Infra-Red Absorption of Solutions of Hydroxides and Hydrolyzing Salts. E. K. Plyler.

P. J. STEELE. The Infra-Red Absorption Spectra of the Hydrolyzing Salts of Cobalt and Nickel in Solution. E. K. Plyler.

1936   E. S. BARR. The Infra-Red Absorption of Aqueous Solutions of Acids from 1.7μ to 6.5μ. E. K. Plyler.

SHERWOOD GITHENS, JR. The Striking Potential of High Frequency Discharges in Hydrogen as Conditioned by Frequency. Otto Stuhlman, Jr.

F. D. WILLIAMS. The Infra-Red Absorption of the Cyanides. E. K. Plyler.

1938   G. E. CROUCH, JR. The Infra-Red Absorption Spectra of Nitrobenzene-Benzene and Ethyl Alcohol-Benzene Mixtures. E. K. Plyler.

M. W. HODGE. The Statistical Behavior of Geiger-Müller Tube Counters. A. E. Ruark.

Ph.D.

1938   C. C. JONES. Energy Loss in the Nuclear Scattering of Electrons in the Energy Range from 0.3 to 2.6 Million Electron Volts. A. E. Ruark.

KATHERINE WAY. Photoelectric Cross Section of the Deuteron. J. A. Wheeler.

J. W. WHITE. The Infra-Red Absorption of Phenol and Ethyl Alcohol. E. K. Plyler.

1940   E. I. HOWELL. High Energy Secondaries in Nitrogen Gas Produced by Electrons of 1.3 to 2.6 Million Electron Volts. A. E. Ruark.

D. R. McMILLAN, JR. The Infra-Red Absorption Spectra of Methyl and Ethyl Alcohol. E. K. Plyler.

1942   A. C. MENIUS, JR. Calculations on the Rosen Theory of the Electron. Nathan Rosen.

1943   C. K. BECK. Infra-Red Absorption of Solid Ammonium Chloride and Ammonium Bromide. P. E. Shearin.

M.A.

1901   J. E. LATTA. Ether Dynamics.

1902   *L. V. N. BRANCH. Resumé of the Development and Present Status of the Theory of Ionic Dissociation.

1908   P. H. ROYSTER. An Application of the Kinetic Theory to Adiabatic Transformations.

1909   *J. C. HINES. The Flicker Photometer and Other Methods of Measuring Relative Intensities of Colored Light Sources.

1910   *V. C. PRITCHETT. Atmospheric Electricity.

1913   T. S. ROYSTER. Therapeutic Value of Electricity.

1915   C. L. WOODALL. Development of Physical Science.

1924   *D. A. WELLS. Secondary Electron Emission from Metals. Otto Stuhlman, Jr.

M. L. BRAUN. Equipment for the Teaching of Physics in Secondary Schools. Otto Stuhlman, Jr., and P. W. Dike.

1925   J. F. DAUGHERTY. The Electrodeless Ring Discharge In Certain Vapors. A. H. Patterson.

1926   *P. H. CARR. The Recovery of Selenium from the Effect of X-Rays. E. K. Plyler.

---

* Master of Science.

M.A.

1926 *J. DE L. FINKLEA. Some Methods of Generating Alternating Current with the Mercury Arc. E. K. Plyler.

1928 *A. F. DANIEL. Studies in Luminescence of Hiddenite and Kunzite. Otto Stuhlman, Jr.

E. R. MANN. The Distribution on a Surface of Evaporating Parallel Wires for Producing Uniform Metallic Films. Otto Stuhlman, Jr.

H. D. USSERY. Studies in Electrolysis. E. K. Plyler.

1929 THEODORE BURDINE. Infra-Red Absorption Bands in the Alcohols. E. K. Plyler.

*P. J. STEELE. The Infra-Red Absorption Spectra of Organic Nitrates. E. K. Plyler.

M. W. TRAWICK. An Analysis of the Electrodeless Spectrum of Mercury at 20 Microns Pressure. Otto Stuhlman, Jr.

1930 K. Z. MORGAN. The Effect of External Resistance in the Plate-Filament Circuit of Radiotrons. Otto Stuhlman, Jr.

M. D. WHITAKER. The Photometric Characteristics of the Electrodeless Discharge in Air and Mercury Vapor. Otto Stuhlman, Jr.

1931 P. E. SHEARIN. The Relation between the Intensity and Position of the Overtones of Some Organic Liquids. E. K. Plyler.

*H. B. MULKEY. The Effect of External Resistance on the Characteristics of a Dynatron. Otto Stuhlman, Jr.

H. H. ZUR BURG. Characteristics of the Electrodeless Discharge in Nitrogen and Hydrogen. Otto Stuhlman, Jr.

1933 E. S. BARR. Intensity of the Hydrogen β, γ, and δ Lines in the Balmer Series Excited by Electrodeless Discharges. Otto Stuhlman, Jr.

C. J. CRAVEN. The Infra-Red Absorption of Nitrate and Carbonate Ions. E. K. Plyler.

SHERWOOD GITHENS, JR. The Internal Magnetic Field of a Solenoid Oscillating at Radio Frequencies. Otto Stuhlman, Jr.

WALTER GORDY. The Effect of an Electric Field on the Infra-Red Absorption of Molecules. E. K. Plyler.

---

* Master of Science.

M.A.
1933   *R. D. WEATHERFORD. The Surface Energy of Dilute Electrolytes. Otto Stuhlman, Jr.

1934   *ANTONIOS ANTONAKOS. Infra-Red Absorption of Aqueous Solutions of Various Halides, 4-5μ. E. K. Plyler.

*C. M. LEAR. Electrification by Collision of Mercury Vapor with an Iron Collector. Otto Stuhlman, Jr.

M. S. McCAY. The Intensity of the Alpha and Beta Lines of Hydrogen as Conditioned by Pressure and Tube Diameter when Excited by Electrodeless Discharge. Otto Stuhlman, Jr.

F. D. WILLIAMS. Infra-Red Absorption of Alcoholic Solutions of the Hydroxides of the Alkali Metals. E. K. Plyler.

1936   F. B. BREAZEALE. On the Use of Wire Screens as Neutral Light Diminishers. Otto Stuhlman, Jr.

R. L. DRISCOLL. An Apparatus for Automatic Analysis of Fluctuations in Radioactive Disintegrations. A. E. Ruark.

TIMOTEO GATICA. The Infra-Red Absorption of Mixtures of Water and Alcohol. E. K. Plyler.

W. L. SMITH. Disintegration of the Beryllium Nucleus by Gamma Rays; Search for Photo-Disintegration of Potassium; Decay Periods of Neutron Induced Activity of Silver; Ratio of Silver Activities Produced by Fast and Slow Neutrons. A. E. Ruark.

*J. W. WHITE. The Infra-Red Absorption of Ethyl Alcohol and Phenol. E. K. Plyler.

1937   H. G. DORSETT, JR. Infra-Red Absorption of Certain Strong and Weak Acids in Aqueous Solutions. E. K. Plyler.

H. M. PARKER. Stable States of Two Deuterons. J. A. Wheeler.

1939   L. J. WILLIS. Infra-Red Absorption of Certain Ketones and Their Corresponding Thio-Ketones. E. K. Plyler.

L. D. WYLY, JR. Thermoelectric and Resistance Temperature Detectors. E. K. Plyler.

1940   *J. S. BROCK. Close Electron-Electron Collisions at Energies from 0.5 to 2.5 Million Electron Volts. A. E. Ruark.

---
* Master of Science.

DISSERTATIONS AND THESES

M.A.

1940   F. L. HORTON. The Infra-Red Absorption of Dioxane-Water Mixtures. E. K. Plyler.

*W. A. PAGE. The Use of Thorium Oxide as a Source of Infra-Red Radiation. E. K. Plyler.

1941   *G. A. HORNBECK. High Energy Secondaries in Nitrogen Produced by Electrons of 0.67 to 1.32 Million Electron Volts. A. E. Ruark.

T. E. PARDUE. Electron-Electron Collisions in the Primary Energy Range from 1.3 to 2.6 Million Electron Volts. A. E. Ruark and P. E. Shearin.

1944   *LAWRENCE FELDMAN. Lower Limits for the Energy Levels of Helium. Nathan Rosen.

*IRVING RESNICK. Boundary Perturbations in Acoustics. E. J. Hellund.

DEPARTMENT OF PHYSIOLOGY

M.S.

1943   VIRGINIA SUHRIE. The Effect of Small Doses of Alcohol upon the Growth and Reproduction of Rats. H. W. Ferrill.

1944   M. E. DARK. Plasma Volume Restoration Following Acute Hemorrhage. A. T. Miller, Jr.

DEPARTMENT OF PLANT PATHOLOGY
(State College)

Ph.D.

1945   D. E. ELLIS. Anthracnose of Dwarf Mistletoe Caused by *Septogloeum gillii* N. Sp.

DEPARTMENT OF POLITICAL SCIENCE

Ph.D.

1938   D. C. CORBITT. The Colonial Government of Cuba. W. W. Pierson.

1941   C. O. LERCHE, JR. The Guarantee of a Republican Form of Government to the States: A Study of Action and Interpretation by the Legislative, Executive, and Judicial Departments of the United States Government. W. W. Pierson and W. S. Jenkins.

1942   C. C. CARTER. The Inferior Courts of North Carolina Created by Legislative Enactment. W. S. Jenkins.

1943   M. C. HUGHES. County Government in Georgia. P. W. Wager.

---

* Master of Science.

M.A.

1938   W. S-J. BLACKSHEAR. Efforts and Achievement in the Codification of International Law by the American States since the World War. K. C. Frazer.

1939   W. N. RAIRIGH. The English Law in Maryland, 1634-1689. E. J. Woodhouse.

1940   A. M. BANNERMAN. A Plan of Government for a Southern Highland Community. P. W. Wager.

A. D. ELLISON. A Study of Municipal Civil Service in North Carolina. J. W. Fesler.

W. A. MITCHELL. The County Legislative Delegation in South Carolina County Government. P. W. Wager.

1941   W. H. O'BRIAN. Legislative Councils in the United States. W. S. Jenkins.

J. L. WITHERS. State Personnel Administration in North Carolina. J. W. Fesler.

1942   D. H. CARLISLE. Cuba, Haiti, and the Dominican Republic in the League of Nations. K. C. Frazer.

ANDREW SZPER. The International Legal Status of Refugees and Stateless Persons. K. C. Frazer.

E. F. WINNINGHAM. Japan's Attitude toward Disarmament Efforts of the League of Nations. K. C. Frazer.

1943   F. H. HARRIS. The Grand Jury in North Carolina: Its Role as a Poltical Institution. C. B. Robson.

DEPARTMENT OF PSYCHOLOGY

Ph.D.

1926   W. W. ROGERS. Factors Involved in the Formation of a Multiple Habit from Disparate Activities. J. F. Dashiell.

1930   K. L. BARKLEY. The Development and Demonstration of a New Method for Determining the Relative Efficiencies of Advertisements in Magazines, with Three Subsidiary Studies: Commodity Preferences, False Recalls, Sex Differences. H. W. Crane.

J. H. McFADDEN. Differential Responses of Normal and Feebleminded Subjects of Equal Mental Age on the Kent-Rosanoff Free Association Test and the Stanford Revision of the Binet-Simon Intelligence Test. H. W. Crane.

1931   A. G. BAYROFF. The Effect of Varying and Stable Environments on Behavior in the Direction Test Box. J. F. Dashiell.

Ph.D.
1931 G. B. DIMMICK. The Effects of Certain Distracting Conditions upon Habit Integration. J. F. Dashiell.

W. D. GLENN, JR. The Fehlers: A Social and Psychometric Study of a Cacogenic Family. H. W. Crane.

J. R. PATRICK. The Effect of Emotional Excitement on Rational Behavior as Demonstrated by the Quadruple-Choice Method. J. F. Dashiell.

1933 H. N. DE WICK. The Relative Recall Effectiveness of Visual and Auditory Presentation of Advertising Material. H. W. Crane.

G. G. KILLINGER. Emotional Judgments of Music. J. F. Dashiell.

1934 R. H. PRESTON. The Retracing Factor in Reversed Maze Learning by the White Rat. J. F. Dashiell.

1937 D. D. WICKENS. The Transference of Conditioned Excitation and Conditioned Inhibition from One Muscle Group to the Antagonistic Muscle Group. J. F. Dashiell.

1938 H. V. BICE. A Study in Word Association. H. W. Crane.

H. W. MARTIN. Effects of Practice on Judging Various Traits of Individuals. J. F. Dashiell.

DOROTHY RETHLINGSHAFER. Behavior of Feebleminded and Normal Subjects Following the Interruption of Activities. J. F. Dashiell.

D. K. SPELT. The Establishment of a Conditioned Response in the Human Fetus *in utero*. J. F. Dashiell.

1939 M. C. MENDENHALL. The Effect of Sodium Phenobarbital on Learning and Reasoning in White Rats. J. F. Dashiell.

1940 A. C. CORNSWEET. Recovery Sequence after Anesthetization. J. F. Dashiell.

HALSEY MACPHEE. The Inter-relational Influences of Three Different Adjunctive Stimuli on Human Maze Performance. J. F. Dashiell.

1942 W. J. DANIEL. The Development of Cooperative Problem Solving in Rats. A. G. Bayroff.

R. C. ROGERS. Response Errors in Conditioned Discrimination. A. G. Bayroff.

Ph.D.
1944   P. S. SIEGEL. An Experimental Examination of Hull's Conceptual Treatment of Simple Trial-and-Error Learning. R. J. Wherry.

CAROLINE TAYLOR. An Experimental Investigation of Improving Defective Color Perception. R. J. Wherry.

M.A.
1921   E. W. ATKINS. The White Rat's Reaction to Multiple Stimuli in Temporal Orders. J. F. Dashiell.

1922   W. D. GLENN, JR. Correlation of the Terman Individual Intelligence Test with Group Intelligence Tests. J. F. Dashiell.

J. H. MCFADDEN. Racial Differences Measured by the Downey Will-Temperament Test. J. F. Dashiell.

1923   F. M. DULA. Methods and Problems in the Measurement of Personality. F. H. Allport.

H. A. HELMS. The Learning by White Rats of an Inclined Plane as a Cue. J. F. Dashiell.

1924   *A. B. CULBERTSON. Some Experimental Work in Mental Set. J. F. Dashiell.

*H. W. MARTIN. Radical Modification of the Maze Problem. J. F. Dashiell.

W. W. ROGERS. Correlations between Estimated Interests, Estimated Abilities, and Measured Abilities of High School Pupils. J. F. Dashiell.

1925   W. M. LINKER, JR. Regularity of Learning in a Multiple Unit Maze. J. F. Dashiell.

1926   *K. C. GARRISON. Some Experimental Work in Mental Set. J. F. Dashiell.

L. C. SPEARS. An Experimental Study of the Ability of Children to Interpret Facial Expression of Emotions. J. F. Dashiell.

1927   *J. C. BAGWELL. Study of Direction Trends in Maze Learning of White Rats. J. F. Dashiell.

K. L. BARKLEY. A Method for the Demonstration of Some Principles Determining the Efficiencies of Magazine Advertisements. J. F. Dashiell.

1929   A. G. BAYROFF. Orientation and Posturing Behavior of the Albino Rat in the Multiple-U Maze. J. F. Dashiell.

---

* Master of Science.

M.A.

1929   M. W. FITZGERALD. A Study of the Validity of the Norms and Standardization of the Wells-Martin Method of Memory Examination Adapted to Psychotic Cases. H. W. Crane.

R. E. HAMILL. Behavior of White Rats in Mazes of Constant Pattern and Varying Distances to be Traversed. J. F. Dashiell.

1933   BLANCHE ZORN. Human Reactions in a Foot Maze. J. F. Dashiell.

1934   A. L. CHADBOURN. Studies in Testimony. J. F. Dashiell.

M. F. PORTER. Psychasthenic Mechanisms. English Bagby.

1935   S. K. BERWANGER. The Relation of Preference to Choice Time in Paired Comparisons of Colors. J. F. Dashiell.

H. V. BICE. Some Preliminary Studies of the Word Association Technique Preparatory to Standardization of a Test. H. W. Crane.

1938   E. U. GLASER. Distribution of Errors Made by Rats on an Elevated Maze before and after Rotation. A. G. Bayroff.

M. E. ROBINS. Reminiscence in the Learning of a Punch Board Maze. J. F. Dashiell.

1941   P. L. POLLOCK. Some Traits which Influence Preferences of Associates in a Woman's Dormitory at the University of North Carolina. J. F. Dashiell.

1942   W. F. DUKES. Constant Factors in the Learning Curve and Their Relation to Intelligence. R. J. Wherry.

CAROLINA TAYLOR. Negative After-Images of Dichromats. J. F. Dashiell.

S. C. WEBB. An Item and Factor Analysis of the Davidson College Mathematics Test. R. J. Wherry.

1943   DOROTHY SIMRALL. A Factor Analysis of Focussed Perception. R. J. Wherry.

1944   MARGERY O'KELLEY. Age-Group versus Serial Testing for Adults with the Revised Stanford-Binet. H. W. Crane.

M. R. WESTROPE. Certainty and Item Analysis. R. J. Wherry.

M.A.
1945   M. B. Ashby. An Experimental Study of the Effect of Shifting the Starting Point in Memorizing a List of Nonsense Syllables. J. F. Dashiell.

D. B. Gray. The Effect of Imposed Rates of Choice on the Learning of a Punchboard Maze. J. F. Dashiell.

DEPARTMENT OF PUBLIC ADMINISTRATION
M.S.
1933   R. B. Henry. A Study of Emergency Relief of the Unemployed in Orange County, North Carolina, October 1, 1932, to March 31, 1933. W. B. Sanders.

1934   Charlotte Califf. Wage Differentials between Negro and White Workers in Southern Industry. H. D. Wolf.

1935   H. B. Wilson. Financial Aspects of City Planning. Clarence Heer.

1938   R. K. Bailey. A Follow-Up Study in Juvenile Delinquency: The Careers of Eighty-Eight Delinquent White Boys Committed to Jackson Training School by the Durham, North Carolina, Juvenile Court (1922-1935), and Their Post-Adjustment. W. B. Sanders.

DEPARTMENT OF PUBLIC HEALTH
Ph.D.
1942   T. J. Brooks, Jr. The Treatment of Canine Filariasis with Anthiomaline, with Special Reference to the Clinical Reactions, Physiology, Pathology and Haematology Produced by This Drug in Dogs, and with Notes on the Possible Application of the Drug to the Treatment of Human Filariasis. H. W. Brown.

W. W. Taylor, Jr. Epidemiological, Pathological, and Life Cycle Studies on the Giant Kidney Worm, *Dioctophyme renale*. H. W. Brown.

*M.S.P.H.
1940   A. E. Williamson, Jr. An Investigation of Natural Disappearance of Bacteria in Air, Effect of Chemical Disinfection on Air-borne Bacteria, and Efficiencies of Air-borne Bacteria Sampling Instruments. H. B. Gotaas.

1941   E. T. Chanlett. The Time Factor in Chlorine and Chloramine Disinfection of Contaminated Swimming Pool Waters. H. B. Gotaas.

---
* Master of Science in Public Health.

DISSERTATIONS AND THESES

M.S.P.H.

1942 C. A. HANSEN. The Treatment of Domestic and Industrial Wastes by Flotation. H. B. Gotaas.

R. K. HORTON. Recovery of Dyes and Coagulants from Chemically Precipitated Textile Wastes. H. B. Gotaas.

1943 H. M. DECKER. Studies on the Cleansing and Sanitation of Eating Utensils. H. G. Baity.

1944 V. E. PEREZ-BERNAL. A Sanitation Program for the Dominican Republic. M. J. Rosenau.

*1945 F. G. BOQUIN. MRS. B. S. BRODY. R. W. BROSSMAN. T. H. BUTTERWORTH. L. E. CARSON. ANGELES CEBOLLERO. MERCEDES CEDO. M. D. CHAVEZ Y ARANGO. M. L. CLARK. M. E. DAVIS. E. H. ELLINWOOD. F. B. FERRAZ. E. H. FREEMAN. J. G. B. GONCALES DA SILVA. N. E. GRAY. N. J. GUTHNE. JANIE HERNDON. R. M. HILDEBRAND, JR. D. A. HUSKEY. MRS. M. J. IDEMA. M. J. JONES. W. L. JOYNER. M. L. KING. FRANCES KORNEGAY. M. E. KOSSACK. C. L. LANKFORD. M. H. LEONARD. M. F. LEWIS. CATALINA LUBE. E. M. MAST. M. E. MATTHEWS. MRS. A. L. MCDONALD. D. E. MELVIN. J. J. ORRANTIA. M. B. OUSLEY. M. H. PARKS. V. L. POTTS. D. E. D. RESTANO. C. B. RICKMAN. A. F. SEIKEL. C. B. SMITH. E. M. SPAHR. L. L. SPELL. J. D. STOUT. M. DE LOS A. VAZGUEZ. M. E. VIERA. A. F. VINCES. DAVID YACOEL.

DIVISION OF PUBLIC WELFARE AND SOCIAL WORK

Ph.D.

1941 V. L. DENTON. An Introductory Study of Interrelationships among Federal, State, and Local Public Relief Administrations. R. M. Brown and H. L. Herring.

1942 D. G. JONES. Youth Adjustments in a Rural Culture: Rockville Community, Hanover County, Virginia. R. M. Brown.

†M.S.S.W.

1940 ROBERTA ENLOE. An Appraisal of the County as an Administrative Unit in the Administration of Public Welfare. G. H. Lawrence.

LUCILLE HINTON. A Study of Some of the Problems of Tuberculosis Patients in Orange County. I. K. Carter.

---

* In this year a thesis was no longer required for the degree of Master of Science in Public Health.
† Master of Science in Social Work.

M.S.S.W.
1940   M. J. MacMillan. A Social Study of Child Care in the Baptist Orphanage of North Carolina. W. B. Sanders.

E. P. Welborn. Eugenical Sterilization in the United States, with Particular Attention to a Follow-up Study of Non-institutional Sterilization Cases in North Carolina, April 5, 1933, to January 1, 1939. W. B. Sanders.

1940   Grace Williams. The Use of Function in Social Case Work in a Rural Area. I. K. Carter.

M. S. Yarbrough. One Hundred Old Age Assistance Cases: A Study of the Expenditures of One Hundred Old Age Assistance Recipients in Leon County, Florida. G. H. Lawrence.

1941   V. W. Gulledge. The North Carolina Conference for Social Service: A Study of Its Development and Methods. S. M. Brown and H. L. Herring.

B. M. Mandelkorn. A Study of the Parole Systems in Seventy-Two State Institutions for Juvenile Delinquents in the United States. W. B. Sanders.

1942   M. G. Bain. Some Medical Problems of Old Age Assistance Recipients in Orange County. I. K. Carter.

M. H. Wilson. WPA: A Study of Some of the Measurable Characteristics of Work Relief Recipients in Eight North Carolina Counties. M. J. Hagood.

1943   Mrs. M. H. Lebey. Vocations for Orphanage Girls. W. B. Sanders.

M. F. Mason. The Negro Community Center of Chapel Hill, North Carolina: A Study of the Process of Community Organization. R. M. Brown.

J. L. Wallace. Children in Wartime from a Social Work Point of View. W. B. Sanders.

M. H. Wright. The Administration of Public Welfare in Kentucky. R. M. Brown.

1944   S. P. Theimann, Jr. An Analysis of Methods of Establishing Birth of Servicemen's Dependents as Indictated by Cases Handled by the Chapel Hill, North Carolina, Chapter of the American Red Cross from January 1, 1943, to June 30, 1943. G. H. Lawrence.

M.S.
1944   A. W. TILLINGHAST. A Statistical Study of the Social Work Personnel in the North Carolina County Departments of Public Welfare, November, 1941. M. J. Hagood.

1945   MRS. R. T. HARTMAN. Children in Jail in North Carolina. W. B. Sanders.

DEPARTMENT OF ROMANCE LANGUAGES

Ph.D.
1927   J. C. LYONS. The Poetic Theory of Obscurity in French Literature of the Sixteenth Century. W. M. Dey.

1928   L. L. WENHOLD. La Chanson des chétifs, an Old French Crusade Epic: An Edition with Introduction, Notes, and Variants. U. T. Holmes, Jr.

1929   G. W. FENLEY. The Roman de la rose in the Middle French Period. U. T. Holmes, Jr.

1930   M. I. BARKER. The Style and Literary Tendencies of Stendhal in His Novels. W. M. Dey.

W. C. SALLEY. The Attitude of the Spanish Romantic Dramatists toward History. N. B. Adams.

S. A. STOUDEMIRE. The Dramatic Works of D. Antonio Gil y Zárate. N. B. Adams.

1933   J. M. GALLARDO. The Individuality of Baltasar Gracián. S. A. Stoudemire and S. E. Leavitt.

R. W. LINKER. La Chevalerie de Ogier de Danemarche (lines 1-6000): A Critical Edition, with Notes, Variants, and Glossary. U. T. Holmes, Jr.

W. M. MCLEOD. The Consaus d'amours, and the Poissance d'amours of Richard de Fournival. U. T. Holmes, Jr.

A. K. SHIELDS. The Madrid Stage, 1820-1833. N. B. Adams.

1935   W. P. SMITH. Jesús Castellanos, His Life and His Works. S. E. Leavitt.

L. B. STABLER. Initiatory Study of Middle French Syntax, with Check-List. U. T. Holmes, Jr.

C. G. TAYLOR. French Tragedy and Tragic Theory, 1690-1715. W. L. Wiley.

1936   F. C. HAYES. The Use of Proverbs in the Siglo de oro Drama: An Introductory Study. S. E. Leavitt and R. S. Boggs.

Ph.D.
1937   D. E. FRIERSON. A Historical Study of the Language of Venice XIII, Franco-Italian MS. of the Fourteenth Century, with a Glossary. U. T. Holmes, Jr.

J. A. THOMPSON. Alexandre Dumas (*père*) and the Spanish Romantic Drama up to 1850. N. B. Adams.

W. R. WEAVER. An Introductory Study of Stage Devices in the *Siglo de oro* Drama. S. E. Leavitt.

1938   L. L. BARRETT. The Supernatural in the Spanish Non-religious *comedia* of the Golden Age. S. E. Leavitt.

C. M. WOODARD. Words for Horse in French and Provençal: A Study in Dialectology. U. T. Holmes, Jr.

1939   J. A. DOWNS. French Lyric Poetry, 1790-1820. W. M. Dey.

H. S. TREANOR. Le Roman de Sydrac, fontaine de toutes sciences. U. T. Holmes, Jr.

1940   D. S. WOGAN. The Indian in Mexican Poetry. S. E. Leavitt.

1941   A. G. ENGSTROM. The French Artistic Short Story before Maupassant. W. M. Dey.

J. W. HASSELL, JR. A Study of the Sources of the First Forty-Five of the *Nouvelles récréations et joyeux devis* of Bonaventure des Périers, with a Bibliography of the French *conteurs* of the 16th Century. J. C. Lyons.

E. D. HEALY. A Critical Edition of the Works of Lanfranc Cigala. U. T. Holmes, Jr.

E. McR. STAGG. Lexicon of the Novels of the Goncourts. U. T. Holmes, Jr.

1942   NITA ANDREWS. A Lexicographical Study of the Early French Farces. U. T. Holmes, Jr.

C. D. ELDRIDGE. An Introductory Study of the State of Secular Letters at the Court of Champagne in the Twelfth Century. U. T. Holmes, Jr.

1943   FRANCIS GHIGO. The Vocabulary of Mellin de Saint-Gelays. U. T. Holmes, Jr.

1943   D. F. MCDOWELL. The Nature of Old Spanish Vocabulary as Determined by an Etymological and Semantic Analysis of the Verbs in the *Primera parte* of the *General estoria* of Alfonso el Sabio. R. S. Boggs.

Ph.D.

1945   W. R. LANSBERG. Words of Doubtful and Unknown Origins in Old French and Provençal. U. T. Holmes, Jr.

M.A.

1908   L. W. PARKER. The Exciting Force in Voltaire's Dramas.

1912   W. R. THOMAS. Innovations of Voltaire in the Tragedy.

1924   M. H. DUNCAN. Brieux: Social Purpose Dominating Art. W. M. Dey.

M. R. LEARNED. The English in the Literature of France to 1550. Oliver Towles.

T. M. MCKNIGHT. Life and Works of Alberto Blest Gana. S. E. Leavitt.

W. A. PICKENS. Some Aspects of the Dramatic Art of Ruiz de Alarcón. S. E. Leavitt.

J. L. SMITH. Some Recent Treatments of the Don Juan Legend in French Drama. W. M. Dey.

S. A. STOUDEMIRE. Longfellow and Spain. S. E. Leavitt.

T. J. WILSON III. Historical Discrepancies in Alfred de Vigny. W. M. Dey.

1925   A. B. ADAMS. The "Pastelero de Madrigal" in Nineteenth Century Spanish Literature. S. E. Leavitt.

K. L. FRAZIER. Estimates of Molière by His Contemporaries. W. M. Dey.

1926   C. A. HOWELL. Guzmán el Bueno in Spanish Literature. S. E. Leavitt.

J. V. MCCALL. The Doña Inés de Castro Legend in Spanish and French Literature. S. E. Leavitt.

L. B. STABLER. Historical Inaccuracies in Certain Plays of Victor Hugo. W. M. Dey.

C. M. WOODARD. A List of Latin Words Containing Open *e* and Open *o* in Accented Open Syllables. H. D. Learned.

T. E. WRIGHT. An Edition of Letters of Henry II of France, 1547-1553. U. T. Holmes, Jr.

1927   M. I. BARKER. Lamartine's Debt to Certain English Poets. W. M. Dey.

A. R. COLLINS. The Comic Tradition of Molière and Beaumarchais in Augier. U. T. Holmes, Jr.

M.A.
1928   S. P. BROWN. The Use of History by Casimir Delavigne. U. T. Holmes, Jr.

J. E. CARROLL, JR. A Study of *Les Amours de Henry Quatre par Louise de Lorraine, princesse de Conti*, an Unpublished Manuscript in the Library of the University of North Carolina. T. J. Wilson III.

R. W. LINKER. Du Bartas' *La Premiere sepmaine* and Pliny's *Naturalis historiae*. U. T. Holmes, Jr.

C. E. POOVEY. Some Aspects of the Dramatic Art of Moreto with Comparisons to Other Playwrights of the *Siglo de oro*. N. B. Adams.

EVELYN WILSON. The Development of Stage Settings in Eighteenth Century French Drama. H. R. Huse.

1929   J. H. ALLRED. A Comparison of Benavente, *Los Intereses creados* and *La Cuidad alegre y confiada*, with Beaumarchais, *Le Barbier de Séville and Le Mariage de Figaro*. S. E. Leavitt.

J. A. DOWNS. François Ponsard and the Decline of the Romantic Drama. W. M. Dey.

E. E. HARPER. Some Aspects of the Dramatic Art of Guillén de Castro. N. B. Adams.

1930   W. D. CREECH, JR. *Histoires des amanz fortunez* and *l'Heptameron*. J. C. Lyons.

C. J. DOUGLAS. The Influence of Don Francisco de Rojas' *Obligados y ofendidos*. N. B. Adams.

K. N. HENDRICKS. Alfred de Musset Portrayed in His Work. W. M. Dey.

F. S. HOWELL. Corneille, Molière, and Racine in the *Recherches sur les théâtres de France* of Beauchamps. T. J. Wilson III.

A. C. JENNINGS. Dramatic Treatments of the Conde Alarcos Legend. S. E. Leavitt.

W. M. McLEOD. Learned Words in French in the Twelfth Century Renaissance. U. T. Holmes, Jr.

A. K. SHIELDS. Adelardo López de Ayala and the Spanish Stage. S. E. Leavitt.

C. G. TAYLOR. Satire in Early Fourteenth Century French Literature in the Time of the Reign of Philippe IV (1285-1314). U. T. Holmes, Jr.

M.A.

1931
G. G. FRAZIER. Jean Regnault de Segrais. J. C. Lyons.

C. C. NEAL, JR. The Originality of Vaugelas and His *Remarques sur la langue françoise*, 1647: A Preliminary Study. U. T. Holmes, Jr.

MRS. DOROTHY NEAL. The Social Drama of Manuel Linares Rivas. S. E. Leavitt.

R. H. PEARSON. The Life and Works of Jean François Sarasin. U. T. Holmes, Jr.

GIOVANNI SPERANDEO. Some Aspects of Juan de la Cueva's Dramatic Art. N. B. Adams.

C. M. STOCKTON. A Historical Survey of Spanish Orthography. R. S. Boggs.

LUCILE VEST. *The Lay of Narcissus:* An Edition with Introduction and Variants Based upon MS. frç. 837 of the Bibliothèque Nationale. U. T. Holmes, Jr.

1932
M. G. BETTS. The Marriage of Ferdinand and Isabella as a Theme in Spanish Literature. S. A. Stoudemire.

A. K. BLOUNT. Notable Folk-Tale Motifs in Old French Literature. U. T. Holmes, Jr.

A. G. EDMUNDS. Georges de Porto-Riche and His *Théâtre d'amour*. W. M. Dey.

R. Y. ELLISON. The *Miracle de le Soucretaine:* An Edition with Introduction and Notes Based upon MS. fr. 375 of the Bibliothèque Nationale. U. T. Holmes, Jr.

L. A. LEWIS. The Thesis Novels of Alfred de Vigny. W. M. Dey.

E. W. LINDSEY. A Translation of the Greek Poems of Gilles Ménage. U. T. Holmes, Jr.

G. R. SULKIN. A History of Judeo-French Literature of the Middle Ages. U. T. Holmes, Jr.

K. B. TOWNSEND. The Medieval Mind as Expressed in Early French Literature. U. T. Holmes, Jr.

E. B. VAUGHN. The Influence of German on Old French Syntax. U. T. Holmes, Jr.

PERCY WISE. The Survival of the Principal Old French Literary Types into the Fourteenth Century. U. T. Holmes, Jr.

M.A.
1933 S. T. BALLENGER. The Legend of the Horse of Don Sancho el Mayor in Spanish Literature. N. B. Adams.

J. Y. CAUSEY. A Critical Bibliography of the Spanish Theater, 1850-1898. S. E. Leavitt.

C. J. DISMUKES. The Influence of Friedrich Nietzsche and Arthur Schopenhauer on Pío Baroja. S. A. Stoudemire.

L. E. GRIMSLEY. *Le chevalier au cygne et Godefroi de Bouillon*: A Study of *Le chevalier au cygne et de Godefroi de Boulogne* and *La Naissance du Chevalier au cygne*, with Special Reference to the Sources of the Legends, the Extant Manuscripts and the Versions of These *Chansons*. U. T. Holmes, Jr.

H. R. MADDOX. Paul Meyer's Notices of Unpublished French Manuscripts: An Analysis. U. T. Holmes, Jr.

L. M. MOSS. The Celtic Element in Gallo-Romance. U. T. Holmes, Jr.

B. R. THURMAN, JR. Several Phases of the Exoticism of Théophile Gautier. W. M. Dey.

1934 G. C. S. ADAMS. Malherbe's Principles of Grammar and Rhyme Applied to the Poetry of Jean Bertaut. J. C. Lyons.

DÉLFIDO CÓRDOVA. Some Aspects of the Dramatic Art of Narciso Serra. S. E. Leavitt.

J. D. FROST, JR. A Critical Edition of Pierre du Ryer's *Arétaphile*. U. T. Holmes, Jr.

MRS. A. B. FUNDERBURK. The Character of Esther in French Dramatic Literature, 1450-1689. J. C. Lyons.

1934 J. M. V. HOLT. The New Elements of the French Vocabulary of the Fourteenth and Fifteenth Centuries. U. T. Holmes, Jr.

W. R. WEAVER. The *Curioso impertinente* Theme in Spanish Dramatic Literature. S. A. Stoudemire.

J. L. WILLIAMSON. Malherbe's Lack of Originality as Expressed in the Works of a Predecessor: Guillaume du Vair. U. T. Holmes, Jr.

1935 M. E. ADAMS. A Study of the Heroic Poems of Desmarets de Saint-Sorlin. J. C. Lyons.

M.A.

1935

L. G. ALLEN. An Analysis of the Medieval French Bestiaries. U. T. Holmes, Jr.

A. G. ENGSTROM. Gautier and Baudelaire: A Study of Their Similarities and Differences with a Consideration of Their Treatment of Similar Poetic Themes. W. M. Dey.

MAXALYNN MOURANE. The Syntax of *Le Livre du Chevalier de La Tour-Landry*. U. T. Holmes, Jr.

1936

F. J. ALLRED. Malherbe and Jean Passerat: An Application of the Former's Principles of Grammar and Rhyme to the Poetry of the Latter. J. C. Lyons.

DOROTHY BRADLEY. Satire in the Works of Alfred de Musset. W. M. Dey.

R. F. CAMPBELL. Life and Social Customs of the Sixteenth Century as Seen in the *Contes et Discours d'Eutrapel* of Noël du Fail. J. C. Lyons and U. T. Holmes, Jr.

C. H. CANTRELL. *El Gran Capitán* as a Theme in Spanish Drama. S. A. Stoudemire.

M. B. COBB. The Dramatic Work of José María Díaz, with Special Reference to Historical Tragedy. S. E. Leavitt.

W. B. NAPIER. The Reception of Victor Hugo in the Restoration Press. W. M. Dey.

I. E. PAYNE. The Sovereign in the Plays of Guillén de Castro y Bellvis. S. E. Leavitt and S. A. Stoudemire.

A. M. SANFORD. Symbolism in the Theatre of François de Curel. W. L. Wiley.

1937

A. L. CHEEK. The Prose Plays of Victor Hugo in Relation to Historical Fact. W. M. Dey.

C. DE W. ELDRIDGE. Hallucination and the Life and Works of Jean-Arthur Rimbaud. W. M. Dey.

R. H. GARDNER. A Supplement to Beaulieux' *Histoire de l'orthographe française*: Punctuation. U. T. Holmes, Jr.

FRANCIS GHIGO. The Provençal Speech of the Waldensian Colonists in North Carolina. U. T. Hòlmes, Jr.

J. W. HASSELL, JR. The Erudition and Ideas of N. de Cholières as Expressed in his *Matinées*. J. C. Lyons.

M.A.
1937   E. D. HEALY. The Views of Ferninand Lot on the Origins of the Old French Epic. U. T. Holmes, Jr.

R. W. KUYKENDALL. A Study of Echegaray's Popularity through His Dramatic Technique. S. E. Leavitt and R. S. Boggs.

W. A. McKNIGHT. The Dramatic Works of Antonio Hurtado y Valhondo. S. E. Leavitt and R. S. Boggs.

E. F. MOYER. A Bibliography of Marie de France, with a Brief Consideration of Certain Theories concerning Her Identity. U. T. Holmes, Jr.

E. I. RIDDICK. Non-medicinal Plant Lore in Old French Literature. U. T. Holmes, Jr.

1938   MARIAN ATKINSON. A Study of Gilles Ménage as an Etymologist. U. T. Holmes, Jr.

J. A. BARRETT. Some Aspects of the Dramatic Technique of Francisco de Rojas Zorrilla. S. E. Leavitt.

G. A. BREWER. A Study of the Norse Element in the French Vocabulary. U. T. Holmes, Jr.

A. R. BURKOT. Chrétien de Troyes' *Perceval* and Its Continuators. U. T. Holmes, Jr.

ATTILIO DICOSTANZO. The Literary Patronage of the Angevine Dynasty of Naples during the Reign of Charles I. U. T. Holmes, Jr.

C. V. DIEHL. An Analysis of the Medieval French Lapidaries. U. T. Holmes, Jr.

RACHEL JOHNSON. Life and Social Customs of the Sixteenth Century as Seen in the *Apologie pour Hérodote* of Henri Estienne. J. C. Lyons.

ALBERTA LOSH. Animate Nature in the Works of Saint François de Sales. U. T. Holmes, Jr.

D. L. MARTIN. Onomastics: A Study of Proper Names in the *Chansons de geste* Period. U. T. Holmes, Jr.

JEAN MORRISON. *Les Prophecies de Merlin;* Edited from Manuscript Arundel 57, British Museum. U. T. Holmes, Jr. and R. W. Linker.

J. R. PRINCE. A Composite System of French Semantics. U. T. Holmes, Jr.

T. E. SCOTT, JR. A Semantics Study of Certain Common Verb Concepts in Vulgar Latin. U. T. Holmes, Jr.

M.A.

1938　R. D. WHICHARD. The Celtic Elements in French Morphology, Syntax, and Phonology. U. T. Holmes, Jr.

N. V. AVERITT. *De passione Judas*; Edited from Manuscript Oxford Laud misc. 471, Bodleian Library. U. T. Holmes, Jr., and R. W. Linker.

1939　A. L. D'ELIA. A Provisional Bibliography of Italian Dialect Dictionaries. U. T. Holmes, Jr.

JOHN DE NOIA. Enrique Gil y Carrasco's Treatment of History in *El Señor De Bembibre*. N. B. Adams.

R. B. FREEMAN. Evidences of Literary Activity in France in the Reign of Charles V, 1364-1380. U. T. Holmes, Jr.

H. H. HILTON, JR. *Seth*: Edited from Manuscript 66, Corpus Christi Library, Cambridge. U. T. Holmes, Jr. and R. W. Linker.

R. G. LEWIS. The Symphonic Technique in Marcel Proust's *A la recherche du temps perdu*. W. M. Dey.

A. E. LINDSAY. Life and Social Customs in France in the Sixteenth Century as Seen in Book One of *Les serées* of Guillaume Bouchet. J. C. Lyons and U. T. Holmes, Jr.

A. G. MACMULLIN. Some Aspects of the Dramatic Technique of Juan de Ariza, with Special Emphasis on His Historical Plays. S. E. Leavitt.

E. L. MUELLER. Jean de Mairet's Use of the Classical Unities. W. L. Wiley.

E. D. TURNER, JR. Some Aspects of the Dramatic Art of Quiñones de Benavente. S. E. Leavitt.

A. H. YARROW. Classification of the Folk-Motifs in the Fabliaux. U. T. Holmes, Jr., and R. S. Boggs.

1940　F. M. DUFFEY. Juan de Grimaldi and the Pre-Romantic Drama in Spain. S. E. Leavitt.

G. R. KEYS. The Dramatic Technique of Tirso de Molina in His Palace Plays. S. E. Leavitt.

W. R. LANSBERG. *Le Pèlerinage de Charlemagne*, Edited from Koch's Copy of the Original MS. U. T. Holmes, Jr.

M. C. S. OLIPHANT. Some French Names in Charleston District, South Carolina. U. T. Holmes, Jr.

M.A.

1940   D. H. WALTHER. Sensory Phenomena in the *Sonatas* of Valle-Inclán. N. B. Adams.

1941   HAZEL DONEGAN. Cervantes' *La ilustre fregona* as a Theme in Spanish Drama. S. A. Stoudemire.

JACQUES HARDRÉ. The Poetic Art of Leconte de Lisle. W. M. Dey.

C. F. HOLGATE. *L'ordenance de médecine et de diète.* U. T. Holmes, Jr., and R. W. Linker.

J. M. SMITH, JR. An Analysis and Comparison of the Burlesque Techniques of Scarron and d'Assoucy. J. C. Lyons.

D. E. STARNES. The Originality of Malherbe's *Remarques* on French Grammar. U. T. Holmes, Jr.

J. W. WHITTED. A Classification and Analysis of the Folk-Motifs in the *Buen aviso y portacuentos* and the *Patrañuelo* of Juan Timoneda. R. S. Boggs.

H. H. WILHELM. Classification of the Folk-Motifs in the Works of Jean Renart. U. T. Holmes, Jr.

1942   J. W. BANNER. The Drama of Ildefonso Antonio Bermejo. S. A. Stoudemire.

G. A. FOSTER. *La Chirurgie de Roger de Salerne.* U. T. Holmes, Jr., and R. W. Linker.

FRANCES MOOSE. *Comment le médecin doit se comporter auprès du malade.* U. T. Holmes, Jr.

W. E. STRICKLAND. A Semantic Study of Certain Common Verb Concepts in Vulgar Latin. U. T. Holmes, Jr.

1943   MRS. R. B. HALL. A Further Semantic Study of Certain Vulgar Latin Verb Concepts. U. T. Holmes, Jr.

T. V. THOMPSON. Boursault: Dramatist of the Late Seventeenth Century. W. L. Wiley.

1944   R. N. ANDES. The Theatre of Hervieu. W. M. Dey.

MRS. S. F. BELL. The Theatre of Émile Augier. W. M. Dey.

G. R. HERNÁNDEZ. The Dramatic Works of Enrique Gaspar. S. E. Leavitt.

M. H. THOMPSON. Franklin and French Society. H. R. Huse.

1945   E. M. HORTON. Albert Samain and the Elements of Romanticism, Parnassianism, and Symbolism in His Poetry. W. M. Dey and A. G. Engstrom.

DEPARTMENT OF RURAL SOCIAL ECONOMICS

Ph.D.

1927   P. W. WAGER. County Government and Administration in North Carolina. E. C. Branson.

1931   J. L. CLARK. Two Major Ills of Southern Farm Civilization. E. C. Branson.

S. M. DERRICK. Economic History of the South Carolina Railroad. E. C. Branson.

1934   W. P. YOUNG. A History of Agricultural Education in North Carolina. S. H. Hobbs, Jr.

1938   COLUMBUS ANDREWS. Administrative County Government in South Carolina. E. C. Branson and S. H. Hobbs, Jr.

M.A.

1915   J. M. DANIEL, JR. Three Typical Farm Systems of North Carolina.

1915   J. T. DAY. Forsyth County, Economic and Social.

G. L. LAMBERT. The National Government's Interest in Agriculture.

1916   WALTER PATTEN. Negro Churches and Sunday Schools, Orange County, North Carolina.

1917   S. H. HOBBS, JR. Gaston County: Economic and Social.

1925   H. H. HUFF. Negro Education in North Carolina. S. H. Hobbs, Jr.

BRANDON TRUSSELL. County Government in Stanly County, with Suggestions for its Improvement. S. H. Hobbs, Jr.

1927   J. L. CHARLTON. Buckingham County, Virginia: A Social Survey. E. C. Branson.

1928   COLUMBUS ANDREWS. The Economic and Social Foundations and Possibilities of Caldwell County, North Carolina. E. C. Branson.

1933   D. S. MATHESON. Farm Movements in North Carolina and Their Significance. S. H. Hobbs, Jr.

1940   B. J. DOWNEY. The Roanoke Farms and the Roanoke Farms Mutual Association. S. H. Hobbs, Jr.

DEPARTMENT OF SOCIOLOGY

Ph.D.

1927 G. B. JOHNSON. Study of the Musical Talent of the American Negro. H. W. Odum.

J. J. RHYNE. Studies of Mill Village Population in North Carolina: An Aproach to the Study of Southern Industrial Development. H. W. Odum.

1928 H. C. BREARLEY. A Study of Homicides in South Carolina, 1920-1928. H. W. Odum.

J. R. STEELMAN. A Study of Mob Action in the South. H. W. Odum.

R. B. VANCE. Human Factors in Cotton Culture: A Study in the Social Geography of the American South. H. W. Odum.

1929 L. M. BROOKS. A Study of Primary Group Isolation. E. R. Groves.

R. M. BROWN. Public Poor Relief in North Carolina. E. R. Groves.

F. W. HOFFER. Counties in Transition: A Study of County Public and Private Welfare Administration in Virginia. E. R. Groves.

KATHARINE JOCHER. Studies of Methods in Social Research. E. R. Groves.

1930 H. P. BRINTON. The Negro in Durham: A Study of Adjustment to Town Life. H. W. Odum.

M. P. SMITH. Municipal Development in North Carolina, 1665-1930: A History of Urbanization. H. W. Odum.

1931 RUTH LINDQUIST. The Family in the Present Social Order: A Study of the Needs of American Families. E. R. Groves.

J. P. MCCONNELL. The After-Prison Life of Released White Prisoners in North Carolina. E. R. Groves.

A. R. RAPER. Two Black Belt Counties: Changes in Rural Life since the Advent of the Boll Weevil in Greene and Macon Counties, Georgia. E. R. Groves.

1932 C. H. HAMILTON. The Role of the Church in Rural Community Life in Virginia. E. R. Groves.

1934 P. W. SHANKWEILER. A Sociological Study of the Child Welfare Program of Worcester, Massachusetts. E. R. Groves.

Ph.D.

1935   L. G. SHIVERS. The Social Welfare Movement in the South: A Study in Regional Culture and Social Organization. H. W. Odum.

1936   B. M. MOORE. Age and Sex Distribution of the People as Conditioning Factors in Cultural Participation: A Study in Regional Demography of the United States. E. R. Groves.

H. E. MOORE. Theories of Regionalism. H. W. Odum.

R. Y. SCHIFFMAN. Occupations in the United States and the South, 1910-1930. M. R. Trabue.

1937   M. J. HAGOOD. Mothers of the South: A Population Study of Native White Women of Childbearing Age of the Southeast. H. W. Odum and Katharine Jocher.

J. M. MACLACHLAN. Mississippi: A Regional Social-Economic Analysis. H. W. Odum.

1938   KENNETH EVANS. Changing Occupational Distribution in the South, with Special Emphasis on the Rise of Professional Services. H. W. Odum.

H. L. GEISERT. The Balance of Interstate Migration in the Southeast, 1870-1930, with Special Reference to the Migration of Eminent Persons. R. B. Vance.

M. R. MELL. A Definitive Study of the Poor Whites of the South. H. W. Odum.

1939   O. M. STONE. Agrarian Conflict in Alabama: Sections, Races and Classes in a Rural State from 1800 to 1938. R. B. Vance.

1940   M. A. EATON. The Climate of the Southeast: A Preliminary Investigation of the Theoretical and Factual Problems of Southern Climate. H. W. Odum and F. C. Erickson.

1941   G. W. LOVEJOY. The North Carolina Youth Survey, 1938-1940. H. W. Odum.

1942   A. W. DAVIS. The Growth of the Technicways: A Study in Societal Change. H. W. Odum.

O. F. HOFFMAN. Culture of the Centerville-Mosel Germans in Manitowoc and Sheboygan Counties, Wisconsin. G. B. Johnson.

S. C. MAYO. Rural Poverty and Relief in the Southeast, 1933-1935. R. B. Vance.

SOCIOLOGY

Ph.D.

1942 D. H. TISDALE. Urbanization: A Study of the Process of Population Concentration in the United States and its Relation to Social Change. H. W. Odum.

1943 W. G. BROWDER. The Pattern of Internal Mobility in Texas as Revealed by the School Census. R. B. Vance.

1944 V. H. WHITNEY. The Pattern of Village Life: A Study of Southern Piedmont Villages in Terms of Population, Structure, and Role. R. B. Vance.

1945 J. E. IVEY, JR. State Planning: Experiments in the American Planning Process. H. W. Odum.

M.A.

1921 R. M. BROWN. Development and Correlation of Social Agencies in North Carolina. H. W. Odum.

A. B. PRUITT. Programs for the Correlation of Home, School, and Community. H. W. Odum.

W. B. SANDERS. An Attempt to Determine the Modes of Adaptation to Human Environment. H. W. Odum.

1922 J. A. DICKEY. Organization and Administration of Public Welfare in the United States. J. F. Steiner.

1923 R. R. ANDERSON. Development of the Social Sciences in Secondary Education. H. W. Odum.

M. E. HARMAN. Child Labor with Special Reference to the Industrial Home Work of Children in Mill Villages. J. F. Steiner.

1924 G. W. MANN. Institutional Factors in Social Change. H. W. Odum.

J. F. STURDIVANT. Status of the Small Mill Village: A Concrete Study of Carrboro, North Carolina. H. W. Odum.

1925 M. F. BOYSWORTH. Leisure Time Activities of Adolescents in North Carolina. H. D. Meyer.

R. E. BROWN. Town Government in North Carolina. H. W. Odum.

CORDELIA COX. Study of the Need of Rural Elementary Educational and Vocational Guidance. H. W. Odum.

R. L. FRITZ. Survey of the Hertford Community, Perquimans County, North Carolina: A Sketch of the Life, Trade Areas, and Parishes of One of the Oldest Towns in North Carolina, a Part of "Ancient Albemarle." H. W. Odum.

M.A.

1925   L. K. FULTON. Adolescent Leisure Time Activities in Mississippi. H. W. Odum.

*C. E. MOORE. Social Aspects of County Organization: A Study of Rural Leadership in Orange County, North Carolina. H. W. Odum.

J. J. RHYNE. The Place of the Social Studies in Mill Village Schools. H. W. Odum.

*E. G. SMITH. Public Welfare Problems of Chapel Hill. H. W. Odum.

OLANDO STONE. Reading Habits of North Carolinians as Indicated by Several Indexes. H. W. Odum.

1926   M. B. BRIDGERS. A History of Social Work in Durham County. H. W. Odum.

L. M. BROOKS. The Administrative Cost of Crime with Special Reference to Durham County. J. F. Steiner.

A. G. MACGILL. A Statistical Analysis of Crime in North Carolina Based on Sheriffs' Monthly Jail Reports from Twenty-One Counties for the Year 1924. J. F. Steiner.

CLYDE RUSSELL. Folk Interpretation of Social Values as Found in Folk Songs and Ballads. H. W. Odum.

F. S. WILDER. Types of Crime in North Carolina: A Statistical Analysis of Superior Court Records for Two Years Ending June 30, 1925. J. F. Steiner.

1927   M. C. BRIETZ. Case Studies of Delinquent Girls in North Carolina. H. W. Odum.

C. V. KISER. Liquor Law Violations in Durham and Person Counties: A Statistical Analysis of the Durham Recorder's Court Records for Four Years Ending July 1, 1926, and the Person County Court Records for Eighteen Months Ending Feb. 1, 1927. H. W. Odum.

G. E. PANKEY. Life Histories of Rural Negro Teachers in the South. H. W. Odum.

M. P. SMITH. Physical Education in North Carolina with a Comparative Study of State Physical Education Laws, Programs, and Departments. H. D. Meyer.

1928   W. P. BEANS. The Influence of Music on the American Family. H. W. Odum.

---

* Master of Science.

SOCIOLOGY

M.A.

1928 M. H. GARFIELD. Unmarried Mothers: A Study in Attitudes. H. W. Odum.

G. H. LAWRENCE. The Organization and Administration of Public Welfare in Orange County, North Carolina. H. W. Odum.

HANNAH PLOWDEN. Present Trends in Chinese Family Life. H. W. Odum.

1929 H. E. HERMANCE. Economic and Educational Development in the South, 1900-1925: A Comparison. H. W. Odum.

JANET QUINLAN. A Study of Rural Illegitimacy in Orange County, North Carolina, 1923-1927. W. B. Sanders.

1930 MRS. LILIAN BRINTON. Keeping Time. H. W. Odum.

V. L. DENTON. Social-Economic Characteristics of the Mississippi Delta. H. W. Odum.

M. K. FLEMING. A Follow-up Study of Juvenile Court Cases in Orange County, North Carolina, 1919-1929. H. W. Odum.

B. C. HIPP. A Gaston County Cotton Mill and Its Community. T. J. Woofter, Jr.

GERTRUDE VAILE. Some Aspects of Family Social Work in Rural Communities in Iowa. H. W. Odum.

HARIETTE WOOD. The Kentucky Mountaineers: A Study of Four Counties of Southeastern Kentucky. L. L. Bernard.

1931 H. N. BROWN III. A History of the Influence of Family Life on Recreation in the United States. E. R. Groves.

W. C. EZELL. Tillman and Blease as "Popular" Leaders in South Carolina. T. J. Woofter, Jr.

S. S. STEVENS. A Critique of the Climatic Theories of Ellsworth Huntington, with Special Reference to the South. R. B. Vance.

L. M. WILLIAMS. Crime in North Carolina: A Study by Counties, 1900 to 1930. R. M. Brown.

I. V. YOUNG. Problems of the Small Town of North Carolina. T. J. Woofter, Jr.

1932 J. VAN R. JOHNSON. A Study of Attitudes and Problems Connected with the Adoption of Young Children. L. M. Brooks.

M.A.

1932 Mrs. Emily MacLachlan. The Diet Pattern of the South: A Study in Regional Sociology. R. B. Vance.

J. M. MacLachlan. Compensatory Characteristics of the Negro Press. G. B. Johnson.

L. O. Toler. The Negro and Communism. G. B. Johnson.

Edith Webb. Farm Life of the Upper Middle Class in Piedmont North Carolina after the Civil War. T. J. Woofter.

N. C. Young. A Case Study of the Tarboro Lynching. T. J. Woofter, Jr.

1933 G. W. Blackwell. State Public Welfare in the Southeast: An Approach to Regional Planning in the Field of State Public Welfare. H. W. Odum.

V. K. Crawford. Student Attitudes on the Race Problem. G. B. Johnson.

J. H. Johnson. West Southern Pines: An Experiment in Negro Self Government. G. B. Johnson.

J. B. Knox. Recreation in Penal Institutions: A Survey of the United States with Special Emphasis on North Carolina. H. D. Meyer.

S. M. Smith. A Social Study of High Point, North Carolina. L. M. Brooks.

1934 Mrs. J. R. Butler. A Study of Some Reformatory Systems for Women Offenders in the United States, with Particular Reference to the Industrial Farm Colony at Kinston, North Carolina. L. M. Brooks.

1935 Frances Hampton. New Leisure: How Is It Spent? H. D. Meyer.

E. D. Hancock. A Sociological Study of the Tri-racial Community in Robeson County, North Carolina. G. B. Johnson.

F. B. Parker. A Study of the Social Adjustment of the Adopted Child. L. M. Brooks.

R. N. Woodworth. Population as an Area of Study in Social Planning. R. B. Vance.

1936 C. G. Adams. Recent Trends in Applied Human Biology: A Study of the Possibilities of Improving the Race by Means of Sterilization and Birth Control. R. B. Vance.

M.A.

1936   E. W. DONOVAN. The Theory of Social Control since Edward Allsworth Ross, 1901-1936: A Study in the Development of a Sociological Concept. R. B. Vance.

Mrs. L. A. GODBOLD. The Contribution of Women in the Development of American Religion. E. R. Groves.

1936   C. L. LASTRUCCI. Marriage Adjustment as a Condition of Marital Happiness: Personality Adjustment in Marriage. E. R. Groves.

M. P. MIZELL. State Differences in the Southeast as Indicated in a Decade of State Bibliographies. H. W. Odum.

O. B. THOMASON. Commercial Recreation of the Southeast: A Study of Commercial Recreation of a Region. H. D. Meyer.

1937   K. L. BARRIER. Seventeen Hundred Economically Handicapped Families: A Study of Families in Orange County, North Carolina, Aided by Federal Emergency Relief. R. M. Brown.

J. P. BECKWITH. A Sociological Study of Police in North Carolina with Special Reference to Personnel Selection. L. M. Brooks.

J. McL. BENSON. Sterilization with Special Reference to Orange County, North Carolina. E. R. Groves.

E. E. DOAN. A State and Its Children: North Carolina, 1900-1936, as Measured by the Children's Charter. Katharine Jocher.

*M. R. McGINNIS. A Social Analysis of the Delinquent Children Appearing Before the Juvenile Court. W. B. Sanders.

JEAN McCAIG. An Analysis of Public Welfare Services to 422 Cases in Orange County, North Carolina, January 1 to December 31, 1936. Katharine Jocher.

M. K. PERRY. A Study of Social and Legal Changes of Status of Women Following the Civil War. E. R. Groves.

V. H. WHITNEY. Social Resources of the Southeast: A Definition and Classification of Agencies and Institutions, Public and Private. H. W. Odum.

---

* Master of Science.

DISSERTATIONS AND THESES

M.A.

1938 RICHARD ASHBY. Florida, 1920 to 1935: A Case of of Interstate Migration. R. B. Vance.

FRED FLETCHER. Curriculum Training for Recreational Leadership in Institutions of Higher Learning in the Southeastern Region. H. D. Meyer.

E. C. HAWKINS. Family Discipline as a Conditioning Influence in the Development of Children during the First Six Years. E. R. Groves.

W. H. LEVITT. The Occupational Distribution of the Jews in North Carolina. R. B. Vance.

RAYMOND McCLINTON. A Social-Economic Analysis of a Mississippi Delta Plantation. R. B. Vance.

1939 A. F. BROWN. The Negro Churches of Chapel Hill: A Community Study. G. B. Johnson.

A. M. GRANT. The Changing Status of Women as Reflected in American Family Legislation since 1930. E. R. Groves.

J. G. HUTCHINSON. The Modern Planned Community Movement in England and the United States. L. M. Brooks.

1940 ALLINE CAMPBELL. Care of the Aged in the Piedmont Sub-Region. D. S. Klaiss.

P. B. CANNON. Illustrations of How the Technicways in the Modern Community Modify the Folkways. H. W. Odum.

A. L. COLEMAN. What is American?—A Lexicographic Analysis of Alleged American Characteristics, Ideals, and Principles. H. W. Odum.

R. W. CROWELL. The Administration of the National Labor Relations Act in North Carolina. H. L. Herring.

J. T. DRAKE. The Negro in Greenville, South Carolina. G. B. Johnson.

C. M. LOOMIS. A Study of the Durham Recreation Department. H. D. Meyer.

ELIZABETH ZACHARY. A Study of Recent Trends in Training for Social Competence through Eleven Years of Development in One Preparatory School. H. D. Meyer.

1941 W. G. BROWDER. The Population of Texas, 1900-1930: A Preliminary Study. H. W. Odum.

M.A.
1941 M. F. CORBETT. A Preliminary Study of the Planter Aristocracy as a Folk Level of Life in the Old South. H. W. Odum.

JERRY DANIEL. A Study of Differential Fertility in North Carolina. M. J. Hagood.

J. D. RICE. The Negro Tobacco Worker and His Union in Durham, North Carolina. G. B. Johnson.

P. C. SCHINHAN. The Case of the South in Milk Production: An Introduction to a Proposed Study of the Milkshed of the Piedmont South. M. J. Hagood.

R. V. SOWERS. A History of the Growth and Development of the Florida Congress of Parents and Teachers: Its Social Contribution to the State. H. D. Meyer.

T. P. YEATMAN. A Population Study of the Youth of the Southeast Region. R. B. Vance.

1942 HAROLD GARFINKEL. Inter-racial and Intra-racial Homicide in Ten Counties in North Carolina, 1930-1940. G. B. Johnson.

E. K. KARCHER, JR. The Measurement of Social Adjustment by Comparison of Self-Ratings and Group-Ratings of the Same Individuals. M. J. Hagood.

R. J. MILLIKEN. Rural Social Subregions of North Carolina: An Application of Factor Analysis to the Problem of Subregional Delineation. M. J. Hagood.

D. O'H. PRICE. Analysis of Occupational Characteristics and Their Social and Economic Correlates for the 93 Metropolitan Centers, 1930. M. J. Hagood.

M. I. WOLF. A Compilation and Analysis of Statistics Relating to American Marriage in 1930. D. S. Klaiss.

1943 F. T. COOKE. Government Participation in Recreation. H. D. Meyer.

W. H. DAVIS. The Organization, Administration, and Program of the Recreation Commission of Greensboro, N. C. H. D. Meyer.

M. McD. DOUGLAS. A Survey of Certain Defense Publications with Special Reference to Their Utilization in Community Institutions. L. M. Brooks.

M.A.

1943
A. L. FERRISS. The Social Participation of Part-Time Farmers in North Carolina. H. L. Herring and H. W. Odum.

E. H. NEFF. Underregistrations of Births, United States, 1939: Regional, Race, and Rural-Urban Differences. H. W. Odum.

D. M. ROYER. A Comparative Study of Three Experiments in Rural "Community" Reconstruction in the Southeast. L. M. Brooks.

W. A. SUTTON, JR. An Approach to a Sociological Analysis of the Consolidated School. L. M. Brooks.

1944
C. M. FREEMAN. Growth and Plan for a Community: A Study of Negro Life in Chapel Hill and Carrboro, North Carolina. H. W. Odum.

MRS. A. B. HASKINS. The Sociological Approach to a Clothing Study. H. W. Odum.

R. G. LYNCH. Some Aspects of the Consumer Cooperative Movement in the Southeast since 1920. L. M. Brooks.

G. L. SIMPSON, JR. Some Aspects of Man and Nature Patterns in North Carolina. H. W. Odum.

L. W. SYRON. An Inquiry into the Pattern of College and University Leadership in the South since 1900: A Preliminary Study of College Presidents. H. W. Odum.

1945
JOSEPH DEUTSCH. Rural Electrification in North Carolina. S. H. Hobbs, Jr.

R. W. KERNODLE. The Origin and Development of Marriage Counseling Facilities in the United States. E. R. Groves.

MRS. B. V. W. MARION. A Study Guide to Family Relations. E. R. Groves.

C. C. PETERS. An Analytical Critique of the Literature in the Field of Marriage Written during the Two Decades 1924-1944. E. R. Groves.

M. N. PRICE. The Development of Leadership by Southern Women through Clubs and Organizations. Edith Williams.

A. I. RIEDEL, JR. The Aged as a Family Problem. E. R. Groves.

K. K. SEBASTIAN. A Statistical Analysis of Selective Service Rejection in North Carolina. H. W. Odum.

ZOOLOGY

M.A.
1945   E. V. STONE. Social Planning for the Reduction of Tuberculosis in the Southeast. G. W. Blackwell.

L. E. WILEY. The Chinese Cooperative Movement. L. M. Brooks.

DEPARTMENT OF ZOOLOGY

Ph.D.
1918   W. C. GEORGE. Sponges of Beaufort (N. C.) Harbor, and Vicinity. H. V. Wilson.

1929   J. T. PENNEY. Cell Behavior in the Regeneration of Sponges from Dissociated Cells. H. V. Wilson.

1934   E. M. DEVINEY. The Behavior of Isolated Pieces of Ascidian (*Perophora viridis*) Stolon as Compared with Ordinary Budding. H. V. Wilson.

1936   M. I. BOLIEK. Syncytial Structures in Sponge Larvae and Lymph Plasmodia of Sea Urchins. H. V. Wilson.

1939   J. A. FINCHER. The Origin of the Germ Cells in a Tetraxonid Sponge (*Stylotella heliophila* Wilson). H. V. Wilson and D. P. Costello.

G. H. TUCKER. The Histology of the Gonads and Development of the Egg Envelopes of an Ascidian (*Styela plicata* Lesueur). H. V. Wilson and R. E. Coker.

L. L. WILLIAMS. A Comparative Study of the Development of the Liver in Teleost Fishes with Special Reference to the Relation Between Liver and Yolk-Periblast. H. V. Wilson.

M.A.
1897   *R. E. COKER. (Special project substituted for thesis.)

1902   C. A. SHORE. (No title available.)

1903   *I. F. LEWIS. On Maturation in *Ascaris megalocephala*.

1911   O. W. HYMAN. Present Status of the Concrescence Theory.

1912   W. C. GEORGE. Evolution of Sex.

J. W. HARRIS. Parasitic Worms of Man.

1918   BLACKWELL MARKHAM. Asymmetry and Regulation in the Spina Bifida Embryos of Some Amphibia.

1920   W. W. KIRK. The Comparative Anatomy and Embryology of the Pronephric System in the Vertebrates. H. V. Wilson.

---
* Master of Science.

DISSERTATIONS AND THESES

M.A.

1921   H. S. EVERETT. Germ Cells of Hydra. H. V. Wilson.

1922   C. D. BEERS. Bud Development in Simple Ascidians. H. V. Wilson.

1924   *W. R. EARLE. Development of the Eye in the Salamander *Amblystoma punctatum*. H. V. Wilson.

N. M. SMITH. Behavior of the Embryonic Cells of the Sea-Urchin (Arbacia) in Lymph Plasmodia outside and inside the Sea-Urchin's Body. H. V. Wilson.

1925   J. T. PENNEY. Comparative Study of the Origin of the Yolk Protoplasm Nuclei in the Bony Fishes. H. V. Wilson.

1928   J. L. BAILEY. Segmental Sense Organs and Their Development in Teleost Fishes. H. V. Wilson.

L. L. HILL. The Mesoblastic Somites in Teleost Fishes. H. V. Wilson.

S. McC. LEE. The Development of the Alimentary Canal System in Teleost Fishes. H. V. Wilson.

1929   *J. P. REYNOLDS. Origins of the Germ Cells in Some Beaufort Sponges. H. V. Wilson.

1930   *T. C. WATKINS. Some Points in the Life Cycle of the Gregarine Monocystis. C. D. Beers.

1931   W. O. PUCKETT. The Embryonic Origin of the Heart, Blood Vessels, and Blood in Teleost Fishes. H. V. Wilson.

L. L. WILLIAMS. The Embryonic Origin of the Axial Skeleton in Teleost Fishes. H. V. Wilson.

1932   J. S. DENDY. The Development of the Liver in the Amphibia. H. V. Wilson.

1933   M. I. BOLIEK. Some Points in the Development of the Eye of Fishes and Amphibia. H. V. Wilson.

1934   H. H. ADDLESTONE. Influence of Temperature on Form and Development of *Daphnia longispina*. R. E. Coker.

J. W. CULBERTSON. Effect of Physico-Chemical Changes in the Environment on Embryo-Formation in the Frog. H. V. Wilson.

1936   E. P. ODUM. The History of the Germ Cells in the Toadfish, *Opsanus tau*. H. V. Wilson.

---

* Master of Science.

M.A.

1936 HARRIET TAYLOR. An Inquiry into the Conditions Governing Cyclomorphosis in Daphnia. R. E. Coker.

1938 C. McL. COKER. A Study of the Genital Rachis of an Echinoid, *Arbacia punctulata*. H. V. Wilson.

1939 N. G. HAIRSTON. Reduction and Regeneration in the Young Hydranths of *Pennaria tiarella* (Ayres). H. V. Wilson and R. L. Taylor.

1940 J. H. ALLEN, JR. The Effects of Certain Salt Solutions on the Unfertilized Eggs of *Thalassema mellita*. D. P. Costello.

L. I. GARDNER. The Cytology of the Mutant Infrabar. R. D. Boche.

Q. R. MURPHY, JR. The Effects of Temperature on the Viscosity of *Amoeba dubia* Protoplasm. D. P. Costello.

1942 DOROTHY AYCOCK. Influence of Temperature on Size and Form of *Cyclops vernalis* Fischer. R. E. Coker.

J. H. PERLMUTT. Estrogenic Nature of Extracts from Ovaries and Fertilized Eggs of the Blue Crab, *Callinectes sapidus*. D. E. Copeland.

H. C. YEATMAN. A Critical Study of the Cyclopoid Copepods of the *viridis-vernalis* Group, with a Description of *Cyclops carolinianus*, n. sp. R. E. Coker.

1943 D. N. GROVE. Differential Distribution of Riffle Fauna in Three Major Watersheds in Western North Carolina. W. L. Engels and R. E. Coker.

E. L. RYDER. Environment Factors Affecting the Germination of Statoblasts of Plumatella (Bryozoa). R. E. Coker.

1944 H. E. LEHMAN. A New Rhabdocoele Parasite of the Sea Urchin, *Strongylocentrotus franciscanus*, (*Syndisyrinx franciscanus* n.gen., n.sp.). D. P. Costello.

INDEX

Abbot, W. R., 78
Abell, S. H., 60
Abernathy, J. R., 121
Abernethy, C. E., 93
Abernethy, C. M., 56
Abernethy, R. F., 23
Abernethy, W. E., 52
Achurch, R. W., 80, 111
Adams, A. B., 142
Adams, C. G., 156
Adams, C. R., 58
Adams, G. C. S., 145
Adams, Louise, 123
Adams, M. E., 145
Adams, R. W., 77, 84
Adams, R. W., 53
Adcock, LeR. M., 67
Adcox, L. B., 63
Addison, L. M., 27
Addlestone, H. H., 162
Addlestone, Jacob, 13, 21
Aderholdt, C. H., 54
Aderholt, V. V., 110
Adler, A. V., 44
Ahern, K. C., 105
Ahner, F. E., 89
Aibara, Kazue, 40
Aid, G. C., 27
Akers, J. McC., 42
Albright, R. M., 114
Albritton, G. G., 13
Alexander, A. L., 24
Alexander, C. B., 106, 110
Alexander, F. M., 87
Allen, E. M., 60
Allen, F. F., 39
Allen, J. H. Jr., 163
Allen, L. G., 146
Allen, M. E., 35
Allen, M. T., 95
Allen, R. E., 11
Allen, R. T., 102
Alley, J. M., 95
Allred, F. J., 146
Allred, J. H., 143
Amaya-Valencia, Eduardo, 33
Amick, H. C., 103
Amick, T. C., 56
Anderson, A. E., 71
Anderson, C. E., 7
Anderson, E. H., 37
Anderson, Geneva, 90
Anderson, H. A., 92
Anderson, H. M., 98
Anderson, J. P., 50
Anderson, L. W., 63
Anderson, R. R., 153
Andes, R. N., 149
Anding, C. E. Jr., 22
Andoe, Josephine, 126

Andrews, Columbus, 150
Andrews, E. R., 16
Andrews, Nita, 49, 141
Andrews, T. M., 12, 19
Andrus, H. S., 116
Ange, F. M., 123
Anscombe, F. C., 106, 110
Anson, C. P., 38
Antonakos, Antonios, 131
Appeldoorn, John, 27
Arey, W. F., 17
Ariail, J. M., 76, 85
Armfield, B. B., 87
Armfield, Frank, 92
Armstrong, Ray, 50
Arnold, F. H., 37
Arnold, G. H., 63
Arrowood, F. M., 49
Ashby, M. B., 137
Ashby, Richard, 158
Ashcraft, E. S., 124
Ashley, F. W., 119
Askew, S. H., 111
Atkins, A. J., 7
Atkins, E. W., 135
Atkins, J. A., 44
Atkinson, Marian, 147
Atkinson, Minnie, 53
Atkinson, W. H. Jr., 84
Aull, L. B. Jr., 73
Austin, Katherine, 69
Austin, L. E., 28, 30
Avera, T. A., 36
Averitt, N. V., 148
Aycock, A. C., 25
Aycock, Dorothy, 163
Aycock, J. L., 84
Aycock, W. B., 115
Babb, J. S., 103
Backenstoss, R. E. Jr., 105
Bacon, M. L., 48
Bagby, W. M., 119
Bagwell, J. C., 135
Bailey, H. V., 48
Bailey, J. L., 162
Bailey, J. O., 78, 86
Bailey, K. B., 109
Bailey, R. K., 137
Bailey, R. W., 34
Bain, M. G., 139
Baker, C. T. Jr., 44
Baker, H. R., 23
Balch, J. McC., 43
Ballard, C. C., 43
Ballenger, S. T., 145
Banner, C. R., 89
Banner, J. W., 149
Bannerman, A. M., 133
Barber, I. W. Jr., 112
Barden, I. L., 30

INDEX

Barker, M. I., 140, 142
Barkley, K. L., 133, 135
Barksdale, Lane, 11
Barnes, B. N., 54
Barnett, Josephine, 125
Barnett, R. W., 42
Barnette, Mrs. E. L., 67
Barnette, Walker, 110
Barnhardt, C. L., 63
Barnwell, J. F., 118
Barr, E. S., 128, 130
Barrett, J. A., 147
Barrett, L. L., 141
Barrier, K. L., 157
Barrington, Sybil, 84
Bartz, W. F., 15
Baskervill, W. H., 24
Baskerville, Charles, 11
Bass, L. A., 17, 21
Battle, H. B., 11
Battle, W. J., 28, 29
Baugh, E. I., 54
Baum, A. E., 60
Baynes, Eloise, 32
Bayroff, A. G., 133, 135
Bazemore, A. W., 27
Beach, E. K., 99
Beans, W. P., 154
Beatty, H. C., 60
Beavers, E. M., 16
Beck, C. K., 129
Beckwith, J. P., 157
Beerbaum, A. W., 105
Beers, C. D., 162
Behrman, J. N., 45
Belcher, R. H., 23
Bell, F. M., 73
Bell, L. J., 105
Bell, Martha, 31
Bell, M. C., 124
Bell, Mrs. S. F., 149
Benbow, C. F., 39
Bender, J. A., 20
Bennett, D. P., 126
Bennett, T. B. Jr., 74
Benson, C. H., 121
Benson, J. McL., 157
Berger, Bernard, 15
Berkeley, A. R., 82
Bernard, M. T., 32
Bernard, W. S., 29
Bernhardt, H. A., 16
Bernhart, G. W., 33
Berwanger, S. K., 136
Betts, A. H., 71
Betts, M. G., 144
Beust, Nora, 53
Bezanson, W. B., 95
Bice, H. V., 134, 136
Bird, C. R., 50
Bitting, M. E., 94
Bivens, W. P., 82
Blackshear, W. S-J., 133
Blackwelder, Mae, 63

Blackwelder, Ruth, 111
Blackwell, G. W., 156
Blackwell, R. C., 120, 121
Blaine, J. C. D., 38, 43
Blair, Elizabeth, 36
Bland, L. E., 32
Bland, M. C., 32
Blankenburg, W. L., 76
Blaylock, F. R., 19
Bloomer, R. O., 101
Blount, A. K., 144
Blythe, F. L., 29
Boger, W. J., 65
Bohlinger, J. H., 71
Bolce, B. L., 36
Boliek, M. I., 161, 162
Bone, J. B., 119
Bonner, Brant, 38
Bonner, J. C., 108
Booker, N. B., 96
Boone, W. E., 115
Boquin, F. G., 138
Bost, R. W., 12, 20
Bourne, W. R., 86
Bowditch, M. F., 119
Bowen, Anne, 34
Bowie, A. Y., 88
Bowman, J. O., 50
Bowman, Wayne, 96
Boyazis, A. C., 74
Boyce, H. S., 103
Boyette, E. T., 50
Boylan, Hannah, 27
Boyle, E. R., 34
Boysworth, M. F., 153
Brabham, H. J., 34
Bracy, William, 95
Braddy, A. W., 89
Bradley, Dorothy, 146
Bradshaw, G. W., 47
Brainard, H. G., 42
Bramlett, A. L., 106
Branch, L. V. N., 129
Brandon, W. P., 110
Brashear, M. M., 77
Braun, M. L., 128, 129
Brawley, D. J., 13, 24
Brearley, H. C., 151
Breazeale, Elizabeth, 29
Breazeale, F. B., 131
Breibart, Soloman, 116
Brenner, Edward, 75
Brett, S. M., 94
Brewer, F. L., 63
Brewer, G. A., 147
Brice, E. C., 39
Bridgers, M. B., 154
Bridges, Clementine, 54
Bridgforth, Betty, 71
Brietz, M. C., 154
Briggs, D. H., 45, 49
Brimley, R. F. W., 63
Brinton, H. P., 151
Brinton, Mrs. Lilian, 155

INDEX

Broadfoot, T. M., 39
Brock, J. S., 131
Brody, Mrs. B. S., 138
Brookes, E. G., 67
Brooks, C. P., 124
Brooks, F. P., 12, 20
Brooks, I. P., 90
Brooks, L. M., 151, 154
Brooks, M. B., 55
Brooks, T. J. Jr., 137
Brossman, R. W., 138
Browder, W. G., 153, 158
Brown, A. F., 158
Brown, C. C., 81
Brown, C. K., 37, 40
Brown, D. A., 90
Brown, H. N. III, 155
Brown, J. L., 34
Brown, L. A., 82
Brown, L. A., 116
Brown, O. M., 110
Brown, R. E., 153
Brown, R. F., 127
Brown, R. M., 151, 153
Brown, S. P., 143
Brown, W. A., 107, 114
Brown, W. H., 117
Browne, A. L., 69
Browning, H. D. Jr., 67
Brownson, A. R., 102
Bruton, G. S., 121
Bruton, M. J., 122
Bryan, N. G., 60
Bryan, T. C., 112
Bryan, W. F., 82
Bryant, L. Y., 93
Bryson, H. J., 103
Buck, H. M., 112
Bullitt, J. B. Jr., 21
Bullock, A. R., 51
Bullock, R. C., 122
Bundrick, O. W., 54
Bundy, V. M., 63
Bunn, B. D., 51
Bunting, F. H., 37
Burdett, P. H., 15
Burdine, Theodore, 130
Burkot, A. R., 147
Burns, S. S., 65
Burton, M. G., 10
Burton, W. F. Jr., 117
Burwell, C. J., 127
Busby, F. F., 36
Bush, G. C., 51
Bush, L. E., 121
Bush, S. J., 31
Butler, A. D., 88
Butler, G. B., 16
Butler, Mrs. J. R., 156
Butler, M. H., 99
Butt, W. H., 103
Butterworth, T. H., 138
Byerly, K. R., 104
Byers, Kansas, 85

Bynum, E. M., 63
Bynum, J. C., 103
Bynum, M. C., 29
Byrd, Mrs. I. O., 69
Byrd, Jess, 95
Byrd, R. E., 113
Byrd, R. M., 13, 21
Caldwell, Elizabeth, 112
Caldwell, J. R. Jr., 115
Califf, Charlotte, 137
Cameron, E. A., 120, 122
Campbell, Alline, 158
Campbell, M. S., 74
Campbell, R. F., 146
Candler, T. T., 81
Cannon, C. V., 16
Cannon, L. S., 60
Cannon, P. B., 158
Cantey, Harry Jr., 73
Cantrell, C. H., 146
Capps, J. A., 48
Cardwell, G. A. Jr., 78
Carlisle, D. H., 133
Carmichael, Colin, 75
Carmichael, K. J., 88
Carmichael, P. A., 127
Carpenter, B. F., 32
Carpenter, C. C., 47
Carr, E. P., 35
Carr, I. N., 110
Carr, P. H., 129
Carroll, C. L., 120
Carroll, C. L. Jr., 124
Carroll, H. A., 54
Carroll, J. E. Jr., 143
Carroll, N. L., 57
Carroll, R. W., 115
Carson, B. G., 12, 21
Carson, L. E., 138
Carter, C. B., 11, 19
Carter, C. C., 132
Carter, E. J., 46, 60
Carter, R. McK., 69
Carter, S. M., 114
Carver, J. E., 89
Cason, E. W., 115
Caubie, F. P. Jr., 78
Causey, J. Y., 145
Cauthen, C. E., 107
Cebollero, Angeles, 138
Cedo, Mercedes, 138
Cerney, A. M. S., 61
Chace, W. E., 108
Chadbourn, A. L., 136
Chamberlain, O. H., 127
Chandler, G. W. Jr., 94
Chandler, W. J., 90
Chanlett, E. T., 137
Chapin, E. M., 23
Chapman, M. C., 116
Charlton, J. L., 150
Chatham, Katherine, 116
Chavez y Arango, M. D., 138
Cheek, A. L., 146

Cheek, J. M., 127
Cheek, P. M., 28, 30
Chen, Mrs. W-H. W., 27
Chesley, Elizabeth, 88
Chester, H. M., 55
Childs, Floyd, 35
Chreitzberg, Margaret, 87
Chrisco, H. F., 75
Christenberry, G. A., 8, 10
Christenbury, E. S., 58
Church, G. L., 26
Clair, J. R., 102
Clanton, B. R., 15
Clark, C. B., 108
Clark, G. K., 125
Clark, I. S., 41
Clark, J. L., 45, 50, 150
Clark, M. L., 138
Clark, N. L., 99
Clark, O. S., 104
Clark, S. F., 15
Clarke, D. L., 82
Clary, M. S., 65
Clayton, O. M., 87
Clegg, E. M., 109
Clegg, Marie, 84
Clifford, A. T., 13, 22
Clough, E. M., 33
Coates, K. D., 90
Cobb, E. G., 16
Cobb, J. T., 82
Cobb, L. M., 86
Cobb, M. B., 146
Cobb, W. B., 101, 102
Cobb, Whitfield Jr., 128
Coble, H. E., 67
Cody, S. S., 27
Coenen, F. E., 105
Cohnstaedt, M. L., 44
Coker, C. McL., 163
Coker, E. C. Jr., 122
Coker, E. R., 89
Coker, J. W., 110
Coker, R. E., 161
Colehour, J. K., 25
Coleman, A. L., 158
Coleman, H. E., 91
Coleman, W. M., 127
Colley, J. C., 69
Collins, A. B., 56
Collins, A. R., 142
Collins, H. W., 121
Collins, R. S., 105
Collins, S. C., 12
Coltrane, W. G. Jr., 42
Congleton, J. E., 79
Conn, M. W., 13, 23
Conrad, L. J., 27
Conrad, W. E. Jr., 59
Constable, E. W., 13, 20
Cook, D. L., 17
Cook, J. F., 105
Cooke, F. T., 159

Cooper, A. J., 65
Copenhaver, Harris, 40
Corbett, M. F., 159
Corbitt, D. C., 107, 132
Cordle, Rachel, 114
Cordova, Delfido, 145
Cornatzer, W. E., 7, 8
Cornette, J. C. Jr., 105
Cornsweet, A. C., 134
Corrie, G. B., 44
Corry, A. B., 125
Cory, A. A., 73
Costner, J. M. Jr., 121
Couch, E. C., 112
Couch, J. N., 8, 9
Coulter, J. L. Jr., 94
Coulter, V. A., 11, 19
Coulter, W. S., 39
Councill, G. McN., 65
Covington, W. B., 49
Coward, E. R., 63
Cowles, J. H., 57
Cox, A. L., 82
Cox, Cordelia, 153
Cox, E. H., 79
Cox, F. M., 54
Cox, H. T., 10
Cox, R. C., 47
Cox, R. C., 43
Crabtree, B. G., 117
Craig, E. J., 50
Craig, Marjorie, 93
Craig, W. G., 50
Crane, C. LaC. Jr., 95
Craven, C. J., 128, 130
Crawford, V. K., 156
Creech, W. D. Jr., 143
Crew, Elsie, 88
Crissman, Curtis, 51
Crissy, W. J. E., 46
Crockford, H. D., 12, 20
Crosby, R. L., 61
Crossen, H. J., 89
Crouch, G. E. Jr., 128
Crow, E. P., 34
Crowe, F. C., 96
Crowell, R. W., 158
Crum, C. H., 35
Crutchfield, K. H., 21
Crutchfield, R. W., 43
Cubbage, S. C., 23
Cubine, M. V., 99
Culbertson, A. B., 135
Culbertson, J. W., 162
Cunningham, H. H., 117
Cunningham, M. S. R., 119
Curlee, A. T., 122
Currie, D. J., 29
Currie, L. W., 113
Curry, B. F., 44
Curtis, J. L., 98
Curtis, W. R., 41
Cutlar, L. F. P., 12

Cutler, A. T., 41
Daggett, G. H., 80
Daily, J. N., 83
Daniel, A. F., 130
Daniel, A. M., 70
Daniel, E. M., 94
Daniel, Jerry, 159
Daniel, J. M. Jr., 150
Daniel, R. McC., 119
Daniel, W. J., 134
Daniels, J. W., 84
Daniels, V. C., 18
Darden, Mrs. B. S., 54
Darden, W. E., 29
Dark, M. E., 132
Daugherty, J. F., 128, 129
Daughtry, E. L., 47
Davenport, J. E., 21
Davenport, J. S., 78
Davey, L. M., 94
Davis, A. W., 152
Davis, B. W., 29, 32
Davis, C. L., 125
Davis, C. W., 58
Davis, F. W., 22
Davis, H. T., 102
Davis, I. M., 7
Davis, J. B., 83
Davis, Louise, 51
Davis, M. E., 138
Davis, M. J., 102
Davis, R. A. Jr., 48
Davis, R. O. E., 11
Davis, S. I., 100
Davis, W. H., 159
Dawson, Ann, 98
Dawson, P. R., 20
Day, J. T., 150
Dean, P. N., 63
Dean, Virginia, 30
Deans, Clyde, 65
Deans, Clyde, 95
Deans, E. V. Jr., 96
Deason, N. A., 64
DeBerry, Nena, 59
Decker, H. M., 138
Deebel, G. F., 16
Degges, F. McI., 28
Delaney, M. A., 34
D'Elia, A. L., 148
DeLong, C. D., 94
De Lotto, M. J., 65
Dendy, J. S., 162
De Noia, John, 148
Denson, C. A., 123
Denson, C. B. Jr., 29
Denton, V. L., 138, 155
Derrick, S. M., 150
de Schweinitz, E. A., 11
Deskins, S. C., 108, 110
Deutsch, Joseph, 160
De Vault, S. H., 47
Deviney, E. M., 161

De Wick, H. N., 134
Deyton, J. B., 112
Dichmann, M. E., 95
Dickert, H. A., 20
Dickert, Y. J., 26
Dickey, J. A., 153
Dickson, G. L., 111
Dickson, M. R., 112
Dickson, T. W., 39
DiCostanzo, Attilio, 147
DiCostanzo, Nestore, 125
Diehl, C. V., 147
Diggs, Mary, 29
Dillard, Irene, 76
Dillin, H. L., 122
Dimmick, G. B., 51, 134
Dismukes, C. J., 145
Disque, J. G., 99
Dixon, V. K., 113
Doan, E. E., 157
Dobbins, C. N., 102
Dobbins, E. G., 74
Dobbins, J. T., 11, 19
Donegan, Hazel, 149
Donnelly, J. F., 65
Donovan, C. H., 38
Donovan, E. W., 157
Dorsett, H. G. Jr., 131
Dorsett, Wilbur, 94
Dosier, J. P., 24
Doubles, J. A. Jr., 8, 10
Doughton, M. R., 83
Douglas, C. J., 143
Douglas, E. M., 38, 43
Douglas, M. C., 96
Douglas, M. McD., 159
Douglas, T. B., 24
Douty, H. M., 37
Downey, B. J., 150
Downs, J. A., 141, 143
Downs, O. U., 92
Drake, J. T., 158
Drake, W. E., 45, 52
Drane, F. P., 18
Driscoll, R. L., 131
Duckett, A. LeR., 117
Duckett, J. W., 16
Duckett, Margaret, 98
Duffey, F. M., 148
Dukes, W. F., 136
Dukes, W. J., 99
Dula, F. M., 135
Duls, L. de S., 99
Duncan, J. F., 109
Duncan, M. H., 142
Duncan, S. L., 85
Dunning, M. H., 118
Dunston, J. O., 22
DuPuis, Elroy, 94
Dupuy, M. F., 118
Durham, F. M., 33
Dwelle, F. R., 114
Dye, W. T. Jr., 17

Eagles, T. R., 121
Eakins, M. A., 43
Earle, W. R., 162
Early, A. D., 55
Early, J. M., 24
Earp, M. J., 99
Eason, J. L., 83
Eaton, Clement, 83
Eaton, F. H., 121
Eaton, M. A., 152
Echols, C. D., 98
Eddlemen, S. McK., 52
Edelman, A. T., 115
Edmonds, E. D., 52
Edmunds, A. G., 144
Edmunds, W. E., 100
Edney, C. R., 109
Edwards, C. C., 121
Edwards, E. L., 96
Edwards, H. L., 14, 25
Edwards, M. E., 111
Edwards, M. E., 107, 112
Edwards, R. A., 101
Edwards, V. C., 11
Egleston, L. A., 90
Ehrlich, Gertrude, 126
Elder, F. K., 46
Eldridge, C. D., 141, 146
Eldridge, J. G., 40
Eliason, M. H., 79, 87
Eliason, N. B., 9
Ellinwood, E. H., 138
Elliott, A. P., 84
Elliott, F. S., 90
Elliott, P. L., 85
Elliott, R. C., 93
Elliott, Van Courtlandt, 28, 30
Ellis, D. E., 132
Ellis, H. A. Jr., 100
Ellison, A. D., 133
Ellison, R. C., 81
Ellison, R. Y., 144
Ellmore, G. H., 53
Elmore, E. B., 88
English, E. E., 54
Engstrom, A. G., 141, 146
Enloe, Roberta, 138
Epps, P. H., 83
Ergle, D. R., 13, 22
Ericson, E. E., 113
Ertel, Mrs. M. P., 71
Estabrook, Cornelia, 116
Estes, J. A., 27
Esteve Abril, H. A., 119
Eutsler, R. B., 40
Evans, B. F., 40
Evans, Kenneth, 152
Evans, M. W., 117
Everett, H. S., 162
Everett, J. E., 15
Everett, R. V., 66
Everett, T. R., 66
Ezell, W. C., 155

Faires, R. S., 82
Farmer, C. M., 47
Farr, H. O. Jr., 14
Farrior, J. E., 100
Farthing, C. L., 71
Faulkner, R. M., 90
Feldman, Lawrence, 132
Feltner, C. E., 75
Felton, L. J., 42
Fenley, G. W., 140
Fenley, V. M., 87
Ferguson, C. V., 54
Ferguson, Elizabeth, 113
Ferguson, T. W., 39
Ferraz, F. B., 138
Ferree, A. W., 57
Ferriss, A. L., 160
Finch, H. M., 52
Fincher, J. A., 161
Fink, T. R., 66
Finklea, J. DeL., 130
Fitzgerald, M. W., 136
Fitz-Richard, Helen, 7
Fleming, G. H. Jr., 24
Fleming, H. M., 57
Fleming, J. D., 27
Fleming, J. S., 55
Fleming, M. K., 155
Fleming, O. I., 58
Fleming, Ruth, 30
Fletcher, Fred, 158
Fletcher, J. F., 43
Floras, C. L., 74
Floyd, J. S., 45
Floyd, L. H., 55
Flurry, R. C., 67
Fogartie, J. E., 29
Fonville, C. C., 39
Fonville, M. S. B., 68
Ford, L. E., 31
Ford, R. A., 68
Fordham, J. B., 111
Fore, Dan Jr., 14, 25
Fortescue, Z. T. Jr., 122
Foster, G. A., 149
Foster, G. H., 80
Foster, W. O., 117
Foust, F. K., 10
Fowler, Stephen, 64
Franklin, W. McK., 73
Frazer, J. S., 113
Frazer, M. H., 97
Frazier, G. G., 144
Frazier, K. C., 109
Frazier, K. L., 142
Frazier, Meledieth, 66
Freeman, Bernice, 91
Freeman, C. M., 160
Freeman, E. H., 138
Freeman, R. B., 148
Freeman, T. B., 61
Frick, C. H., 120
Frierson, D. E., 141

Fritz, R. L., 153
Frost, J. D. Jr., 145
Frye, J. R., 16
Fulton, L. K., 154
Funderburk, Mrs. A. B., 145
Funderburk, R. S., 112
Furr, C. A., 54
Furr, W. C., 47
Gaddy, C. F., 86
Gaddy, H. C., 66
Gallardo, J. M., 140
Gallent, J. B., 13, 22
Gallman, M. N., 98
Garbee, M. F., 71
Garber, J. M., 66
Gardner, J. H., 98
Gardner, L. I., 163
Gardner, R. H., 146
Garfield, M. H., 155
Garfinkel, Harold, 159
Garner, Collie, 88
Garner, L. L., 122
Garner, W. H., 56
Garrett, R. L., 123
Garrison, K. C., 135
Gaskin, G. C., 58
Gaston, Katherine, 71
Gatica, Timoteo, 131
Gatling, W. E. G., 61
Gault, R. L., 34
Gee, R. E. Jr., 25
Gehrke, W. H., 114
Geiger, V. P., 90
Geisert, H. L., 152
Gentry, Eva, 30
Gentry, J. S., 61
George, W. C., 161
Gerard, F. T. Jr., 98
Germany, A. H., 17
Gerow, Mrs. B. K., 100
Ghigo, Francis, 141, 146
Gibson, E. H. III., 116
Gilbert, H. McT., 59
Giles, I. V., 12, 19
Giles, W. E., 20
Gillam, M. V., 32
Gilman, Rhoda, 35
Gilreath, E. S., 18, 21
Ginnings, R. R., 66
Girlinghouse, F. W., 45, 51
Githens, Sherwood Jr., 128, 130
Glaser, E. U., 136
Glasgow, E. C., 98
Glenn, A. G., 56
Glenn, R. C., 109
Glenn, W. D. Jr., 134, 135
Godbold, Mrs. L. A., 157
Godfrey, J. L., 113
Godwin, F. C., 64
Godwin, J. E., 32
Goldston, W. L. Jr., 102
Goncales da Silva, J. G. B., 138
Goode, Selden Jr., 109

Goodman, L. C., 61
Goodwin, E. B., 51
Goodwin, O. K., 50
Goold, E. H. Jr., 98
Gordon, G. K., 115
Gordon, W. J., 127
Gordy, Walter, 128, 130
Gore, Arabella, 95
Gorham, M. C., 84
Goss, L. C., 99
Graham, E. K., 114
Graham, J. O., 19
Grainger, J. M., 82
Grant, A. M., 158
Grant, F. W., 25
Graves, A. N., 71
Graves, E. H., 41
Graves, N. H., 51
Graves, R. H., 108
Gray, D. B., 137
Gray, N. E., 138
Green, F. M., 106, 109
Green, H. C., 56
Greene, A. G., 117
Greene, A. R., 21
Greene, N. E., 104
Gregory, J. P. Jr., 71
Grier, W. B., 119
Griffin, A. G., 40
Griffin, E. J., 68
Griffin, M. H., 28, 30
Griffin, M. L., 80
Griffith, P. M., 100
Grimes, J. M. Jr., 108, 114
Grimsley, L. E., 145
Grosiak, E. H., 43
Grotyohann, J. W. C., 128
Grove, D. N., 163
Grubb, G. G., 79
Grubbs, W. McK., 112
Gruhn, W. T., 46
Guerry, Alexander Jr., 44
Guess, F. W., 35
Gulledge, H. C., 16
Gulledge, V. W., 139
Gunter, J. W., 38, 43
Gunter, P. G., 109
Guthne, N. J., 138
Gwyn, P. H. Jr., 39
Gwynn, J. M., 30
Gyles, M. F., 120
Hackett, J. B., 44
Haden, W. L. Jr., 16
Hager, O. B., 22
Hagood, M. J., 152
Hagood, M. J., 91
Hair, J. K., 120
Hairston, N. G., 163
Hales, J. D. Jr., 70
Hall, Dan, 122
Hall, J. N., 109
Hall, N. S., 7
Hall, Mrs. R. B., 149

Ham, M. L. Jr., 59
Hamer, B. DuB., 33
Hamill, R. E., 136
Hamilton, C. H., 151
Hamilton, T. H., 84
Hammack, T. T., 71
Hammer, M. L., 101
Hammond, E. A., 108, 116
Hammond, T. T., 44
Hampton, Frances, 156
Hampton, Lelia, 90
Hampton, W. O., 45, 49
Hamrick, S. M., 45
Hancock, E. D., 156
Haniford, C. M., 101
Hansen, C. A., 138
Hansen, P. S., 126
Happoldt, W. B., 16
Harbin, Katherine, 92
Hard, C. F., 85
Hardré, Jacques, 149
Hardy, F. T., 66
Harman, M. E., 153
Harmon, A. O., 86
Harper, E. E., 143
Harper, J. C., 39
Harrell, R. C., 85
Harrill, C. V., 24
Harrill, W. B., 68
Harris, C. R., 12
Harris, F. H., 133
Harris, I. F., 18
Harris, J. W., 161
Harris, J. W. Jr., 77
Harris, R. C., 26
Harris, R. C., 56
Harris, W. D., 113
Harrison, J. B., 111
Harrison, J. G., 81
Harshman, W. V., 22
Hart, O. P., 128
Hartman, Mrs. R. T., 140
Hartsell, E. H., 80, 93
Hartsell, W. W., 70
Harvey, J. V., 9
Haskins, Mrs. A. B., 160
Hassell, J. W. Jr., 141, 146
Hatcher, J. T., 48
Hawfield, S. G., 50
Hawkes, B. G., 26
Hawkins, E. C., 158
Hawkins, J. R., 61
Hawley, F. M., 127
Hawley, F. M. Jr., 44
Hawthorne, Manning, 94
Haynes, Laurine, 28, 30
Haynes, L. L., 97
Hayes, F. C., 140
Hayes, K. R., 33
Hayes, Virginia, 36
Healy, E. D., 141, 147
Heffner, H. C., 84
Heffner, R. L., 86

Heiberg-Jurgensen, K. O., 36
Heldman, Lynette, 33
Helms, H. A., 135
Henderson, Archibald, 120
Henderson, Archibald Jr., 98
Henderson, J. S., 44
Hendricks, C. F., 11
Hendricks, K. N., 143
Hening, E. F., 98
Henry, G. K. G., 28
Henry, Homer, 51
Henry, N. H., 80, 92
Henry, N. Q., 9
Henry, R. B., 137
Henry, Sibyl, 46
Herbert, H. B., 123
Herman, Lila, 101
Hermance, H. E., 155
Hernandez, G. R., 149
Herndon, Janie, 138
Hester, St. Clair, 29
Hewitt, W. C., 10
Hickerson, T. F., 120
Hicks, J. E., 43
Hicks, M. M., 113
Highsmith, E. McK., 45, 47
Highsmith, J. A., 47
Hight, M. E., 112
Hildebrand, C. I., 92
Hildebrand, R. M. Jr., 138
Hill, G. H., 52
Hill, Hampden, 19
Hill, Hubert, 102
Hill, L. L., 162
Hill, M. A. Jr., 121
Hill, M. J., 89
Hillhouse, A. M., 41
Hilton, H. H. Jr., 148
Hines, E. T., 56
Hines, J. C., 129
Hines, M. M., 98
Hines, T. I., 61
Hinshaw, C. R., 49
Hinson, T. E., 40
Hinton, Lucille, 138
Hipp, B. C., 155
Hixson, I. M., 31
Hobart, G. H., 44
Hobbs, S. H. Jr., 150
Hockemeyer, E. A., 60
Hocutt, O. B., 56
Hodge, M. W., 128
Hodges, J. K., 14
Hodges, J. L., 118
Hodgin, D. R., 86
Hoffer, F. W., 151
Hoffman, L. R., 127
Hoffman, O. F., 152
Hogan, W. J. IV., 31
Holder, B. B., 37, 39
Holder, E. M., 111
Holgate, C. F., 149
Holland, A. C., 51

Holland, W. T., 104
Hollett, A. R., 75
Hollingsworth, R. R., 45
Hollowell, Annabelle, 97
Hollowell, Minnie, 112
Holman, A. M., 117
Holmes, H. McC. Jr., 73
Holmes, J. A., 83
Holmes, M. B., 47
Holmes, R. W., 52
Holroyd, G. C., 15, 22
Holt, J. M. V., 145
Hon, R. C., 37
Honeycutt, A. W., 70
Honeycutt, Mrs. M. A., 30
Hood, Robin, 42
Hook, C. W., 122
Hook, M. W., 122
Hooke, Robert, 124
Hopkins, H. M., 48
Hornbeck, G. A., 132
Hornbeck, R. W., 104
Horne, B. C. Jr., 125
Horne, H. H., 29
Horne, McD. K. Jr., 38, 42
Horne, M. M., 92
Horner, G. F., 79
Horney, W. J., 81
Horton, E. M., 149
Horton, F. L., 132
Horton, R. K., 138
Hough, J. M., 61
House, H. C. Jr., 68
Houston, Mrs. F. B., 45
Howard, Claude, 82
Howell, A. C., 76
Howell, C. A., 142
Howell, E. I., 129
Howell, F. S., 143
Howell, I. R., 101
Howell, James, 80, 90
Howell, J. V., 124
Howell, W. W., 43
Hoyle, H. B. Jr., 124
Hoyle, V. A., 121
Hsiang, L. C., 75
Huckabee, M. L., 27
Hudson, A. P., 77
Hudson, C. C., 25
Hudson, H. C., 53
Hudson, W. P., 96
Huff, H. H., 150
Huff, J. B., 82
Huff, J. W., 30
Huffines, A. D., 70
Huffman, E. E., 23
Huffman, E. O., 25
Huggins, M. A., 52
Hughes, A. E., 13, 22
Hughes, H. H., 82
Hughes, M. C., 132
Hume, R. D., 93
Hume, Thomas Jr., 81

Huneycutt, J. E., 61
Hunnicutt, E. H., 113
Hunsicker, F. P., 75
Hunt, L. E., 64
Hunter, E. C., 45, 53
Hunter, F. J., 36
Hunter, J. E. Jr., 25
Hunter, W. F. Jr., 25
Hurley, L. B., 77
Hurt, A. B., 53
Husketh, S. J., 48
Huskey, D. A., 138
Huskins, C. C., 115
Hutchinson, C. R., 54
Hutchinson, J. G., 158
Hutchinson, Marguerite, 125
Hutchinson, R. F., 44
Huth, M. L., 105
Hyman, O. W., 161
Idema, Mrs. M. J., 138
Inglis, M. H., 58
Inghram, M. R., 39
Ingram, L. B., 71
Inman, S. E., 97
Isley, E. B., 56
Ives, C. L., 52
Ivey, J. E. Jr., 153
Jackson, D. H., 19
Jacocks, W. P., 109
James, F. M., 123
Jarman, L. W., 49
Jarratt, Paschal, 100
Jeffrey, R. N., 64
Jeffries, W. L., 11, 19
Jenkins, A. S., 87
Jenkins, E. B., 28, 30
Jenkins, E. L., 125
Jenkins, K. A., 88
Jenkins, S. F., 78, 89
Jenkins, W. M., 64
Jenkins, W. S., 106, 110
Jennings, A. C., 143
Jennings, E. DeW., 12, 20
Jeter, D. DeL., 101
Jimenez-Macias, Rafael, 44
Jobe, L. H., 48
Jocher, Katharine, 151
Johnson, A. B., 57
Johnson, A. T., 76
Johnson, A. W., 97
Johnson, B. L., 13
Johnson, E. D., 118
Johnson, Elizabeth, 124
Johnson, Emilie, 36
Johnson, G. A., 18
Johnson, G. B., 151
Johnson, G. G., 106
Johnson, J. H., 156
Johnson, J. S., 66
Johnson, J. van R., 155
Johnson, Lois, 92
Johnson, M. D., 119
Johnson, M. L., 97

Johnson, Rachel, 147
Johnson, W. C., 73
Johnson, W. H. E., 57
Johnston, C. S., 103
Johnston, F. B., 61
Johnston, J. H., 47
Johnston, Minnie, 66
Johnston, W. R., 25
Johnstone, R. F., 114
Jones, A. E., 29
Jones, C. C., 129
Jones, C. W., 98
Jones, D. G., 138
Jones, F. L., 92
Jones, J. B., 52
Jones, L. N., 34
Jones, M. D., 93
Jones, M. J., 138
Jones, O. W., 82
Joost, N. T. Jr., 96
Jordan, G. W., 68
Jordan, S. S., 11, 18
Joybert, W. H., 38
Joyner, C. R., 71
Joyner, J. B., 23
Joyner, W. L., 138
Justice, J. M., 117
Justice, M. F., 113
Kaczka, E. A., 17
Kampschmidt, W. H., 116
Kani, Ali, 46
Kapp, M. E., 14
Karcher, E. K. Jr., 159
Karlin, J. A., 116
Kaufholz, C. F., 35
Keeler, Caroline, 117
Keelser, E. Y., 73
Keith, A. B., 108
Kelley, A. W., 77, 85
Kendrick, J. W., 43
Kendrick, M. P., 29
Kennard, K. I., 126
Kennedy, E. C., 31
Kenyon, R. L., 17
Kernodle, R. W., 160
Kershaw, P. G. de S., 59
Kesler, T. L., 104
Kestler, C. B., 92
Keys, G. R., 148
Killinger, G. G., 134
Kimbrough, T. R., 26
Kimmel, Herbert, 46
Kimpel, B. D., 80
Kinard, F. M., 88
Kincaid, G. N., 61
King, G. H., 71
King, G. K., 28
King, G. V., 119
King, M. L., 138
King, T. L., 13, 23
Kirk, W. W., 161
Kiser, A. L., 54
Kiser, C. V., 154

Kiser, J. A., 64
Kiser, O. L., 52
Kiser, W. LeR., 61
Kita, Saichiro, 40
Kitasawa, Shinjiro, 39
Knight, B. H., 19
Knight, S. B., 15, 26
Knox, J. B., 156
Knox, W. T., 52
Koch, F. H. Jr., 34
Koch, R. A., 7
Koo, T-Y, 75
Korff, N. M., 105
Kornegay, A. D., 61
Kornegay, Frances, 138
Kossack, M. E., 138
Krahenbuhl, K. M., 94
Kreps, C. H. Jr., 44
Krynitsky, J. A., 17
Kuhlman, C. E., 38
Kurz, Mrs. M. T., 81
Kuykendall, R. W., 147
Kwei, M. T., 56
Kyker, G. C., 15
Lackey, Katherine, 100
Lacy, D. M., 115
Ladu, A. I., 78, 87
Laird, W. M., 104
Lambert, G. L., 150
Lambert, H. D., 102
Lancaster, A. L., 105
Lander, E. M. Jr., 117
Lane, B. B., 82
Lane, E. S., 95
Lang, A. G., 8
Lang, J. A., 112
Langdon, R. M., 119
Langston, A. D. B., 79
Langston, J. H., 16, 26
Lanham, Louise, 79, 87
Lankford, C. L., 138
Lansberg, W. R., 142, 148
Lantham, Lois, 33
La Rocca, J. P., 126
Larson, F. L., 60
Lasley, J. W., 121
Lasley, R. L., 83
Lastrucci, C. L., 157
Latimer, P. H. Jr., 15
Latshaw, H. F., 48
Latshaw, S. L., 84
Latta, J. E., 129
Lawrence, C. G., 53
Lawrence, G. H., 155
Lawrence, M. S., 30
Layton, J. S., 98
Lear, C. M., 131
Learned, M. R., 142
Leath, T. H., 111
LeBaron, P. M., 104
Lebey, Mrs. M. H., 139
LeConte, J. N., 14
Ledbetter, I. B., 48

INDEX

Ledford, R. N., 48
Lee, E. H., 60
Lee, R. A., 70
Lee, Rachel, 68
Lee, R. M., 41
Lee, S. B., 103
Lee, S. McC., 162
Lee, T. H., 124
Lee, V. J. Jr., 33
Leggette, L. P., 33
Lehman, H. E., 163
Leiserson, Lee, 16, 26
Leitner, J. G., 10
Lemmond, W. H. Jr., 21
Lense, F. T. Jr., 26
Leonard, M. H., 138
Leonard, M. L., 71
Leopold, R. S., 26
Lerche, C. O. Jr., 132
Levitt, W. H., 158
Lewis, Dorothy, 34
Lewis, D. P., 8
Lewis, I. F., 161
Lewis, J. B., 96
Lewis, K. P., 34
Lewis, L. A., 144
Lewis, M. F., 138
Lewis, R. G., 148
Lichtenthaeler, R. A., 18
Liddell, A. F., 127
Ligon, Mrs. S. O., 57
Liles, M. S., 59
Lilly, A. E., 91
Lilly, Mrs. G. G., 100
Lindley, C. C., 71
Lindquist, Ruth, 151
Lindsay, A. E., 148
Lindsey, E. S., 76, 84
Lindsey, E. W., 144
Lineberger, A. C., 83
Lineberry, R. A., 13, 21
Lingerfeldt, T. H., 68
Link, A. S., 108, 118
Linker, J. B., 121
Linker, J. D., 123
Linker, R. W., 140, 143
Linker, W. M. Jr., 135
Linton, R. H., 96
Lipscomb, C. C., 64
Little, C. H. Jr., 124
Little, G. P., 53
Little, T. A., 85
Ljung, H. A., 13, 22
Lloyd, W. R., 126
Loaring-Clark, H. E., 36
Lockhart, L. B. Jr., 17
Lockmiller, D. A., 107
Loflin, D. L., 68
Loflin, J. C., 14, 24
Lofton, W. M. Jr., 12, 21
Lohr, B. E., 103
Lohr, L. L. Jr., 47
London, L. F., 107, 114

Long, Edgar, 83
Long, P. G., 92
Long, W. I., 35
Longest, E. C., 66
Loomis, C. M., 158
Looper, T. L., 53
Losh, Alberta, 147
Love, V. M., 54
Lovejoy, G. W., 152
Lowry, R. F., 59
Lube, Catalina, 138
Lumiansky, R. M., 80
Lumpkin, B. G., 81
Lurcy, L. G., 44
Lyon, R. M., 110
Lyons, J. C., 140
Lynch, E. L., 8
Lynch, R. G., 160
McAuliffe, R. G., 114
MacBryde, J. P., 97
McCaig, Jean, 157
McCain, J. W. Jr., 79, 86
McCain, Mrs. L. H., 93
McCall, J. V., 142
McCampbell, J. C., 102
McCanless, Rosamond, 93
McCanless, W. F., 84
McCarthy, C. W., 66
MacCarthy, G. R., 101, 103
McCay, M. S., 131
McClamroch, R. P., 77, 84
McClinton, Raymond, 158
McCluer, J. D., 22
McConnell, J. P., 151
McCormack, J. H., 42
McCoy, S. J., 78
McCracken, J. G., 66
McCullen, J. T. Jr., 96
McCulloch, R. W., 83
McCullough, E. F., 114
McCullough, M. C., 114
McCurdy, H. F., 57
McDaniel, C. Y., 88
McDaniel, J. L., 124
McDaniel, V. M., 88
McDearman, E. B., 25
McDill, J. M., 92
McDonald, A. L., 68
McDonald, Mrs. A. L., 138
McDonald, J. R., 62
McDonald, L. S., 68
MacDowell, D. A., 96
McDowell, D. F., 141
McDuffie, J. B., 72
McEwen, J. L., 20
McEwen, M. M., 7
McFadden, J. H., 133, 135
McFadyen, H. C., 119
McFerrin, J. B. Jr., 37, 42
McGalliard, J. C., 86
McGeachy, J. A. Jr., 115
McGee, B. M., 37, 41
McGehee, Elise, 64

MacGill, A. G., 154
McGinnis, M. R., 157
McGirt, R. M., 54
McGowan, W. T., 121
MacGregor, J. L., 70
McIntosh, C. E., 55
McIntosh, Mrs. Linda, 53
McIver, J. W., 73
McKay, A. A., 83
MacKay, E. S., 90
McKay, H. S., 118
McKay, J. A., 9
McKay, Merle, 35
McKee, Jane, 97
McKee, Jessie, 86
McKie, G. M., 82
McKinney, W. M., 75
McKnight, T. M., 142
McKnight, W. A., 147
Maclachlan, Mrs. Emily, 156
Maclachlan, J. M., 152, 156
McLain, C. R., 52
McLain, R. B., 70
McLean, Frank, 82
MacLean, J. A., 75
McLellan, C. R., 23
McLeod, A. H. Jr., 117
McLeod, J. A., 89
McLeod, M. A., 68
McLeod, W. M., 140, 143
McMillan, D. R. Jr., 129
MacMillan, Genevieve, 48
McMillan, J. B., 89
McMillan, K. M., 92
MacMillan, M. J., 139
McMillan, T. E., 109
MacMillan, W. D., 76, 83
MacMullin, A. G., 148
McNairy, L. G., 42
McNeer, M. W., 93
McNeil, J. M., 113
McNeill, R. F., 117
McNeir, W. F., 80, 91
Macon, H. L., 37
Macon, Mrs. H. L., 72
Macormac, A. R., 14
MacPhee, Halsey, 134
McPherson, E. G., 108, 110
McPherson, M. B., 116
McQueen, W. B. Jr., 91
McSwain, H. E., 72
Maddox, H. R., 145
Maddry, C. A., 127
Maddry, C. K., 111
Mahler, A. J., 79
Mandelkorn, B. M., 139
Maner, W. L. Jr., 36
Mangum, E. P., 81
Mann, E. R., 130
Mann, G. W., 153
March, F. A., 75
Marion, Mrs. B. V. W., 160
Markham, Blackwell, 161

Marley, Mrs. C. J., 37
Marsh, H. E., 102
Marsh, L. A., 99
Marshall, R. E., 124
Marshburn, R. F., 49
Martin, D. F. Jr., 38, 41
Martin, D. L., 147
Martin, Flossie, 70
Martin, H. W., 134, 135
Martin, I. L., 103
Martin, L. D., 109
Martin, R. J., 104
Martin, S. M. Jr., 23
Martin, S. W., 108
Martin, V. C., 31
Martínez-Ponte, J. R., 74
Martone, J. D., 27
Marvin, J. R., 75
Mary, Virginia, 97
Masi, J. F., 18
Mason, M. F., 139
Massey, M. E., 117
Mast, E. M., 138
Masten, J. T., 38
Masterson, J. R., 47
Matheson, D. S., 150
Mathews, A. C., 8, 9
Matthews, M. E., 138
Matthews, V. D., 8, 9
Mattocks, J. E., 102
Mattox, W. J., 13, 23
Mauldin, W. L., 26
Mauney, S. A., 40
Maurice, C. S., 104
Maxwell, Baldwin, 83
Mayo, S. C., 152
Meares, K. deR., 28, 30
Mears, H. F., 118
Mebane, W. M., 12, 21
Medlin, L. R., 66
Meibohm, E. R. H., 26
Meisen, A. F., 108
Mell, M. R., 152
Melvin, D. E., 138
Mendenhall, M. C., 134
Mendenhall, M. S., 108
Mendenhall, M. S., 57
Menius, A. C. Jr., 129
Mercer, C. M., 62
Mereno-Enriquez, M. De L.A., 7
Merryfield, Fred, 74
Metz, G. E., 52
Meyer, F. E., 34
Meyers, Frederick, 38, 43
Michie, O. E., 45
Midgett, E. L., 76
Miller, C. E., 103
Miller, E. S., 81
Miller, H. C., 47
Miller, J. B., 103
Miller, L. L. B., 72
Miller, Vida, 93
Millican, C. B., 85

INDEX 177

Milliken, R. J., 159
Mills, J. E., 11
Mills, M. S., 95
Millsaps, V. D., 8, 49
Milne, David, 15
Milner, C. F., 64
Minakuchi, Yutaka, 127
Mitchell, Adolphus, 74
Mitchell, Mavis, 70
Mitchell, Rex, 70
Mitchell, W. A., 133
Mizell, Mrs. L. G., 99
Mizell, M. P., 157
Mock, H. B., 76, 85
Moehlmann, E. O., 20
Moffatt, J. S., 76, 83
Momiyama, Hiroshi, 40
Monk, Vivian, 85
Monroe, M. K., 88
Montgomery, M. J., 72
Mooneyhan, Mildred, 64
Moore, B. M., 152
Moore, C. A. P., 95
Moore, C. E., 154
Moore, C. M., 39
Moore, Mrs. G. R., 62
Moore, H. E., 152
Moore, J. A., 47
Moore, J. H., 55
Moore, M. A. Jr., 87
Moose, Frances, 149
Moran, K. F., 34
Morgan, E. C., 80, 90
Morgan, E. W., 62
Morgan, Gladys, 22
Morgan, Mrs. G. S., 70
Morgan, K. Z., 130
Morgan, R. R., 62
Morgan, W. W., 56
Morris, A. C., 80
Morris, J. A., 95
Morris, J. E., 59
Morris, M. E., 47
Morrison, F. W., 83
Morrison, Jean, 147
Morrison, J. S., 42
Morrison, Mrs. L. H., 72
Morrison, R. W., 45, 51
Morse, Mildred, 21
Morton, L. M., 98
Morton, R. J., 73
Moseley, M. E., 72
Moser, A. M., 50
Moses, W. L., 92
Mosher, E. S., 110
Moss, B. T., 29, 31
Moss, C. J., 110
Moss, D. B., 97
Moss, L. M., 145
Mourane, J. H., 21
Mourane, Maxalynn, 146
Mouzon, O. T., 38
Moyer, E. F., 147

Mueller, C. H., 105
Mueller, E. L., 148
Mulkey, H. B., 130
Mullis, C. E., 62
Mumford, Dorothy, 89
Munch, J. F., 124
Munch, M. E., 7
Munch, M. F., 33
Munch, R. H., 24
Murphy, Andrew, 22
Murphy, Elisabeth, 90
Murphy, G. M., 21
Murphy, Q. R. Jr., 163
Murphy, S. C., 68
Murphy, W. A., 95
Murray, Paul, 108
Murray, W. L., 108
Muse, M. McC., 58
Mutniah, S. N. A. A., 41
Myers, G. T., 64
Nagano, Kiyoshi, 40
Nahikian, H. M., 120, 124
Naiman, Barnette, 20
Naito, Yasushiro, 40
Nance, R. B., 105
Napier, W. B., 146
Nash, T. P. Jr., 19
Naylor, H. P., 111
Neal, C. C. Jr., 144
Neal, Mrs. Dorothy, 144
Neal, S. A., 67
Neale, C. M., 72
Neely, Jack, 125
Neff, E. H., 160
Neiman, Ernest, 19
Newborne, Anne, 125
Newby, G. E. Jr., 41
Newell, E. J., 19
Newell, O. E., 93
Nicholes, R. M. Jr., 15, 25
Nicholson, Catherine, 101
Nicholson, G. F. Jr., 125
Nicholson, G. W., 120
Nickell, J. P., 36
Niggli, J. M., 33
Nims, F. B., 29, 30
Nims, Horace, 31
Nix, W. V., 57
Noblin, Stuart, 115
Noe, T. P. Jr., 74
Nolen, Herman, 42
Norburn, M. E., 101
Norfleet, T. F. Jr., 117
Norman, G. C., 114
Norman, N. B., 68
Norment, O. L., 70
North, N. C., 93
Norton, C. C., 106
Norton, R. D., 13
Nowell, A. E., 34
Nowell, J. W., 18
Oates, M. N., 73
O'Brian, W. H., 133

Odum, E. P., 162
Ogburn, S. C. Jr., 12
O'Kelley, Margery, 136
Oldham, J. E., 81
Oliphant, M. C. S., 148
Olive, L. S., 9, 10
Olive, W. J., 79, 88
Oliver, J. B., 32
Oliver, G. M., 24
Olsen, W. A., 87
Oncley, Ruth, 36
Orr, J. L., 109
Orr, H. E., 11
Orrantia, J. J., 138
Osborne, A. M., 88
Osborne, F. M., 81
Osborne, M. H., 99
Osborne, R. S., 97
Ousley, M. B., 138
Owen, W. W., 15
Owens, J. J., 42
Owl, H. McC., 111
Pace, C. J., 99
Padgett, J. A., 106
Padgett, J. B., 73
Page, W. A., 132
Paige, D. D., 100
Pangle, M. G., 40
Pankey, G. E., 154
Pardue, T. E., 132
Park, C. B., 27
Park, H. V., 120, 123
Park, J. G., 23
Parker, D. P., 29
Parker, F. B., 156
Parker, Haywood Jr., 23
Parker, H. M., 131
Parker, J. A., 53
Parker, J. W., 33
Parker, L. W., 142
Parker, R. E., 83
Parker, W. G., 58
Parker, W. R., 127
Parker, W. V., 121
Parkhurst, A. J., 46
Parks, M. H., 138
Parlett, M. M., 78
Pass, C. E., 34
Patrick, J. R., 134
Patrick, R. W., 108, 114
Patrick, T. L., 64
Patten, Lawrence, 97
Patten, Walter, 150
Patterson, E. V., 109
Patterson, P. M., 9
Patton, J. W., 106, 110
Payne, I. E., 146
Payne, W. D., 65
Peacock, W. H., 62
Pearce, E. P. Jr., 67
Pearsall, F. E., 124
Pearson, L. W., 109
Pearson, R. H., 144

Peel, J. C., 48
Peeler, E. N., 52
Peery, William, 33
Peery, W. W., 81
Peet, T. B., 88
Pegg, C. H., 106, 111
Pegg, H. D., 49, 107
Pelton, M. C. S., 82
Penn, M. B., 32
Pennekamp, A. H. C., 94
Penney, J. T., 161, 162
Perez-Bernal, V. E., 137
Perian, John, 118
Perine, K. B., 21
Perkerson, F. S., 17
Perlmutt, J. H., 163
Perritt, L. G., 42
Perry, E. J., 39
Perry, L. J., 57
Perry, M. G., 29
Perry, M. K., 157
Perry, W. A., 26
Peters, C. C., 160
Pettigrew, M. M., 95
Pettigrew, R. C., 86
Pettis, B. J., 124
Pettis, M. L., 97
Pfaff, E. E., 114
Pfaff, K. T., 118
Pfeiffer, K. G., 79
Pharis, G. M., 34
Philips, C. T., 102
Phillips, C. L., 70
Phillips, E. H., 90
Phillips, K. G., 68
Phillips, L. B., 31
Phillips, M. O., 37, 41
Phillips, W. B., 11
Pickens, W. A., 142
Pickens, W. M., 49
Pickett, H. G., 12, 20
Pickler, D. A., 25
Pierce, J. Le R., 62
Pigott, C. A., 25
Pinner, C. H., 51
Pithon-Pinto, Antonio, 68
Pittana, J. B., 74
Pittman, C. L., 79, 91
Plemmons, W. H., 46
Plowden, Hannah, 155
Plumblee, M. Q., 70
Plyler, M. T., 82
Pochmann, H. A., 77
Pogue, J. E. Jr., 18
Polhill, E. F., 113
Pollock, P. B., 52
Pollock, P. L., 136
Pool, E. I. D., 55
Poovey, C. E., 143
Pope, D. B., 35
Popper, Estelle, 115
Porter, G. B., 85
Porter, M. F., 136

Porter, Mrs. R. C., 72
Posey, J. W., 32
Potter, R. R., 76
Potts, V. L., 138
Pound, M. B., 107
Powell, C. P., 110
Powell, E. L., 27
Powell, M. A., 31
Powell, T. E. Jr., 103
Prazeres, A. C., 75
Presnell, W. C., 41
Preston, R. H., 134
Preston, S. W., 37, 41
Price, D. O'H., 159
Price, M. N., 160
Prince, J. R., 147
Prince, L. McD., 86
Pritchard, H. C., 99
Pritchard, Maude, 83
Pritchett, F. G., 100
Pritchett, V. C., 129
Proffit, E. Q., 57
Proffit, G. T., 57
Pruette, D. B., 65
Pruitt, A. B., 153
Puckett, J. W. Jr., 67
Puckett, M. A., 69
Puckett, W. O., 162
Pugh, J. T., 29
Pyburn, N. K., 46
Quinlan, Janet, 155
Rabb, W. W., 65
Rabe, A. D., 62
Rabun, J. W., 116
Raddatz, W. L., 93
Radimersky, G. W., 105
Radoff, M. L., 32
Rairigh, W. N., 133
Randolph, E. E., 18, 76
Randolph, E. O., 102
Randolph, M. C., 79
Ranes, Arthur, 49
Rankin, E. R., 47
Rankin, H. A. Jr., 87
Rankin, W. W., 121
Raper, A. F., 151
Raper, J. R., 10
Ray, H. R., 102
Raynor, W. R., 62
Read, J. B., 33
Reaves, H. M., 85
Reckendorf, Angelika, 67
Redfern, V. S., 105
Redmond, B. B., 65
Reece, J. T., 127
Reece, Sanford, 35
Reep, A. R., 49
Reeves, C. G., 41
Reid, L. P., 84
Reid, P. A., 116
Reidel, A. I. Jr., 160
Renegar, H. C., 49
Resnick, Irving, 132

Restano, D. E. D., 138
Rethlingshafer, Dorothy, 134
Reynolds, C. E., 90
Reynolds, J. O., 125
Reynolds, J. P., 162
Reynolds, J. S., 97
Reynolds, W. N., 59
Rhodes, L. B., 19
Rhyne, J. J., 151, 154
Rhyne, O. P., 82
Rhyne, W. L., 116
Rice, Mrs. J. C., 58
Rice, J. D., 159
Rice, J. G., 99
Richardson, Howard, 35
Richardson, N. B., 58
Richardson, R. R. Jr., 99
Richardson, W. B., 25
Richmond, T. W., 24
Rickman, C. B., 138
Ricks, Mrs. M. B., 69
Riddick, E. I., 147
Riddick, T. M., 75
Riess, M. E., 89
Rigley, R. L., 31
Rigsby, E. P., 126
Ritchie, D. D., 10
Robbins, G. B., 48
Roberts, E. W., 92
Roberts, Frances, 91
Roberts, W. P., 119
Robertson, D. W. Jr., 81, 95
Robertson, J. B., 55
Robins, M. E., 136
Robson, C. B., 106
Roesel, D. M., 28
Rogers, C. R., 122
Rogers, E. S., 122
Rogers, Pauline, 115
Rogers, R. C., 134
Rogers, W. W., 133, 135
Roome, E. M., 53
Rose, N. V., 95
Ross, J. A., 128
Ross, J. K., 82
Ross, L. W., 59
Ross, O. B., 127
Roth, H. D., 126
Roth, S. G., 123
Royall, S. L., 93
Royer, D. M., 160
Royster, J. H., 47
Royster, P. H., 129
Royster, T. S., 129
Rudisill, W. A., 19
Rulfs, D. J., 80
Russell, Clyde, 154
Russell, F. H., 27
Russell, H. K., 77, 87
Ruth, E. B., 67
Ryder, E. L., 163
Ryland, R. T., 52
Sabbagh, M. A., 36

Sadler, A. G., 43
Salek, J. T., 35
Sallee, Hilmar, 36
Salley, W. C., 140
Sample, A. B., 8
Sams, H. W., 80
Sanders, J. H., 23
Sanders, J. P., 13
Sanders, W. B., 153
Sandmel, F. F., 35
Sanford, A. M., 146
Santora, A. C., 17
Sappington, N. O., 111
Sartain, Mrs. C. P., 90
Sasscer, R. G., 103
Saunders, J. A. L., 122, 123
Saunders, J. M., 110
Sawyer, G. L., 58
Sawyer, J. E., 53
Sawyer, J. R., 72
Scales, M. L., 34
Scarborough, J. B., 121
Schaff, W. R., 50
Schaible, V. M., 122
Schiffman, R. Y., 152
Schiller, I. P., 117
Schinhan, P. C., 159
Schmeisser, L. G., 126
Schmitt, H. A., 74
Schneider, D. L., 115
Scholz, Herbert Jr., 122
Scholz, Ruth, 9
Schroeder, P. B., 115
Schultze, H. C., 16
Schwenning, C. H., 87
Scott, J. W., 12
Scott, J. W., 91
Scott, S. E., 89
Scott, T. E. Jr., 147
Seay, Dorothy, 116
Sebastian, K. K., 160
Seckinger, D. L., 83
Seebeck, C. L. Jr., 120
Seelye, M. A., 100
Seikel, A. F., 138
Self, R. H., 100
Sellars, W. B., 22
Sellers, J. B., 107
Sensabaugh, G. F., 78, 89
Sessums, A. C., 86
Setzer, E. G., 11
Seward, D. M., 123
Sewell, S. W., 96
Shanks, H. T., 106
Shankweiler, P. W., 151
Shanor, Leland, 8, 10
Sharpe, D. R., 100
Shaw, Chandler, 107, 112
Shearer, R. D., 103
Shearin, P. E., 130
Shelton, N. W., 59
Shepard, F. C., 46, 50
Sherard, Catherine, 53

Sherwin, H. S., 11
Shields, A. K., 140, 143
Shiki, Seiji, 40
Shine, L. S., 86
Shine, W. H., 78, 86
Shivers, L. G., 152
Shockley, M. S., 79
Shohan, C. J., 42
Shore, C. A., 161
Shreve, C. G., 65
Shreve, O. D., 18
Shuford, R. H., 39
Shugar, G. J., 26
Sides, L. R., 49
Sieber, S. M., 100
Siegel, P. S., 135
Silliman, W. W. Jr., 92
Simkins, T. M. Jr., 32
Simkins, V. B., 32
Simmons, N. L., 14
Simons, M. A., 57
Simpson, E. S., 69
Simpson, G. L. Jr., 160
Simpson, H. H., 55
Simpson, M. B., 59
Simrall, Dorothy, 136
Simril, V. L., 17
Sinclair, F. McP., 43
Sinclair, T. B., 62
Siniavsky, B. M., 42
Sink, W. G., 15
Sipe, B. W., 40
Sipe, E. C., 60
Sisson, C. N., 107
Sitterson, J. C., 107, 113
Sitterson, N. L., 72
Skaggs, M. L., 107, 111
Skinner, R. J., 98
Slade, J. J. Jr., 123
Slavens, M. D., 104
Sledd, A. P., 15, 20
Slicer, D. H., 98
Smart, M. E., 53
Smedley, Katherine, 113
Smiley, T. B., 74
Smith, A. R., 21
Smith, A. S., 112
Smith, B. E., 9
Smith, C. B., 138
Smith, C. G., 84
Smith, C. M., 125
Smith, E. G., 154
Smith, E. R., 31
Smith, F. S. Jr., 69
Smith, H. P., 46
Smith, J. L., 142
Smith, J. M. Jr., 149
Smith, J. N., 97
Smith, J. W., 104
Smith, K. B., 92
Smith, K. K., 91
Smith, M. H., 59
Smith, M. J., 28

Smith, M. P., 151, 154
Smith, N. C., 126
Smith, N. M., 162
Smith, N. R., 70
Smith, R. E., 124
Smith, S. C., 12, 20
Smith, S. D., 107
Smith, S. M., 156
Smith, T. E., 8
Smith, T. H., 65
Smith, W. F., 23
Smith, W. L., 131
Smith, W. P., 140
Smithdeal, E. O., 49
Smithey, I. W., 12, 19
Smoot, W. B., 20
Snider, A. M., 111
Snider, E. M., 89
Snodderly, D. M., 62
Snoddy, C. E., 86
Solem, E. K., 37
Southard, L. G., 102
Southern, J. A., 15
Sowers, R. V., 159
Spahr, E. M., 138
Spainhour, J. F. Jr., 84
Sparger, C. B., 41
Sparks, L. A., 35
Sparrow, M. S., 83
Spearman, Walter, 33
Spears, L. C., 135
Spears, M. T., 127
Speas, J. W., 121
Speck, J. C., 17
Spell, L. L., 138
Spelt, D. K., 134
Sperandeo, Giovanni, 144
Spiers, H. S., 91
Spiers, M. T., 94
Spivey, G. C., 77, 86
Spivey, H. E., 79, 89
Spruill, J. C., 110
Spruill, M. J., 84
Stabler, L. B., 140, 142
Stacy, L. E. Jr., 19
Stacy, M. H., 120
Stagg, E. McR., 141
Stainback, R. F., 74
Stallings, N. A., 67
Stanley, J. A., 62
Stansell, Dorothy, 97
Stansell, Frances, 31
Starling, R. B., 116
Starnes, C. J., 26
Starnes, D. E., 149
Starr, H. W., 76
Steele, P. J., 128, 130
Steelman, J. R., 151
Steely, Mercedes, 94
Stein, S. I., 36
Stephens, H. E., 56
Stephenson, I. J., 123
Stevens, Mrs. E. P., 24

Stevens, G. P., 120
Stevens, S. S., 155
Stevenson, H. A., 77
Stevenson, Reston, 18
Stewart, A. B., 116
Stewart, J. W., 56
Stewart, L. M., 10
Stirewalt, E. N., 27
Stockard, S. W., 108
Stockton, C. M., 144
Stone, E. V., 161
Stone, O. M., 152
Stone, Orlando, 154
Stoner, Irwin, 125
Story, T. E., 48
Stoudemire, S. A., 140, 142
Stout, Agnes, 77
Stout, J. D., 138
Stout, W. W., 76, 84
Straley, H. W. III., 101
Strickland, Mrs. H. E., 69
Strickland, W. E., 149
Stroup, T. B., 78, 87
Stuckey, J. L., 102
Sturdivant, J. F., 153
Suhrie, Virginia, 132
Sulkin, G. R., 144
Sullivan, Rodman, 38
Sumerford, S. D., 14, 24
Surprenant, L. C., 16
Suskin, A. I., 29, 31
Sutton, C. McK., 85
Sutton, W. A. Jr., 160
Svarlien, Oscar, 108
Svendsen, J. K., 80, 93
Swain, H. L., 67
Swedenberg, H. T. Jr., 79
Swor, C. E., 93
Syron, L. W., 160
Szper, Andrew, 133
Talmage, M. B., 99
Tanner, H. A., 14
Tanner, M. S., 32
Tapp, Eleanor, 119
Tapp, Louise, 99
Taylor, A. E., 118
Taylor, Caroline, 135, 136
Taylor, C. G., 140, 143
Taylor, G. F., 112
Taylor, Harriet, 163
Taylor, H. E., 47
Taylor, H. M., 12, 20
Taylor, J. L., 18
Taylor, L. B., 59
Taylor, Martha, 58
Taylor, R. H., 109
Taylor, T. C., 109
Taylor, W. F., 77
Taylor, W. W. Jr., 137
Teachey, G. B., 72
Tebbens, W. G. Jr., 17
Tebeau, C. P., 17
Temple, E. S., 56

Templeton, M. McC., 125
Terry, A. W., 94
Tharrington, B. H., 63
Theimann, S. P. Jr., 139
Thomas, C. L., 23
Thomas, H. C., 24
Thomas, H. L., 50
Thomas, L. C., 14, 25
Thomas, M. B., 91
Thomas, M. O., 100
Thomas, R. E., 22
Thomas, W. R., 142
Thomasson, L. F., 60
Thompson, F. T., 76, 85
Thompson, H. T., 104
Thompson, J. A., 141
Thompson, L. S., 105
Thompson, M. A., 122
Thompson, M. H., 149
Thompson, O. B., 157
Thompson, S. H., 46, 49
Thompson, T. V., 149
Thornton, M. L., 119
Thorpe, J. E. Jr., 95
Thurman, B. R. Jr., 145
Tillinghast, A. W., 140
Tisdale, D. H., 153
Toler, L. O., 156
Tomberlin, B. M., 118
Torian, J. P., 124
Totten, H. R., 8, 9
Towell, E. E., 18
Townsend, K. B., 144
Toxey, C. B., 125
Trabue, E. S., 86
Trawick, M. W., 130
Treanor, H. S., 141
Tremain, R. L., 50
Trimble, R. McC., 73
Tripp, G. A., 60
Trotman, L. E., 36
Trott, G. R., 123
Trussell, Brandon, 150
Tucker, G. H., 161
Tufts, M. A., 91
Turlington, S. W., 114
Turner, C. W., 118
Turner, E. D. Jr., 148
Turner, J. O., 14, 24
Turner, Lucile, 89
Turrentine, J. W., 18
Turrentine, S. B., 81
Tuttle, O. A., 55
Tutwiler, T. S., 18
Unangst, D. M., 91
Underhill, F. E., 30
Underwood, Evelyn, 119
Underwood, Henrietta, 31
Unger, R. McI., 60
Upchurch, W. M., 47
Upsher, Littleton Jr., 18
Ussery, H. D., 130
Uzzell, W. E., 111

Uzzle, A. B. Jr., 74
Vaile, Gertrude, 155
Valk, A de T. Jr., 7
Vance, R. B., 151
Van de Luyster, Nelson, 106
Vandiver, E. P., 77, 87
Vann, J. D. Jr., 41
Vanneman, C. R., 28
Vardell, M. L., 9
Vaughan, J. H., 109
Vaughn, E. B., 144
Vazquez, M. de los A., 138
Veach, Vivian, 34
Veasey, W. F., 72
Venable, C. S., 19
Vermont, Adolf, 82
Vernon, H. J., 65
Vest, Lucile, 144
Viera, M. E., 138
Vinces, A. F., 138
Vitz, H. E., 104
Wager, P. W., 150
Walker, A. E., 127
Walker, C. H., 103
Walker, E. C., 100
Walker, J. A., 34
Walker, L. P., 125
Walker, T. E., 65
Walker, T. T., 21
Wall, B. H., 118
Wall, J. G., 123
Wall, W. R., 123
Wallace, J. L., 139
Wallace, J. M. Jr., 27
Wallace, L. De L., 96
Wallace, R. M., 81, 89
Walser, R. G., 92
Walsh, F. G., 35
Walters, E. L., 97
Walther, D. H., 149
Wang, E. T-C., 96
Ward, D. A., 91
Ward, Eloise, 63
Ward, E. R., 23
Ward, L. M., 30
Ward, M. M., 63
Ward, M. W., 10
Ward, Rebecca, 9
Wardlaw, J. G. Jr., 73
Warren, R. S., 60
Warren, W. F., 39
Warshaw, Jacob, 82
Washburn, B. E., 82
Watkins, J. H., 102, 104
Watkins, T. C., 162
Watson, J. D., 75
Watters, D. A., 33
Watters, Mary, 107
Way, E. L., 29, 31
Way, Katharine, 129
Way, William Jr., 41
Wearn, Cornelia, 111
Weatherford, R. D., 131

Weatherly, C. H., 50
Weathers, C. L., 50
Weatherup, Marjorie, 32
Weaver, J. R., 48
Weaver, P. J., 116
Weaver, W. R., 141, 145
Webb, B. D., 7, 26
Webb, C. H., 35
Webb, Edith, 156
Webb, S. C., 136
Webb, S. C., 69
Webb, W. S., 86
Webster, F. W., 55
Webster, J. W., 115
Webster, M. M., 103
Weeks, Mrs. G. E., 101
Weeks, M. S., 69
Weeks, S. B., 76, 81
Wegelin, C. A., 99
Weigand, Erika, 7
Welborn, E. P., 139
Welborn, E. S., 39
Wellons, L. D., 67
Wells, D. A., 129
Wells, E. M., 10
Wells, Mrs. H. E., 59
Wells, J. R., 69
Wells, M. P., 78, 90
Wenhold, L. L., 140
Wertz, S. M., 30
West, E. A., 118
West, H. G., 127
Westby, J. M., 46
Westrope, M. R., 136
Wetherell, E. L., 70
Wharton, V. L., 108, 112
Whichard, R. D., 148
Whichard, W. G., 116
Whiffen, A. J., 9, 10
Whipple, A. A., 101
Whitaker, B. L., 109
Whitaker, M. D., 130
White, Clemon, 35
White, Elizabeth, 31
White, H. E., 56
White, J. W., 129, 131
White, Locke Jr., 17
White, V. C., 78
White, W. A., 101, 104
Whitehead, A. C., 29
Whitener, D. J., 107, 110
Whitener, R. W., 49
Whitener, T. A., 49
Whitfield, J. V., 40
Whitley, D. P., 51
Whitley, G. T., 82
Whitney, V. H., 153, 157
Whitted, J. W., 149
Wickens, D. D., 92, 134
Wideman, S. A., 16, 25
Wiggins, R. L., 69
Wike, C. E., 72
Wilburn, H. I., 10

Wilder, F. S., 38, 154
Wiley, L. E., 161
Wilhelm, H. H., 149
Wilkin, H. D., 118
Willard, E. P. Jr., 28, 85
Williams, A. J., 124
Williams, A. L., 78, 89
Williams, Alton, 94
Williams, C. C., 72
Williams, C. C., 124
Williams, F. D., 128, 131
Williams, F. T., 122
Williams, Grace, 139
Williams, H. H., 29
Williams, J. W., 117
Williams, L. C., 39
Williams, L. L., 51, 161, 162
Williams, L. M., 155
Williams, M. C., 31
Williams, M. H., 127
Williams, M. L., 44
Williams, R. H., 26
Williams, W. W., 14, 23
Williamson, A. E. Jr., 137
Williamson, J. L., 145
Williamson, M. L., 45
Williard, C. W., 19
Willis, L. J., 131
Willis, S. H., 85
Wills, G. S., 81
Wilson, C. B., 58
Wilson, Evelyn, 143
Wilson, Mrs. F. P., 55
Wilson, G. P. Jr., 36
Wilson, H. B., 137
Wilson, J. B., 80
Wilson, J. C., 114
Wilson, K. E., 77, 85
Wilson, Mrs. Lottie, 123
Wilson, L. R., 76, 82
Wilson, M. H., 139
Wilson, R. B., 91
Wilson, T. J. Jr., 28, 29
Wilson, T. J. III., 142
Wilson, W. L., 88
Windell, G. T., 63
Winkler, E. W., 75
Winn, Lily, 87
Winningham, E. F., 133
Winslow, R. S., 37
Wise, Percy, 144
Wismer, L. H., 36
Withers, J. L., 133
Witten, C. H., 27
Wittmeyer, H. F., 96
Wogan, D. S., 141
Wolf, M. I., 159
Wolfe, J. H., 107, 113
Wolff, K. McK., 111
Wolff, M. H., 109
Wolff, W. E., 36
Womble, Frances, 83
Wood, Harriette, 155

Wood, J. E., 121
Wood, J. H., 14
Wood, R. H., 67
Wood, T. W., 38
Woodall, C. L., 129
Woodard, C. M., 141, 142
Woodard, Mrs. F. P., 100
Woodward, C. V., 107
Woodworth, R. N., 156
Workman, J. H. A., 46, 56
Wormell, H. E., 91
Worth, A. M., 74
Wright, E. A., 40
Wright, F. M., 28
Wright, I. C., 109
Wright, L. B., 76
Wright, L. B., 85
Wright, M. H., 139
Wright, T. E., 142
Wyche, M. C., 118
Wyly, L. D. Jr., 131
Wynn, M. M., 98
Yacoel, David, 138

Yapar, N. F., 43
Yarbrough, Gustie, 112
Yarbrough, M. S., 139
Yarrow, A. H., 148
Yates, E. W., 119
Yeatman, H. C., 163
Yeatman, T. P., 159
Yoder, E. M., 55
Yoder, F. R., 39
Yoffie, L. R. C., 80
York, G. A., 124
Young, I. V., 155
Young, N. C., 156
Young, W. P., 150
Yount, M. A., 81
Yount, M. H., 127
Zachary, Elizabeth, 158
Ziegler, A. W., 11
Zimmerman, H. J., 119
Zorn, Blanche, 136
zur Burg, F. W., 22
zur Burg, H. H., 130

www.ingramcontent.com/pod-product-compliance
Lightning Source LLC
Chambersburg PA
CBHW030113010526
44116CB00005B/226